AF352266

Go ahead, laugh to see me haunting all these shipwrecks, a salvager leaving
sumptuous silver plate behind, not too handy with the net, rather clumsy with
fishhooks, bending over you with such care and concern ...
Patrick Chamoiseau, *School Days*

Landscape With Shipwreck is dedicated to the late Marian McMahon.

LANDSCAPE WITH SHIPWRECK

first person cinema and the films of philip hoffman

edited by karyn sandlos and mike hoolboom

Co-editors: Karyn Sandlos and Mike Hoolboom
Project Coordinator: Kelly Langgard
Production Manager: Chris Gehman
Technical Assistant: Larissa Fan
Design: f. duran productions
      Franci Duran
      Steven Casey
      With Simon Rojas and Kika Thorne
Copy Editor: Sharon English
Proofreader: Scott McLeod
Financial Support: The Canada Council for the Arts

Cover photo: *Sweep*, photo by Alli Anttilainen
Full page photo credits
page 17: *Chimera*
page 41: *?O,Zoo!*, photo by Marian McMahon
page 75: *river*
page 137: *passing through/torn formations*
page 166: *Kitchener-Berlin*
page 200: Philip Hoffman, polaroid by Carl Brown
page 245: *What these ashes wanted*
page 253: *What these ashes wanted*
page 257: *What these ashes wanted*

Typeset in bodoni BE light, light italic, bodoni BE regular and medium. Printed on Accent Opaque 70 lb. Smooth,White
Printed in Canada by AGMV Marquis, Cap-St-Ignace, Québec

ISBN 1-894663-00-4

National Library of Canada Cataloguing in Publication Data
Main entry under title: *Landscape with shipwreck : first person cinema and the films of Philip Hoffman*
Includes bibliographical references.

1. Hoffman, Philip - Criticism and interpretation. 2. Experimental films - Canada - History and criticism.
I. Sandlos, Karyn Elizabeth, 1968-
II. Hoolboom, Michael. III. Images Festival of Independent Film & Video.
PN1998.3.H63L36 2001   791.43'0232'092   C2001-930329-7

Co-published by Images Festival of Independent Film and Video and Insomniac Press

Images Festival of Independent Film and Video
401 Richmond St. West, Suite 448
Toronto, Ontario, Canada M5V 3A8
info@imagesfestival.com
www.imagesfestival.com

Insomniac Press
192 Spadina Ave., Suite 403
Toronto, Ontario, Canada M5T 2C2
www.insomniacpress.com

ACKNOWLEDGEMENTS

Landscape With Shipwreck would not exist without the help of those who believed it essential that Philip Hoffman's work become the focus of our collective ruminations on first-person cinema in Canada. Special thanks goes to Mike Hoolboom for inspiring and jet fuelling this project. Kelly Langgard has been instrumental in coordinating production, and Chris Gehman and Larissa Fan have attended to the countless details that have ensured the completion of this book. I am indebted to many others who have offered their talents and expertise: Franci Duran, Marc Glassman, Ellen Flanders, Sharon English, and all of the writers and artists who have lifted this collection up to the light of day. Finally, thanks to Mike Cartmell for his wonderful title, and to Beth Easton and Deirdre Logue for their understanding of shipwrecks.

Love and gratitude to Philip Hoffman for his light and shadows.

Karyn Sandlos

This book was made possible through financial assistance from the Canada Council for the Arts.

The Canada Council | Le Conseil des Arts
for the Arts | du Canada

CONTENTS

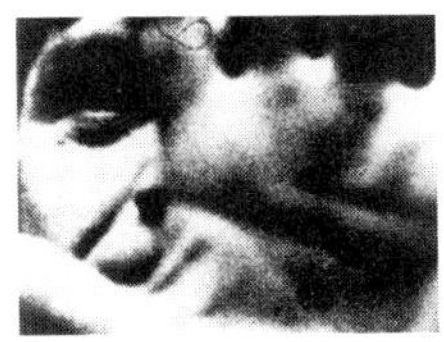

stills (top to bottom): *passing through/torn formations, river, What these ashes wanted.*

photo: Hoffman's mother with
the triplets before he was born.

INTRODUCTION

I met him at the equipment crib of Sheridan College, primal hearth of the
Escarpment School, though that name had not even made its way into rumour
then. He always wore flannel, and jeans that would never come quite clean, no
matter how often washed, as if part of the world was always sticking to him. He
wasn't Philip Hoffman then, he was just Phil, dishing out light meters and grip-
stands with a smile, rubbing together the dimes to make rent on his basement digs.

He was serious, even then. Working summers at a hog plant will do that to
you. On a clear night you could still smell the blood on him, the muscles working
overtime just to keep him still. He never talked much, soaking it all in, and wher-
ever he went his camera was sure to follow. He was a diary filmmaker, collecting
moments of his own life the way others collect rare stamps or hockey cards. He
didn't work off a script, never believed in plans or Daytimers, knowing the places
he was headed would never make it onto anyone's map but his own.

Phil Hoffman is my friend. And I am afraid for him.

When I reread this collection of writings, it's hard to shake off the funereal
air, the sense that something is over. The book is closed. The project is finished.
In biblical times, there circulated rumours of a book so fearsome, so awful, that its
reading would occasion the events it described, and end the world as it was known.
I have no doubt that for Phil, this is that book. I pray he never reads it.

Phil Hoffman makes personal documentaries, which is to say he strains
history through his own fictions. His work takes on some formidable themes:
memory, the family, the making of official and unofficial histories, the ethics of
representation, love and loss in the time of AIDS. He has devoted his life to examining the narrow aperture each of us uses to bring our own experience into focus.
Some might call this personality. Or style. Subjectivity. A sense of immediacy
emanates from work that means more than it knows, and in arriving at Hoffman's
films, many of the writers in this volume have taken up the same beat, making

confessions of their own, allowing their ghosts to haunt this inscription. This
memorial.

Whatever may be recognized has already passed.

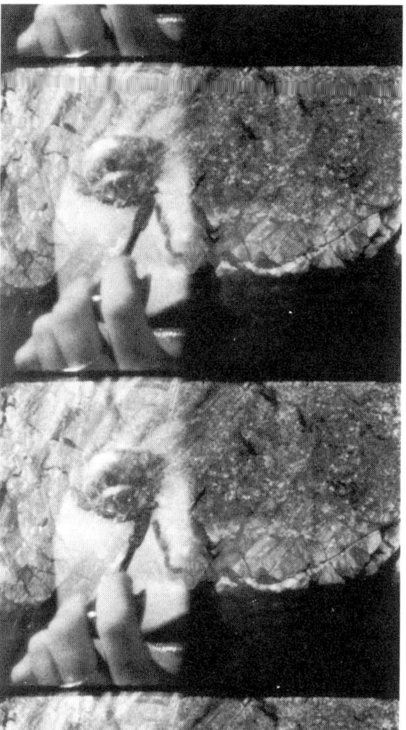

I met him four years ago in a darkened theatre. I was looking for something,
though I didn't know it then. He was sitting behind me and we were introduced
moments before the Marian McMahon Award was granted to filmmaker Jennifer
Reeves. At that time I didn't know about the Film Farm or the films that are made
there. But there was something in the way people spoke about the workshop, and
about Phil and his late partner, Marian. I got on the list.

In 1992 Phil and Marian moved to a farm north of Toronto and started the
Independent Imaging Retreat. This is a no-logo film school: no computers or hi-
tech gear, just some wind-up cameras, some DIY film chemicals, two makeshift
darkrooms, and a few flatbeds. In pouring over the contents of this book these
past months, I realize that each year I go back to the farm because I'm working
on something that will never be finished.

I've learned many things from Phil Hoffman, one being that I have a few
friends who are also my teachers. These are difficult people to know. Friends like

Phil make demands; they rub up against parts of me that would be easier to ignore or forget. But these friendships anchor me to the world even as they break my heart. If I'm afraid for Phil, it's because in knowing him, I fear for myself.

As many of the writers in this volume will attest, telling personal stories is dangerous work. This book is an untidy stew of gravediggers and critics, architects and builders. In their conversion of pictures into words, each has used the secret history of their own naming as compass and guide. There are explications here, of course. We have riven the maker, taken him apart like a motor car, peered into the secret life of the body. There is also a posse of artists' projects, some by folks who swore off movies long before Phil ever picked up his father's super-8 camera, still clinging to the dream of family. These photographs and scripts speak alongside the written word, not to fill in the gaps but to deepen them, not to make the strange seem more familiar, but to turn towards the secret task of this volume: to write what cannot be written. To write what must not, must never be written. To uncover a kind of writing that is beside itself, and without regret.

While tending the wounds that remain imprinted on this collection I have often thought of the gift of the corner mirror that Leesa receives from her estranged father in *passing through/torn formations* (1988). This is a gift that asks Leesa to look at herself, though it offers not the solace of transparency, but the possibility of an infinitely varied reflection. Caught in the suturing of two faces, Leesa's image shatters. By reading this book, you risk making this story your own.

Landscape With Shipwreck: First Person Cinema and the Films of Philip Hoffman is dedicated to Marian McMahon, Phil's partner for thirteen years. Her legacy underlines the dictum that she followed to the end: "A self to which it would be worth her while to be true." Marian might have written this book. Instead, she is its first witness.

Karyn Sandlos and Mike Hoolboom

THIN ICE

by Karyn Sandlos

In my mid-thirties I realized I had slipped past a childhood I had ignored and not understood.
Michael Ondaatje, *Running in the Family*

Beginnings can be awkward, because they ask us to do things before we know how. I read somewhere that we can't learn our personal histories off by heart. Memory is fickle; it doesn't fade with time, it shape shifts. And although memory is a central preoccupation in Philip Hoffman's work, his first film, *On the Pond*, suggests that telling personal stories requires a degree of amnesia. In 1978, while a student at Sheridan College, Hoffman tape-recorded a family gathering as material for a personal documentary film. The occasion was his birthday, and the Hoffman family had assembled for a celebratory slide show. Following his own diaristic work in writing and photography, Hoffman recalls that his aim, in making *On the Pond*, was to begin with what he knew. What could be more familiar than one's own family history, retrieved from an archive of Kodak mementos? Yet, in *On the Pond*, tensions between what can be revealed and what must remain hidden behind a veil of propriety suggest a much deeper layer of prohibition at stake in the telling of personal stories. In this film, pictures of home give provisional shape to an indeterminate longing and make the familiar an uneasy place to return to. At our most personal, it would seem, we are never quite at home.

Memory, the thirst for presence ...
Octavio Paz, *A Tree Within*

In *On the Pond*, Hoffman brings the truth-making apparatuses of the still and moving image to bear on that most colloquial of historic documents: the family anecdote. The film opens with a series of black-and-white stills, underscored by a family's exclamations of delight. A number of voices proffer the details of time and place. There is the cottage and the pond. Children fish in summer and skate in winter. There is Princess, the family dog. The photographs are animated by the usual snippets of commentary: "Oh, that's a good one of you!" "Do you remember when we …?" "I wish I knew you better then … " Amidst the convivial clamor of the soundtrack, a daughter's wish to have known her mother better captures my attention, for she speaks to her mother with the quiet resignation of one who has arrived too late. In this moment, the family's exuberance for the factual details of a past life together belies the tones and shadows of their shared recollections. Through fleeting disclosures they tell stories of longing using a past—or at least a version of the past—that might temper all that is unbearable about the present.

I often wonder whether I have any actual memories of my own childhood, or whether access to my past is made possible only by the stories of others. There are few things I find more frustrating than being left to my own failed recollections. Lost keys, forgotten directions, and misplaced bits of information are the hints that trying too hard to remember makes us forget. Perhaps most images are like tools that relieve us of this kind of difficulty by giving shape to a past that is largely made up of traces, impulses, flashes of colour, and fragments in need of a structure. *Tell me a story that will help me forget what I want from a past that is lost to me.* Images aren't lies exactly, but they may work like screens that shield us from the discards of our lives. To preserve the past, to give meaning to these fragments, is at once the work of a magician and the practice of an embalmer. With a wish to give order to the refractory pull of desire, the archive snatches memory from the flow of time.

On the map of history, perhaps the water stain is memory.
Anne Michaels, *Fugitive Pieces*

But even anesthesia can be administered in uneven doses. *On the Pond* cuts between family photographs and the recurring scene of a boy playing hockey on a frozen pond—the clamour of the domestic drama and the stillness of a frozen landscape. At night, backlit by the windows of the cottage, his father prepares the ice with buckets of water. The water will be solid by morning, but first it leaves a stain. While most stains have only a material presence, this one lingers in the mind with a haunting intractability, there and not there at the same time. Amidst images of landscape and childhood that beckon with a nostalgia echoed in the words of Hoffman's older sister intoning "Oh, I want to go back," traces of uncertainty pierce through ordered time. If there is a true picture of the past, it must be like these fleeting glimpses when they surface like a photograph that could easily have been discarded or returned from the lab stamped "print no charge." In *On the Pond*, these are moments when, just as the negative image gives birth to the positive print, amnesia gives memory its contours.

To articulate the past historically does not mean to recognize it the way it really was. It means to seize hold of a memory as it flashes up at a moment of danger. Walter Benjamin, *Illuminations*

In *On the Pond*, there is a strange image of the back of Hoffman's mother's head, framed by a figure in motion on the left and the small face of a very young Hoffman lower down. The voice-over tells us that this photograph was taken on Thanksgiving Day, when Hoffman's mother was "feeling lousy." While the emotional tone of the day is admitted, Hoffman's effort to cheer his mother up becomes the focus of this conversation. But the seconds of silence that surround the tiny image of a child's smiling face tear at the delicate suturing between meaning and image, between memory and the psychic cost of bringing the past to light. The family gathers in an act of forgetting. It is not the picture itself that leaves a stain, but the layers of affect and meaning that linger unresolved in the silence that follows their conversation about a day that is lost to them. Forgotten, perhaps, but not gone: the image is as permanent and imperfect as the conflicts it serves to disguise, and it glances off the viewer with the tug of retrospective desire. This is, as Benjamin might have put it, a moment of recognition in which the past flashes up as an image, never to be seen again.

On the Pond is a study in still and moving images, and the flow of the past through preserved moments in time. Pictures of home and family are intercut with photographs of Hoffman's hockey team, the silence of the pond broken by the clamour of an audience, a coach's obsessive words of encouragement, and the encroaching chant of Ca-na-da! Ca-na-da! A young Hoffman surveys a collection of trophies alongside team photographs that herald his departure from the family. Through a laboured series of push-ups, he measures his stamina against the ice. Photographs of Hoffman's own childhood provide a measure of the distance between home and the world, and the small rituals of the pond reveal their larger purpose: Hoffman gains strength in order to leave, and distance so that he may one day return.

It is no accident that many of us become fascinated by our family histories long after we have left home. For years after my own leaving, I asked my family not to pose for photographs taken at our annual reunions. I stopped taking pictures, however, when I realized that we didn't know how not to perform in front of a camera. Not posing was more awkward than posing. Perhaps this was my way of trying to call attention to a certain distance of my own—to manipulate the conventional time of family portraits as a way of trying to live outside the ordered traditions of home and family. And it may be that going home requires this measure of distance, this lapse of memory, that most pictures afford us. If absence clears a path for our return, a little amnesia may be the price of presence. Like trying to hold light between two hands.

As in childhood we live sweeping close to the sky, and now what dawn is this.
Ann Carson, *Autobiography of Red*

It is possible that the process of making a personal film relies more on memory lapses than it does on memory. My own first film began as a disparate collection of stories that I had been repeatedly told about my childhood, until I was old enough to wonder where the stories ended and my own experience began. The images I made didn't lend themselves to an easy or obvious ordering, and so I experimented with one version and then another, wondering why I felt compelled to tell stories that seemed to fill in the spaces where memory failed me. There was a period in which mastery over the film's unfolding gave way to a strange sense of disorientation. The film began to unmake the maker, like a dream that was nudging me forward in search of artifacts, vestiges, echoes.

Toward the end of *On the Pond*, Hoffman, now in his twenties, reclines on a bed flipping the pages of an old hockey album. Next to the bed, a projector reel rotates and a turntable revolves. The film has ended and the music has stopped, but the silence is disturbed by the skip of the needle and the incessant hum of the projector. If memories are like water staining ice, then the best replicas of memory must glimmer even as they disappear. The problem is that we make films when we wake to the knowledge that we have been sleeping, but we also make films in order to help us sleep better. And if we do, in fact, sleep through much of our childhoods, it is not just the familiar that we reach for later on, but the urgent flashes of ourselves that can't be explained, or understood, or fully retrieved. Hoffman glances intently at the camera as he moves off of the bed, leaving the photo album behind. Emerging from the cottage, he makes his way back to the pond.

photo: *On the Pond.* Production still by Dan Swim.

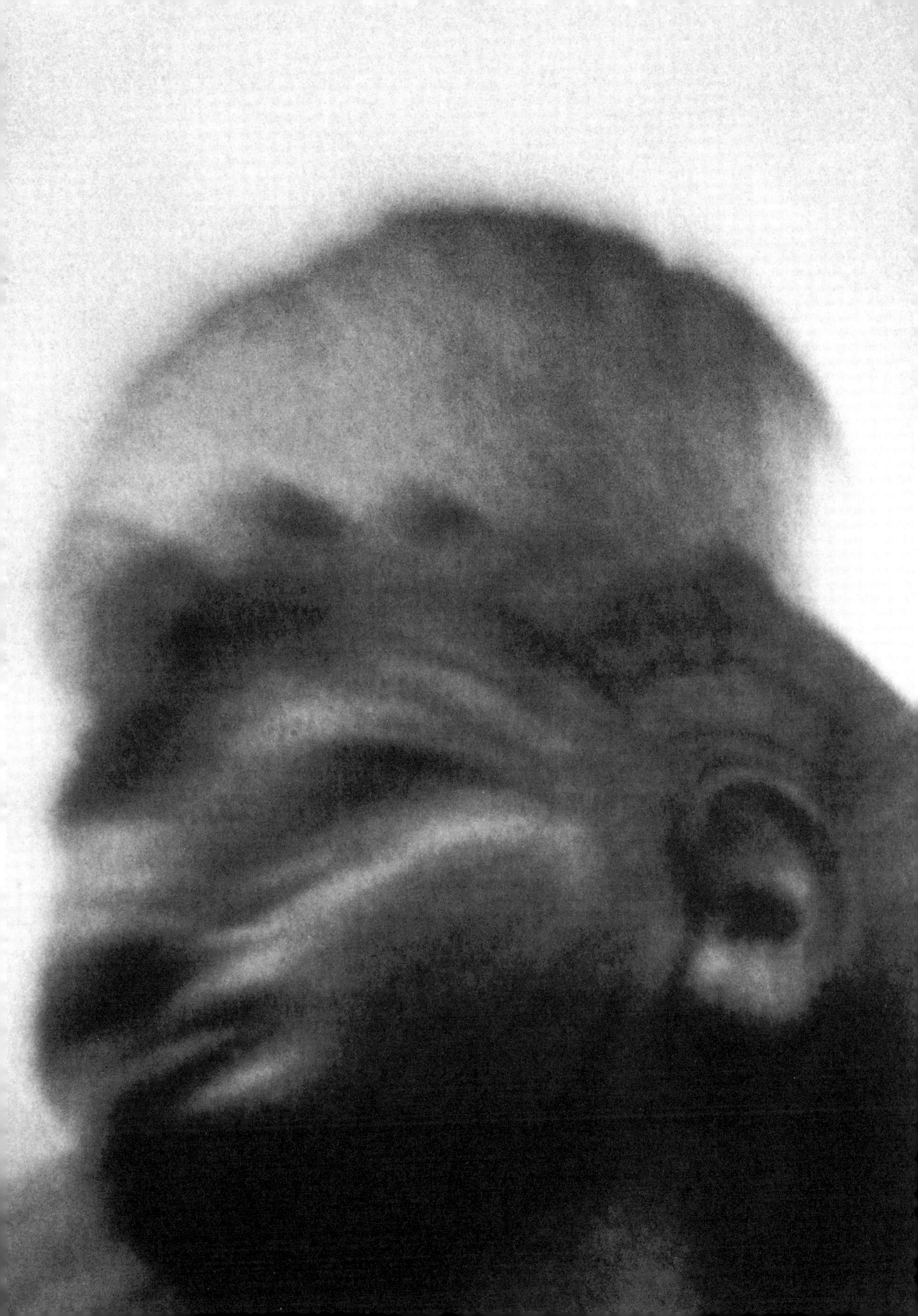

ALL THIS FALLING

by Daniel Reeves

I can't help thinking how unspontaneous it is to prop open a book of old family photographs and sit awkwardly at a keyboard trying to breathe life back into the past, which although forever here, is also hidden by time. The earliest photographs are two-by-two inch black-and-whites that could almost pass for big postage stamps, with their square frames, crinkle-cut edges and tidy compositions. I will use them to launch this letter of inquiry, moving with their crisply outlined silver halides and chiaroscuro clouds toward that part of my life that is largely hidden: memories obscured by sadness and my mother's inability to sketch out even the broadest strokes.

It is possible that the shame of her own weakness and irresolution, galvanised by our step-father Milton's abhorrence of what existed before him, keeps her commentary bound to the litany of how much she loved my father, and how handsome and despicable he was. Oddly enough, I can't even name this man at the moment. I want to call him John, or Charles, yet I cannot speak with any certainty. Perhaps this amnesia is the inevitable product of the choking dilemma I find myself in: to be unable to name or even say the thing which, however dim, is here before me like a tree or house. I am reminded of those dust devils in the desert: you never see them plainly, no matter how fast you whip your skull around, since they live only in the periphery of vision. So here they are before me, these slightly browning blacks and blank whites, hidden from view until my brother Tom and I were well into our thirties.

My brother asked if I wanted to see any photographs of my REAL father? Who disappeared from view so long ago but could have been living just around the corner for all we know? Yes, Tom, I said, I suppose I would like to see them, as well as read the clumsy letters of protest he wrote to my mother when she (as the story goes) discovered he had another wife and family. Whether my father was actually married to my mother at the time, I cannot be sure. It has only recently occurred to me what a shadow of half-told stories and hidden plots lies behind me.

My real father is bereft of any redeeming or endearing qualities, apart from his so-called handsome visage and seductive charm. I conjure up his vanity and deceit in my own deluded wandering. It's true, we look a bit alike, moulds from the same press. Yet this tiny silver image has an appropriately tilted horizon, as if everything on earth were already in full slide and I am being held up by this wayward rascal in baggy pants with the clumsy potato-sack ineptitude of men who can't be bothered with parenting. In spite of what little I have heard about this boozing womaniser, I really like him. I like my father for his cockiness and nonchalance, the way I also admire detective heroes.

In these little squares my mother Suzanne is desirable, with her handsome face, white-ribbon-decked curls, fine big bones adrift in satin, and her shy, cloth coat. With little effort, I can imagine her opening again and again like a warm flower to the men who knew how to love her, but not live with her.

I find three other shots from the same roll. They share the same light, and the cold spring air of temporary grace that precedes the deep well of disappointment and shame known only to the truly abandoned. I am looking at my brother's early face, usually so animated and intelligent. Here, it is blank, as if he is seeing into an altogether different movie or shadow world. As if he already sees the familial drift and slide in all its vain, glorious tumult and banal horror—the years of harsh oppression and control that were to besiege the tiny forts we built around our hearts to barricade ourselves from darkness.

Rilke once wrote, "Oh look, it's in this one, it's in them all. And yet there is someone who holds up all this falling." This feeling of being held is in these photographs for me, and not just because they are rooted in who I am. I find it in all old photographs, the older the better. It is born fresh in the Polaroid as it slips into this very morning—only it is not ripe yet. Ripening requires time. How much time is determined by the viewer. For me, it is a long time, and it is mostly a black-and-white time, since colours seem to trick and glamourize vision. Looking now at two new-baby photos, it is clear that the one left uncoloured is full of light and presence, while the other looks like a child who never existed. Gazing at the first, my eyes fill with love for this chubby, smiling face and curling hands. I want to pick him up gently and walk slowly around the room with him cradled in my arms, singing the world outside.

For years I have thought about the boys who died in the water alongside me on the only day I can really remember from Vietnam. My feelings are a mixture of anger, anguish and pure astonishment at my survival. I think of those soldiers as lost children, like those in the limbo preached to my brother and me in childhood. Like us, the boys in bloodied uniforms never had a chance to live, and like these photographs, they remain frozen in time. In my deeper understanding I can see that the boys have moved on. I have tried to move on as well, but in this

moment I can't help but think of them like glass shattering at my feet as it tumbles from my frozen hand—so quickly without warning. I see them with all their time stolen, snatched from their eternally open arms, and I see myself walking out of this arrested moment and going forward into promise, into light. Yet there is something I have left behind with the boys in that crystallised stillness.

The Japanese word for mysterious, *shinpiteki*, is pronounced "shimpi-teki." This is a perfect sound to describe the qualities found in these old photographs. In this mood I discover the early photographs of my brother. Dressed in white, like a sacrifice or an inmate, this baby appears abandoned, hollering and clutching toward the closest edges of the frame. The camera is barely off the squared perspective of tiled floor, and its gaze charges the room with the tensile feel of a huge mouth about to spring shut. This tension is heightened by the soft, out-of-focus jitter caused by the nervous hand of the photographer during a sluggish sweep of the shutter.

In this photograph I see a wee boy in trouble, and I cannot break into this lost space. As much as I might wish to soothe him, there is no way into this room, for it is locked inside him. I have a teacher who says that sometimes it is difficult to be solid; it is hard to stand upright in times of fierce wind and hard weather, when there seems to be nothing at all of substance or strength to cling to. I believe the real lesson is that there is truly nothing to hold onto.

In the christening shot of my brother (who was born almost two years after the war, in June of 1947), my mother is looking down with a bemused smile at his tiny face, which is dwarfed by the comet tail of an unbelievably large white christening gown. My mother's torso, shoulders and Slavic head (adorned with a bad hat and ugly glasses), are encircled by a shiny church window that rises on two arches of brick window framing. The secret of the photograph is this mirroring circle of glass that opens into a world left behind. This is another universe, another family cosmology that trails off behind my mother and back through the 40s into the Depression and other beginnings.

There are other photographs that are gone, lost, buried, or that have otherwise disappeared in our shifting lives. In that window I see another family. There is my mother's husband (Charles Derman, I believe) and two children of that union: Robert and Jaqueline. The children walked out of the picture of my dear mother's life and never turned back. This is the true mystery and, I suspect, the proper key to all that remains so obscure and illogical in this fractured history. It is the story line and the detail behind all those times and places that my mother fails to talk about. If my view was wider and more perfectly aware, then all this would just be noise or dim movement. But for someone still walking, still seeking, these rags tied to branches fluttering in the wind must mark the way back home.

Questions: Why, if our father's name was Merkle, were we brought up and always registered in schools as Derman? Was my mother, in fact, ever married to this man Merkle? Why did my mother's marriage to Charles Derman end? Why did the children go off with him to England and the air force rather than stay with mother, the more socially acceptable thing to do in 1940s Catholic America? Why have the children never made contact with my mother? Why did Milton go through the trouble of using his influence at city hall to get faked birth certificates (which I have used successfully all my adult life), which state that he is our real father? Why would Milton, whenever he really lost control, call us little bastards and the like? Why do Tommy and I look so different, and yet, where similar, look like our mother? Why was the divorce and dispensation such a long and complicated ordeal?

Lately, it has occurred to me that some of these mysteries might be explained by the strong possibility that mother was having an affair with this Mr. Merkle, and that her first husband left with the children when the affair was discovered. Subsequently, my mother never legally married my father (thus keeping the name Derman, which my brother and I had as a last name while we were growing up). All this will remain unclear until my mother cares to share the truth with us. Somehow, I feel that knowing would put some ground under my feet.

Returning to the album, I find a series of shots taken on a summer day in the park. Among them is my favourite image of myself. It is a symbol of all that I would like to be remembered by. In this photograph I am seated beneath a large, wide-brimmed straw hat, enthroned upon a picnic table with my denim-clad legs

splayed out in front. Each leg ends in a fat sneaker, and these look like two mute pages at the court of happy fools. I am looking directly into the lens and holding a can of National Bohemian Beer, a local brand often referred to as National Bo, or in times of urgency, just Bo. The white stem of an unfiltered cigarette perches on my lips, unlit, and awkward as a first erection.

You have seen this photo before. It's the one where the children wield the power symbols; the ruddy Plains Indian boy buried in a mountain of buffalo hide with a feathered pipe and Winchester cradled in his thin brown arms. His eyes are like a frozen lake, and they reel in the future with the pull of a magnet for a herd of pins. The child with the top hat and pipe, the chubby hands that grip the steering wheel, the fingers that stroke the flank of the hanging stag or pitch coal into the steam and brass of forward motion—these children are all acting out parts, filling up the costumed space of those in power, aching for and acting out the future. When I was young and had begun to reason, I yearned for the power of the grown-ups in towering trousers and looming skirts, who filled the lonely horizon of my helplessness with their demands and one-way suggestions.

So much from birth until five lies buried or blocked. What do I remember? Going to a night-club act with Milton and mom and being given all of the baby chicks that the magician had used in his act. I took them home in a cardboard box, where they died one by one during a week-long wake to the tune of *Tammy's In Love.*

I remember two scenes of anger and violence. In the first, my mother and I are walking downtown when a man in a station wagon is rear-ended by a black taxi driver. His car is not really hurt, but the man is consumed by an intolerably powerful rage, and he repeatedly smashes the car behind him by roaring forward and then slamming his car into reverse. His wife, who is clutching a young baby and crying hysterically, flops about in the front seat like a suburban Raggedy Ann. Pieces of both cars tear away and fall with a great, heartbreaking commotion. The whole scene goes by in a minute, but it seems to linger like the slow-motion inferno of *Zabriskie Point.* Finally, the enraged man screeches away and vanishes into traffic, tires howling and burning into the soft, black summer tar. Someone from the dumbstruck crowd yells to the taxi man, "Hey! Don't worry pal, I've got his number!"

I have just turned three. We are in a long line of cars moving slowly and hesitantly through hazy fields, following a weaving drunk whose erratic driving is keeping everyone from passing and forcing oncoming traffic onto the shoulder. Suddenly, as the drunk lurches to the side of the road, a few other cars stop. Men emerge. They surround the drunk and yank him from the car. As we pass, the men can be seen pummelling and kicking the drunk man to the ground. My mother says he is getting what he deserves.

In his last poems, written as he approached an early and certain death, Raymond Carver refers to a picture taken two years before he was informed of his fatal cancer.

> You open a drawer and find inside the man's photograph,
> knowing he has only two years to live. Only he hasn't found
> this out yet. That's why he can mug for the camera.

No matter how tightly I shut my eyes, or how forcibly I peer into the labyrinth of my faint memories of these early years, I can retrieve only fragments. Half a room, the shadowed parts of a hall, the element of fear from an incomplete scene, the eclipsed pattern of a quilt, many faces devoid of names. Where does the *rasa*, the sweetness hide? Where is the juice of the thing? I am certain there must be rooms bulging with books in all the major cities and universities, ready to offer a definitive answer to this mystery of memory, but as Rumi says, "Truth is not a matter for discussion." Thesis upon theory from epistemology to deconstruction and back around the bend in time again. These are shadow studies: bound to language, they are fettered by the expectation of result. For me, what is real must necessarily be signless—without reference or symbol—and while the truly signless cannot be measured or rationally described, like all this falling, it must be held.

THIS IS CINERAMA

by Jeffrey Paull

The war is over. We learn about atomic bombs and concentration camps. We read about the suburbs, even as we are creating them. Since the 20s, my mother's family have been picture-takers, filling candy boxes with snapshots of their New World lives. But there were no pictures of their parents, my grandparents, the old country. It is as if life and images began in Cleveland. By not appearing in photos, the old country was buried and forbidden. (Consider the generation gap when interpreting the phrase "escaping to Cleveland").

The family get-together ritual involved cousins and aunts with handfuls of photos, jumping in and out of each other's stories. Our multiple points of view and sudden story twists brought laughs; nothing bad ever happened. This was a floor activity, away from the civilizing influence of chairs and tables. Our pictures returned us to our bodies, granting us permission to speak, look and act, just like in the movies. By sharing we found a place to belong in each other. And it was a way of celebrating the safe (but unspoken) passage across an ocean and two world wars. Many Jews, we had only recently found out, had not been so lucky—though we rarely spoke about that. When we saw pictures of the camps, we were silent.

The photos weren't arranged in albums or slotted in slide trays. They were in our hands and our laps, taking the place of our faces. While the images stayed the same, the order and emphasis changed as years went by. The distancing of the photographs' semblance allowed us to get closer to intimacy. We orchestrated those evenings as we went along and performed the photos from riffs we had learned long ago, improvising the lyrics, singing the pictures.

None of us were able to be as free with one another when we were without our shared Fanny Farmer boxes of iconic visual aids. The snapshots were important, that is, they "worked," because they resembled the surface of people or things. The photograph's shard of time, that song without music, was the interior time of our imaginations. It lasted for all of us, as long as we made the story last. In this way the snapshots freed us, temporarily, from the implacable domination of the atomic second, from the present that is the "always" part—the mathematics, philosophy, and spirituality part—of Time itself, caught in the act of passing.

Sometime around 1946 I first became aware of images qua images. My family took me to the Loew's Park on 105th and Euclid. The black-and-white movie showed a couple of cops. As we were leaving I saw two real-life cops by the real-life candy counter. Were these, in fact, the black-and-white cops I had seen in the movie? How did they get from the movie screen to this lobby? Though I was just seven, I knew it troubled no one else, so I was afraid to ask. It was my problem. Sadly, that was the dark side of my love for movies. I was safe from having to ask, because the story in a movie answers its own questions. Questions for me weren't entrees to knowledge or people, or for that matter, to myself. They were evidence of weakness and vulnerability, incompetence and shame. Asking questions might disturb some unknown and delicate balance, generating chaos. Except for questions about how things worked. Things: mechanical contrivances, gear, paraphernalia, tech. Human relationships remained, for me, a picture in motion: the mechanical contrivance of the image.

In fifth grade some hip teacher showed Norman McLaren's *Hen Hop* and *Begone Dull Care*. I discovered the aesthetic equivalent of life in an alternative universe. This was the world of primal visual experience: of pressing on my eyelids and seeing shapes; of flying dreams in which I swooped and soared and steered with my shoulders. McLaren's movies showed me a world familiar as a child. The colours and actions demonstrated the energy of life rather than the likeness of snapshots.

I'm in seventh grade. It was a time of twelve-inch, black-and-white TVs and small movie screens. Women wore girdles and gloves, men wore hats, people who got polio lived out their days in iron lungs, everybody knew their place.

photo: Jeffrey Paull's parents.

Unmarried women were spinsters or old maids, toys were wood, and Raggedy Ann was still the doll of choice in this Time Before Barbie. Movies in colour were just for costume fantasies. I read about Cinerama in a *Popular Mechanics* magazine. Cinerama's three-projector array blended left, centre and right film frames onto a huge, semi-circular screen with seven-track stereophonic sound. The works, sensuously speaking. We are dropping off my freshman sister at her Chicago college when I declare that the family will go to Chicago's Cinerama theatre. And we actually do. The show begins with a small-screen rendition of Méliès' *A Trip to the Moon* (which, in 1953, was trip enough for me) and Lowell Thomas' voice-o'-God short history of film. Then the drapes open up the rest of the screen with, "Ladies and Gentlemen, this is Cinerama!" and the spectacle and sensation go on forever. We are on a roller coaster, of course. In one year:

1. My sister leaves the house.
2. I have my Bar Mitzvah.
3. I discover sex.
4. This is Cinerama.

I am nearly sixteen when I see Fellini's *La Strada*. I feel a kinship to the lonely and uncomprehending Gelsomina, and I long to emulate the spirited and inspirational tightrope/clown character played by Richard Basehart. I am moved to tears. Tears as a teen? When I was nine, I remember cutting my hand badly. I didn't cry because I wasn't helpless in my own pain. But in *La Strada*, I was able to experience the plight of a character, and their sufferings returned me to my own. I was a step closer to being a man. (It is only a movie.)

When I was seventeen I went with my pals to see *And God Created Woman*. It starred Jean-Louis Trintignant and Brigitte Bardot's ass, as I remember. Back then girdles obscured the crack of American tushes, and 1957 brassieres turned breasts into cones or bullets. Women's bodies were not of this world. But it was possible, in images, to see women's flesh as warm and yielding to the touch. Just as mine was.

I go through a period of making (pre-"super") 8mm high-school/hijinx movies with my friends and family. Unaware I'm acting out a variation of "ontogeny recapitulates phylogeny," I naively do all sorts of Méliès and Griffiths stuff. I mock drama, and attempt slapstick. I have no feel for editing, but my camera's well-placed.

My next image revelation came after I endured the humiliation of flunking out of university, and at the end of my third year, too. I hated school. My sustainment of it represented one thousand days and nights of avoidance and passivity, reflecting weakness of spirit. It took me three years of managing to accomplish very little and just enough until grades forced the issue I couldn't handle on my own. I was still using somebody else's snapshots to evoke my responses.

But now I'm in film school, at university number two. On the first day, Dr. Steel is talking about Marilyn Monroe, who has recently cashed in her chips. Then it hits me: MY HOMEWORK IS GOING TO THE MOVIES. I lean over to Closest Classmate. "Am I in heaven, or what?"

That semester, I discovered that images can have intense spiritual power. The film was Carl Dreyer's *La passion de Jeanne d'Arc*. We were sitting in the basement of a former booze warehouse, and I remember my wonder that I was experiencing this film in my eyes, chest, knees and legs—not my mind. Not my mind. I remember thinking, "I didn't know! I didn't know!"

Dreyer's film is silent, so the movement of its characters and camera are free of the time required for dialogue. Real-life actions, on the other hand, take as long as distance requires. Speechless people in silent movies are de-corporealized just like snapshots; both suggest a world without gravity.

I've seen hour after delicious hour of movies by Fellini, Bailey, Preston Sturges, Deren, Brakhage, on and on. The movie cafeteria is overflowing with choices as I enter Film Production One and make My First Film. My protagonist walks through endlessly empty streets (remember it's 1963) and finally gets crushed in one of those tall, many-spoked, cylindrical subway turnstiles. To Vivaldi. Never, I think, will another movie have to be made, except maybe a comedy. I show it to my class and the teacher says, "Well, if you want to make an experimental film …" Of course I was crushed. I thought I had done the real thing.

Years later I asked one of my teachers how I was accepted in Boston's film school after previously flunking out. Only one answer in my application set me apart from other applicants. The form asked, "Why do you think you should be accepted in our program?" I bet the farm on just one sentence: "I want to make movies. If I don't get in I will die." They decided to take a chance on me, and after becoming a film teacher myself, I've tried to pass that opportunity along to my students.

My sister gave me the gift of being there first, absorbing my parents' desperation during the Great Depression. There was little work for my father as a new lawyer, and mother's classes swelled to thirty-five. Without daycare, our mother had to arrange a place to park Margery each day. Five years later, when I was born, things were less hectic.

My father gave me the gift of working with my hands and fixing things; my mother gave me the gift of a visual imagination. We had an attic, old clothes to do Let's Pretend, mother's eight albums of classical 78s, and art classes on the weekend. But the drawings I made never meant much to me. Only movies and photos, only images of real things or things that moved made my inner mechanisms emote. Movies and stills extended more of the universe in my direction: ritual belonging, spiritual awareness, an expanded sense of compassion, seemingly hot sex, and (to my amazement) a feeling of joy within the bounds of institutional learning. In film school I became aware that a movie was able to evoke a range and depth of emotions in me that didn't happen when the auditorium lights of the world were on. The further away from people I was, the closer I could get. I had yet to deal with the sentimentality and brutishness inside myself.

There was more to come. In 1963 I saw Eisenstein's *Ivan the Terrible*. I was drawn to its construction in ways that evoked a new sort of response, and I wanted to know why. Such a deeply experienced curiosity had never happened before. I eventually realized that I was used to cutting on action, which is a central part of a movie's illusion of "realness." The scenes, people and objects seem to extend beyond the space of the screen, and have a life independent of the composition. Everything is still there after the cut.

This is not so, however, with parts of Eistenstein's *Ivan the Terrible*. Cutting on action accents the physical forces of the bodies that act. Eisenstein resolved actions inside shots, which left the image de-corporealized, echoing the loss of physicality in a still photo. The kinetically dramatic aspects of the actors were resolved in each shot, and only then would Eisenstein go on to the next. This technique had a couple of effects. The actions themselves seemed realistic, but the shot-to-shot linking wasn't. Time was no longer fluid, but experienced as droplets, discrete elements, mosaic elements. Running your eyes over the length of *Ivan* is like running your fingers over the surface of a Byzantine church mosaic. Temporally, Eisenstein's isolation of motions does what Byzantine church mosaics do spatially. Each image is likened to its physical-world counterpart through metaphor, rather then a necessarily specious resemblance.

And herein lies the idea that has excited me since I saw *Ivan* eighteen or so years ago. I discovered that Time (*Ivan*) and Space (Byzantine paintings and mosaics) are interchangeable. Everyday experience of a time-space continuum has something in common with the seemingly arcane relativity of Einstein and sub-atomic physics. My imagination is taken with implications and fantasies about that. Still images and movies, in fact all gesture and poses, have equivalencies in other forms.

The following semester I make another film. No more experimental films! Now for the Real Thing. I want to make a film about people and feelings. A film about love. I am pleased with how it comes out. The film is about a young couple. He's a student (what else?) and she's pregnant. His studies mean he doesn't have much time for her, and her increasing size makes her self-conscious and lonely. After a playful opening of the couple in bed, and a semi-erotic bread-making sequence, the couple reunite at dinner and resolve nothing. End of movie.

Years later I'm visiting a friend who has showed that film each year in his classes. I hadn't seen it during this time. We're walking down the hall when he says, "Your problem is you fall in love with your friends' wives, and instead of making love to them, you make movies about them." My feet froze to the floor, and the breath of words froze in my mouth. What was, for Ron, an off-handed remark, and an obvious truth, was too dangerous for me to acknowledge all these years. And I thought I was getting somewhere.

I have a picture of my parents on top of the TV. It was taken before they were married, which is about ten years before I would have been old enough to "know" them. It's a long shot of them standing in a field. My mom wears a long skirt and short-sleeved sweater; you can see a large blouse collar framing her neck. Her right arm is partly lifted as she grasps my father's hand, which is around her waist. Her stance and smile are confident; her strong Russian jaw frames her deep-set eyes.

Many years later I'm leaving a live theatre production here in Toronto. I've enjoyed myself immensely and wonder, "Why don't I go to plays more often?" I had been going to movies a lot, but rarely to plays. I pictured myself watching a movie and then a play, imagining back and forth, and realized that live theatre makes me subtly anxious in a way that a movie doesn't. When one watches movies, one is always watching the past. Live theatre, of course, only happens in the present, so the next moment, and all the moments after, are beyond the control of history. Images are safe because they've already happened: they're no longer attached to chance, sudden changes at the last moment, the moment of death in the middle of life.

My dad is a pile of black hair and mustache, full dark lips and alert eyes. His other hand is in his trouser pocket. He wears braces and a tie, and stands ready with his legs apart. Both he and my mother look like fun, ready to go, attached to each other, bright and confident. It is a dream photo of parents. I never knew these people, even though we lived in the same pleasant, well-meaning, upper-middle-class home until I went away to college. We all meant well to each other.

When I was fourteen, we lived three blocks away from the only movie theatre in Cleveland that showed British movies: Alec Guiness, Dennis Price, Glynis Johns, Valerie Hobson, Alistair Sim. One night, a man sitting next to me put his hand gently on my thigh. The complex emotions that generated in me would take years to untangle. The image could touch back.

THE SPY WHO KNEW TOO MUCH

by Richard Kerr

photo: Hoffman and Kerr.
Cinecycle 1993. by John
Porter.

CONFESSION

I have known Philip Hoffman for more than thirty years. We used to travel together, play hockey, make pictures. An old friendship demands loyalty and discretion, a respect for the line between the stories only the two of you can share, and those fit for print. Phil is an autobiographer; that is his muse, his stock-in-trade. Rarely has someone's life and work been so interchangeable: his life is his material, and any pulling back the curtains or insider exposé might threaten this project.

In place of hyper-biography I've relied on exchange and process, a terrain that, as practitioners, we are both comfortable with. We wanted to keep it on the lighter side—there's enough angst in our work after all—and rely on a faux interview dialogue. I wanted to touch on the broad strokes that lay at the heart of Phil's work and process. More importantly, I wanted to know what he is thinking these days in order to reflect on the consistencies and changes in his thinking over the years. This dialogue is necessarily incomplete. What is said is important, but what is left unspoken is more important. That is the way these old friends would have it.

QUESTIONNAIRE

RK: What is your idea of perfect happiness?
PH: It changes daily.

RK: What is your greatest fear?
PH: Hospitals (in Ontario).
Lightning (everywhere else).

RK: What is your greatest extravagance?
PH: 400-foot loads of Double-X negative.

RK: What is your favourite journey?
PH: Inner. It's cheap, fast and out of control.

RK: What do you consider the most overrated virtue?
PH: Confidence.

RK: What is your current state of mind?
PH: It changes as I write.

RK: What do you consider your greatest achievement?
PH: Most Gentlemanly Player, Waterloo Siskins, 1974.

RK: What do you regard as the lowest depth of misery?
PH: Imprisoned in your own life.

RK: What quality do you most like in a man?
PH: Emotion.

RK: What quality do you most like in a woman?
PH: Muscle.

RK: How would you like to die?
PH: At home.

RK: What is your motto?
PH: It changes.

CORRESPONDENCE
August 31, 2000

Hi Richard,

It seemed as Monday morning rolled around there were just too many pressures with J's family
visit outside of Montreal, and the little girl's needs (you know all about that, kids are new for me).
Anyway, it seemed too much. I'm very moved that you are contributing to this book because in
my mind, you are my brother. Our drifting apart was quite painful for me, so your gestures to
reconnect are touching. I want to do the same and am really sorry our meeting didn't work out.

Phil

CONTEXT
In the mid-1970s, when Phil was gearing up the grand project of autobiography as
his life's work, the times were less than encouraging. Especially for a middle-class
white male. And there was a considerable canon of experimentalists who had
forged significant works of cinematic autobiography. Marie Menken, Jonas Mekas,
Stan Brakhage and Robert Frank come to mind, but you can make your own list.
This received history can be heavy for a young maker trying to sort it all out.

The mid-70s also marked a sea change from modernism to postmodernism,
with its libraries of cultural theory and prescriptions of political correctness. It was

uncool, if not politically dangerous, to reflect on the self. These pressures of influence could easily have led a young filmmaker away from his muse. But Phil's clear thinking and thoroughness, his wait-and-watch style and deliberateness, separated him from the rest of us. Day-to-day discipline created his body of work. As Yogi Berra put it, "You can observe a lot just by watching."

MEMORIES THAT WON'T BE MADE INTO FILMS

Teenaged Phil alone in his room, listening to Dylan while family life reverberates around him.

Walking on water wasn't built in a day.
Jack Kerouac

Phil always looked like his father. He was the youngest, with triplet sisters, but he was always the man around the house, possessed of an early quiet confidence and responsibility.

There is no decisive moment. It's got to be created. I've got to do everything to make it happen in front of the lens.
Robert Frank

Phil was small, wiry, strong and tough. He got bigger every year. He was a natural athlete, competitive but clean, and he never backed down. Phil was a crafty pool player, a game he sharpened in the basement with his pool-shark uncle Wally. The darkroom was next door.

I'll play it first and tell you what it is later.
Miles Davis

Things happened fast once we built our first darkroom. Enterprise and imagination. Dylan sings, "You go your way, and I'll go mine."

No poet, no artist of any art has complete meaning alone. His significance, his appreciation, is the appreciation of his relation to the dead poets and artists.
T.S. Eliot

Young Phil at his lake a.k.a. *On the Pond* (1978). Another classic setting in the young man's life. I always imagined he did his big thinking there. The river served a different purpose …

Ideas are one thing and what happens is another.
John Cage

On the banks of the Saugeen River, eighteen-year-old Phil guts a brook trout. Every year the same scene on a different river: Quebec, Nova Scotia, Newfoundland, Alberta … but never Saskatchewan. I lived in Regina for fifteen years. Final note about fishing: I suspect Phil enjoyed fishing by himself, as opposed to in groups. Too much bonding in a boat will drive a young man to the river.

It is a mistake for an artist to speak too often about their job. It releases the tension needed for work.
Jemina Knowles

Phil Hoffman's father is proud of his son. I saw that look in his eye thirty years ago, on the (backyard) pond. I saw it again fifteen years later at the Toronto debut of *passing through/torn formations* (1988). I hope to see that look one more time before I go.

I never heard much about Phil's days in his father's meat-packing plant; they were overshadowed by his father's stories which were fantastical. His roots were German, hardworking, filled with personal sacrifice and just rewards. But it was always clear that the son would go his own way. Solo is vertical. The Hoffman team has the most refined sense of father and son I can imagine.

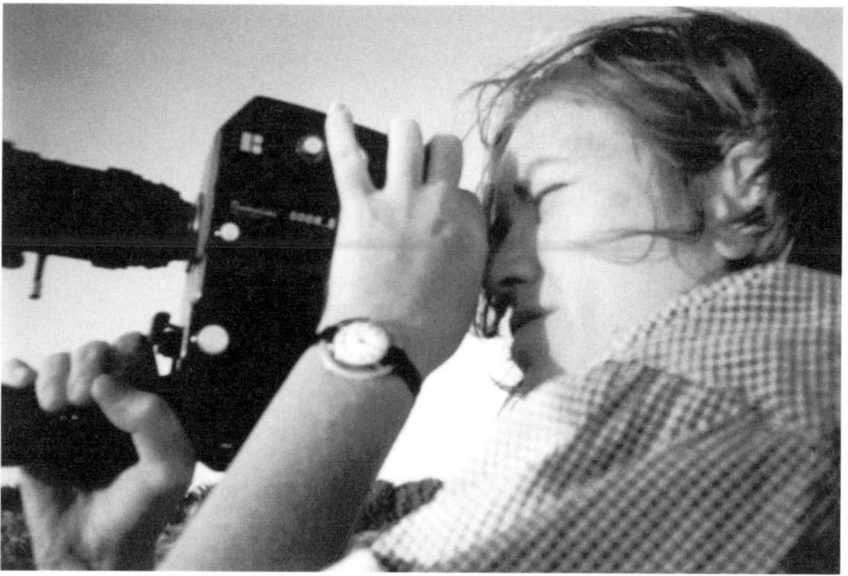

I always say keep a diary and someday it will keep you.
Mae West

There was always cold beer, reefer and a loaded camera on the road trips. But Phil was the only one who could fix a flat tire in the middle of the night.

I write for myself and strangers … The strangers, dear reader, are an afterthought.
Gertrude Stein

The more Phil travels, the more verbal he becomes. He may be the best life observer I know. We took some important research and development trips together. In 1976 we drove to the Allan Ginsberg archives via Ginsberg's New York apartment—a good story, but I've forgotten too much to tell it properly. Phil would be able to, though. Four years later we drove east to find Robert Frank in Mabou, chronicled in *The Road Ended at the Beach* (1983). We took a sci-fi-type journey to Love Canal. Countless rages into the night that I can barely remember. Once again, Phil's memory is better than mine … of the details, at least.

I know with certainty that a man's work is nothing but the longing to recover, through the detours of art, the two or three simple and great images which gained access to his heart.
Albert Camus

In the restless years between high school and university, Phil looks for the way through. We stay tuned in. One day, he shows up at Sheridan College. Things happen fast again. We are living our movies. Here are the first signs of Phil as an image and sound collector, so organized and methodical. His obsessive work patterns are already established: a life of consistent film creation lies ahead.

All art is a more or less oblique confession. All artists, if they are to survive, are forced to tell the whole story, to vomit up the anguish.
James Baldwin

Before photography: many nights out with Phil where nothing is said but much is seen. After photography: even less is said, but pictures are taken, sound recorded. We are pecking, hunting and gathering. Process is process, but where are the negatives? It was never about copyright, but archive. Memory counts. Phil taught me that.

Marian comes to my wedding in Toronto. It becomes a late afternoon lawn party. As a jet passes overhead, I say it's Phil on his way to Holland and Greenaway's zoo. We smile.

We teach together at Sheridan College, huge hours, the beginnings of our second careers. We are dragged into our first academic mutiny, always learning on the job. Today we're still teaching, keepers of some sort of flame.

There are a few industry freelance ventures, promos for Women's College Hospital. I direct, Phil shoots, the piece wins awards, good start! Kevin Sullivan's first effort, *Krieghoff*, is really Phil's story, maybe one of his best. I often wonder if he tells his students about his freelance days. There was a Parachute Club video called *Sexual Intelligence*, good work if you could get it.

The moment you cheat for the sake of beauty, you know you're an artist.
Max Jacob

I moved to Saskatchewan to take a teaching job after Phil turned it down. Phil referred me, I made a cold call, and once again it all worked out. Phil and I weren't seeing much of each other by then, both trying to look after our separate lives.

Personal history (autobiography) is an effort to find salvation, to make one's own experience come out right.
Alfred Kazin

In Saskatchewan I sit with my young family glued to CBC watching the Genies. Phil is up for Best Documentary with *?O,Zoo!* (1986) He wears his comfortable brown cardigan. He has a winner's look.

Autobiography provides insurance against oblivion. But without publicity, oblivion endures. I believe that all careers end in failure, that each of us manages a certain coherence manifest in a particular work, and granted by personality, hard work and luck. But after that moment, our later years are spent in decline. If we are fortunate, we are able to coast with dignity. Life is diamond shaped. In the beginning, opportunities expand: later they contract. Unfortunately, none of us knows where the widest point of the diamond resides until we've already passed it. The big bang theory of careers? This contracting might not be as negative as it appears, because one may retreat from career into home life, perhaps to take care of elders or make gardens. But perhaps there are several diamonds expanding and contracting at different times in your life. Like those party hats you get as a kid, excited to find that as you unfold them, each one is connected to the other, and they go on and on, forever.

SOMEWHERE BETWEEN

by Jeremy Rigsby

Travelogues are films made by tourists. They are defined by their creators' decision to remain on unfamiliar terms with unfamiliar surroundings. These are not documentaries, which presume or strive for some unmediated relation to their subjects. Unless documentaries can demonstrate that they are provisional and selective, they are prone to be mistaken for truth. Unless travelogues can demonstrate that they are art, they are largely the product of hobbyists who can afford vacations. Travelogues may affirm their artfulness by appealing to an aesthetic derived from the lyrical avant-garde, or more frequently, by adopting the discursive strategies of fictional films. *Somewhere Between Jalostotitlan and Encarnacion* (1984) takes the latter route, all the way to a Mexican crossroads of the real and the imaginary.

The fictive convention relied upon by *Somewhere Between* establishes an artificial contiguity between the film's two discrete components: intertitles and images (mostly of Mexico). This convention is associative editing, a neat version of the so-called Kuleshov effect, whereby details noted in the intertitles are presumed to refer to the images they immediately follow or anticipate by the simple virtue of proximity. The dead youth, for example, is nowhere seen or implied in any of the footage. The titles state that Hoffman "put the camera down." But the cop car that speeds by the boy's corpse must be the very one just seen passing the Coke billboard. Likewise, the beggar girl who is conceded a peso is identified as the beggar girl who then appears. And the girl with the big eyes awaiting her dead brother? There she is, her presence lingering by symbolic association with the image of a snail. Much of the film's remaining footage is neutral and irrelevant to the text, but marshalled to support a funereal aura through melancholy slow motion or sepulchral, greenish-black tints.

That the film's apparent coherence of text and image is a construction of cinematic artifice should be obvious, but the film condescends to underline the point. The soundtrack, a plaintive sax solo, twice jars incongruously with footage of musicians playing visibly different tunes—prompting suspicion of any simple

congruence between real events and their remains on screen. And in a sequence quite exceeding the credulity that associative editing might sustain, a funeral procession plods down conspicuously non-Mexican (i.e., Toronto's) streets, a near-parodic intrusion that must be rationalized as a metaphorical digression on the universality of death, or some such thing. All these contrivances and retractions cumulate in a film whose reliability as documentation is severely undermined by its imperative to simulate fiction. *Somewhere Between* thus exploits a special tension inherent to the travelogue as a genre. Conventions that would affirm the continuity of narrative films, or the veracity of documentaries, are here destabilized, indeterminate, somewhere between … where, exactly?

Clearly not the poles of the debate on the film's ethics, which aroused controversy when *Somewhere Between* was first exhibited in 1984. The film's supporters regarded the omission of the child's dead body as a noble refusal of spectacular and exploitative documentary practices. The detractors, conventional "journalistic" documentarians, considered the film irredeemably deprived of the potential impact conferred by such a powerful image.

Both these arguments assume the film's images support the text and signify only the conclusive absence it describes. But the latter position does implicitly contain a more incisive interpretation: footage of the accident or its aftermath would confirm that it actually happened. This shopworn raison d'être of the journalistic documentary finds application here; an appeal to evidence validates the skepticism this film seems designed to provoke. Its issues aren't ethical, but ontological. Did the dead youth exist, or did Hoffman invent him? Given the film's lack of positive evidence, coupled with its protracted insistence that it be acknowledged as a synthetic construction, the question remains. There are two plausible answers. In the first instance, Hoffman sifts through a large amount of Mexican vacation footage to find a few shots that, by chance, contain imagery similar to details he recalled of the accident and to the text he wrote to describe it. Or he returned from Mexico with a relatively small amount of attractive but disparate, mismatched footage, which he united into coherent form by fabricating the accident as a kind of plot device.

Occam's razor might suggest the second option, but that's not the rub. As film critic Rita Gonzàlez writes:

> … international filmmakers have been drawn to the notion
> of Mexico as a transgressive or mythic space, an eidolon
> that they have done their part to perpetuate.

As the avant-garde film canon attests, south of the border has been a popular destination for filmmaking tourists, the special condition of their alienation in Mexico circumscribed by this imperative to solicit visionary experience. The roster of sojourners includes Bruce Baillie, Bruce Conner, Richard Myers and Chick Strand, who made most of her career around Guadalajara and once confidently declared that "Mexico is surrealism." The Mexican travelogue is almost always these filmmakers' projected phantasmata. The "reality" of the death in *Somewhere Between* is akin to the "reality" of, say, the quintessentially Mexican peyote hallucinations in Larry Jordan's *Triptych in Four Parts*: as real as permitted by illusory circumstances. The virtue of *Somewhere Between* is to be conscious of its complicity in this tradition of cultural mystification. It inspires and permits doubt. It doubts the authenticity of the particular experience it describes, the authenticity of Mexico as an experience of the "mythic," and perhaps ultimately the authenticity of experience in general. Typical of the traveler's tale is a tendency to embellish. Rarely is one so evocative, or so obliging, of the tendency to disbelieve its teller.

WORKS CITED

Gonzàlez, Rita.
"The Mexperimental Cinema." *The Mexperimental Cinema*. Guggenheim Museum: 1999.
n. pag.

LETTER

by Peter Greenaway

January 24, 1984

Monique Belanger
Arts Awards Service
Canada Council, Ottawa

Dear Ms. Belanger,

I met Phil Hoffman at the 1984 Grierson Seminar. His films were a breath of fresh air amidst so much conventional material. His films blithely side stepped the orthodoxies so taken for granted by those who believe documentary cinema is an educational rostrum, is about questions of balance, is essentially a dissertation on something described as "truth." Meeting him in the context of his films backed up my impressions of his aims and abilities. His work is an encouragement to those who want to use autobiography as subject matter, personal vision as a trademark, and show how small resources can be a positive virtue.

It was Phil's suggestion in London several months later that he would like to be some sort of witness to the feature production of the film *Zed & Two Noughts* in Rotterdam in the spring of this year—which I am certainly agreeable to—though I will not hide the fact that I believe, as a filmmaker with a personal vision, he is well past the apprenticeship stage. What he needs now is opportunities, encouragement and experience. Since his method is to work with a camera as a constant companion, I would wish he could be encouraged to make a modest film whilst he is in Rotterdam and London, certainly to be encouraged to shoot some two or three thousand feet of 16mm. The desirability of his presenting a script before hand, as far as I can see, is not necessary, considering his work method. In fact, I think it ought to be a condition of his association with the *Zed & Two Noughts* project that he shoot on his own on any subject whatsoever.

Most of the relevant detail of the production of *Zed & Two Noughts* Phil has already mentioned. It is perhaps not so strange a co-production, as seen from a British point of view, but nonetheless will present a nicely complex mixture of finance, production, cast and crew that aptly mirrors the complexity of the film's structure and content—the ambivalent diversity of species and purpose—of beasts and men—both sides of the cages in a zoo. Phil has volunteered not just to stand by and observe but to offer practical help which will always be useful on such a modestly budgeted, ambitious film.

If he (and you) believe that he (and you) can profit by his experience with the production, then I am certainly happy to invite him. If there is anything else you would like to know, I am sure I can help, though I would be obliged, as I am sure you would understand, to keep bureaucracy to a minimum. The production of a feature film is very time-consuming and demanding.

Here's hoping that you can agree to Phil's participation.

Yours sincerely,

Peter Greenaway

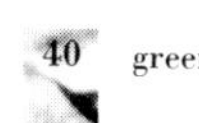

DECEPTION AND ETHICS IN ?O,ZOO!
(THE MAKING OF A FICTION FILM)

by Michael Zryd

still: above, "That old battle-
axe" *?O,Zoo!*.

My thanks to Karyn Sandlos
for her excellent editorial
work on this essay.
Michael Zryd

L̲ike all "anti-documentary" films—those that call into question the documentary genre's easy claims to epistemological certainty—Phil Hoffman's *?O,Zoo!
(The Making of a Fiction Film)* (1986) must be approached in terms of the particular documentary form it questions and the particular context of its maker and
making. In *?O,Zoo!* Hoffman plays off the filmic projects of John Grierson and
Peter Greenaway to furnish an admirably tentative meditation on two knotted ethical problems of film form. One concerns the way that sound/image constructions
attempt to dictate meaning in conventional documentary. The second takes on
film's photographic claims to certainty in one of documentary's favourite subjects:
the representation of death. These intersecting planes of subjectivity and convention, and these ethical meditations, create a turbulence underneath the disarming-
ly simple and elegant surface of *?O,Zoo!*, a turbulence that accounts for the emotional resonance of its ending(s), and for its troubling aftertaste.

FOUNDING FATHERS

?O,Zoo! is, in some ways, atypical of Hoffman's work, being his most directly analytical examination of a set of film conventions. In films like *On the Pond* (1978)
and *passing through/torn formations* (1988), a much more meditative and lyrical
mix of image, sound, and narration offers an intensely personal view of childhood
and family. *Somewhere Between Jalostotitlan and Encarnacion* (1984) deals with
Hoffman's reaction to an isolated incident in Mexico: the death of a small boy in
the street. *The Road Ended at the Beach* (1983) is a diary-quest that follows
Hoffman and some friends "in search of the Beat generation" as they trek across
eastern Canada to find Robert Frank. All these films share an explicit personal
voice (either in voice-over or written text), a voice by turns matter-of-fact, self-
ironic, or poeticized (here, often with less certain success), but always direct and
Hoffman's own.

Robert Frank's influence is central to the development of Hoffman's sensibility. Aware of the filters the apparatus imposes between film and experience, the filmmaker seeks direct contact with his subjects. With Frank, Hoffman shares a concern for the articulation of the filmmaker's subjectivity and for the camera's power to record and reveal events. Unlike Frank, however, Hoffman's approach is tentative; as Blaine Allan puts it, Hoffman places himself "on the temporal and spatial edges of an event" (91). In *The Road Ended at the Beach*, Hoffman ironizes the Frank persona to point, finally, to the folly of attempting to recapture the immediacy of the Beat generation's attitude to "experience." When he finally finds Frank in Nova Scotia, Hoffman is told, in a low key (and utter) deflation of his quest, that Kerouac is dead, the Beat generation is over, go home.

If *The Road Ended at the Beach* can be seen as Hoffman's attempt to exorcise the ghost of Robert Frank, *?O,Zoo!* finds him tackling two more figures of influence: John Grierson and Peter Greenaway. In *?O,Zoo!*, they are paired as the Founding Father and the Grand Inquisitor of the institutional documentary. Hoffman links the two unmistakably, though not explicitly, in a passage in the first sequence of the film:

> That spring, I went to the Netherlands to make a short film
> around the making of a fiction film. I met the director in a
> seminar in my native country in the fall before my grandfa-
> ther's footage was found. This seminar, an annual tradition
> since 1939, is devoted to the documentation and catego-
> rization of all types of wildlife species ever captured on
> film. The seminar grew out of the same institution that
> employed my grandfather as a newsreel cameraman. I can
> still hear my grandfather's remarks about the founder of
> the institution, as he put it, "that old battle-axe."

The "fiction film" is *A Zed & Two Noughts* (1985); the director, Greenaway. Hoffman and Greenaway met at the 1984 Grierson Documentary Seminar held in Brockville, Ontario. The seminar that year, entitled "Systems in Collapse," was devoted to the anti-documentary. The seminar began after Grierson's death and within the fiction of *?O,Zoo!*'s first sequence, Hoffman conflates the seminar with the National Film Board (NFB), founded by Grierson in 1939. "That old battle-axe" is an appropri-ate description of the mythical, crusty Scotch Calvinist; to underscore the point, the phrase appears over a close-up of an ostrich's head. The physical similarity to Grierson is striking.

Grierson hovers as a key figure behind both the Canadian and British docu-mentary traditions, and is thus a point of departure for both Hoffman and Greenaway. Grierson's unique legacy as film director and administrator of openly propagandistic film products in the service of the state makes the "Griersonian" mode of documentary a particularly acute model of what Noël Burch calls an "Institutional Mode of Representation" (1979). Certainly, one can identify an NFB house style, with as many stylistic tics as any Hollywood studio study could muster. Greenaway worked for eight years in the British equivalent of the NFB, the Office of Information. During that time, he produced what he called "soft-core propaganda" (qtd. in Della Penna and Shedden 20) before turning to experimental and narrative-fiction modes of filmmaking. Especially in his hyperbolically parodic anti-documentaries, *The Falls* (1980) and *Vertical Features Remake* (1979), Greenaway works to great advantage off the solidity and recognizability of the government-issue documentary. Systematic in their astonishing mimicry of form and profound in their analysis of the technocratic ideology at the base of Grierson's form, Greenaway's films initiate a full-frontal assault on the Griersonian institutional mode.

Hoffman's confrontation with the Grierson mould and myth and with Greenaway's analytic project is oblique, even affectionate. *?O,Zoo!* adapts the central formal device of Greenaway's critique—a coherent voice-over ordering disparate images to create a hermetic, non-referential fictional universe—to the rhetorical traditions of the narrated, personal diary-film of the independent filmmaker. The fiction of the grandfather frames Hoffman's own penetration of Greenaway's narrative film production, less to satirize Greenaway than to harness the skeptical dynamic of Greenaway's voice-over/image relation.[1] While the extreme artifice characteristic of Greenaway's later cinema is concentrated in his elaborate visual tableaux, in earlier films Greenaway's artifice is concentrated in the complex counterpoint between his soundtrack (Colin Cantlie's voiceover narration and Michael Nyman's music) and "documentary" imagery. Hoffman mobilizes Greenaway's counterpoint, but refuses to capitulate his filmic world entirely to fiction; instead, Hoffman keeps his meditation on events focused on what he calls "lived experiences."

Sound Models

In *The Creative Use of Sound* (1933) Grierson outlines his defence of the freedom and power of sound. Clearly inspired by the 1929 *Statement on Sound* co-signed by Eisenstein, Pudovkin, and Alexandrov, Grierson insists, like the Soviets, that "the final question is how we are to use sound creatively rather than reproductively" (158). Yet, though he maintains the mobility of the sound-montage piece, Grierson prescribes a limit to the possibilities of asynchronous sound:

> Our rule should be to have the mute strip and the sound complementary to each other, helping each other along.

1. In one delicious sequence, Hoffman ironizes Greenaway's move to big-budget feature filmmaking. While Greenaway's crew makes futile attempts to corral a flock of flamingos, Hoffman simply sets up a feed bucket in front of his Bolex. A flamingo approaches and he gets the shot; personal control of the apparatus has its rewards.

That is what Pudovkin meant when he talks about
asynchronous sound. (159)

By invoking Pudovkin instead of Eisenstein, Grierson demonstrates his preference for linear coherence at the expense of a dialectical approach that would expose contradiction. In this respect, when Grierson calls for art to be a "hammer" (qtd. in Morris 41), he is far from Eisenstein's "kino-fist."

Complementary sound/image relations serve the production of coherent, stable meanings in filmic text. Later in his essay, when Grierson speaks of the use of a "chorus", he says it must be in the service of unity: "By the chorus, characters are brought together and a single mood permeates a whole location" (160). Interestingly, he notes of the "recitative chorus" that "the very crudest form of this is the commentary you find ordinarily attached to 'interest' films" (161).[2] Yet even if Grierson favours, at this early point in the 1930s, a voice-over narration "which adds dramatic or poetic colour to the action" (161), that "colour" must not in any way create conflict. Rather, it must enhance meaning. As he says of the general desired effect of the propaganda film, the voiceover should "inspire confidence," not present "problems" (Morris 45). Grierson's dislike of Humphrey Jennings' WWII films demonstrates how the "creative use of sound" must not be in any way disturbing. Moreover, the dominance of the "recititive chorus" in Canadian WWII documentaries made under Grierson's command demonstrates how the route of least resistance to a strong propaganda message is through "authoritative narration" (Elder 157).[3]

The complementary voice-over/image relation is the bedrock of the institutional documentary. The image track is arranged to illustrate the narrator's descriptions, and the indexical power of the photographic image is harnessed to the rhetoric of the soundtrack. Referential authority is thus placed in the service of an authoritative voice-over narrator, usually male, whose vocal performance is coded by standardized diction, pacing, clarity of tone and coherence. Greenaway's mimicry of this convention is superlative. In *Vertical Features Remake*, Colin Cantlie's "BBC voice" explains the attempts of the "Institute for Restoration and Reclamation" to reconstruct a film by a "Tulse Luper." As names and places appear on the soundtrack, photographs, drawings and moving images appear on the image track to illustrate the often convoluted but always self-assured narration. The insistence of the illustration is key to the satire; the film cuts to the same photograph of Tulse Luper no fewer than twenty-three times.

Hoffman's clearest appropriation of Greenaway's method of constructing a fiction in fake documentary form appears in the opening sequence of *?O,Zoo!* Instead of attacking the authority of the institutional narrator (Greenaway's target), Hoffman undermines a different set of conventions: those surrounding the author-

2. "Interest" films refer to educational and industrial lecture films of the 1920s, from which Grierson was at pains to distinguish his "true" documentaries.

3. Kathryn Elder describes the "recurrent features" of the Canadian WWII propaganda films:
" ... authoritative narration, rapid cutting, and close alliance of image and text: features that today can be easily identified as NFB trademarks" (157).

ity of the filmmaker-narrator of the personal diary film. Interestingly, *?O,Zoo!* is the only early film of Hoffman's where he does not read his own narration. Reminiscent of Hollis Frampton's (*nostalgia*) (1971), where Frampton has Michael Snow read the voice-over of his most obviously "autobiographical" film, Hoffman puts himself at one remove from the "revelations" contained in *?O,Zoo!*.

SOUND-IMAGE RELATIONS AND FAKE FRAMING

The film opens in silence on a lion roaring—a joke on the MGM lion announcing the beginning of another, more familiar kind of fiction film. The image is sepia-toned (as will be all the images of this sequence), connoting age. The silence is broken by the voice of the male narrator:

> The footage was found by my sister in my grandfather's loft.
> Having been at one time a newsreel cameraman, grandfa-
> ther knew to keep the canister well sealed, and since the
> loft was relatively cool and dry, there was no noticeable
> deterioration.

The voice is flat and deliberate, not a BBC voice but a voice appropriate to a personal diary film. This explanation of the image's integrity and lack of deterioration makes reference to the filmmaking process, while bringing the viewer into the confidence of the voice-over. The narrator assumes we know that a cool, dry loft and a well-sealed canister will prevent a film from deteriorating. The immediate wedding of image and voice-over, the personal tone, and the reflexive explanations attempt to pull us into the film, which is itself consistently set against the institutional film:

> I recalled seeing my grandfather's old newsreels. There
> was a marked difference between the repetitive nature of
> the news film and the footage found in the loft.

If Hoffman differentiates the "voice" of the institutional newsreel from that of the personal diarist, he also invokes his own tradition: Canadian experimental filmmaking. One shot of the stock footage Hoffman uses had already been incorporated by experimental filmmaker David Rimmer into his film *Watching for the Queen* (1973). The allusion is at first proleptic of the levels of intertextuality in the film, as Grierson, Greenaway, Vermeer and a variety of structural film tropes make "appearances" in *?O,Zoo!* More specifically, the allusion refers to the tradition of Canadian experimental filmmaking that interrogates the photographic image. Rimmer, for example, often uses stock footage to study image degradation through

looping, so Hoffman's term "repetitive" is apt. When Hoffman later implies that
the NFB is an organization devoted to the filming of wildlife, he alludes both to
Greenaway's obsessive filming of animals (and the setting of *A Zed & Two Noughts*
in a zoo) and to the stereotypical NFB nature documentary. The inversion is here
complete: within the fiction, the "personal" images of the grandfather are linked,
by subject, to the institution of the NFB. Meanwhile, the stock institutional images
of the public event allude to the independent experimental tradition.

Another important method of cinematic critique in *?O,Zoo!* is the use of
direct address to set reflexive traps for the spectator. In the next section, the narrator directly addresses the viewer in the imperative:

> There was something peculiar about grandfather's footage.
> Watch. Wait for the flash marking the beginning of the shot
> and then start counting.

Once again, the direct address underlines the reflexivity of the film by acknowledging our presence as spectators, underscoring its apparent honesty and transparency—even as it more forcefully tells us how to interpret the images (there is
something "peculiar" to watch for). But the voice-over tricks us. After the flash,
the narrator falls silent for about twenty seconds over a close up of a camel rhyth-
mically chewing. Following the narrator's orders, we begin to count and fall into
sync with the camel's chewing. But as the shot proceeds, the chewing gets more
and more erratic and our counting struggles to keep its own pace. Finally, the
voice-over returns to rescue the viewer and explain the "peculiarity":

> Most of the shots are exactly twenty-eight seconds in length.

Instructed to count, we are defeated by the rhythm of the image. The narrator's
knowledge further points to our failure:

> I was impressed with both the precision and self-control
> my grandfather expressed in shooting this unusual material
> as compared with the erratic camera work displayed in
> the newsreels.

"Precision and self-control" are qualities of the text and its "maker," but not of
the viewer. Moreover, the "self-control" is an arbitrary limit set by the apparatus;
Hoffman's camera is a spring-wound Bolex, whose full shot length is twenty-eight
seconds at twenty-four frames per second.

In addition to direct address, *?O,Zoo!*'s voice-over plays with codes of documentary evidence, specifically with one of the most banal elements of the camera

person's trade: camera logs. *?O,Zoo!* takes this elementary "document" and uses it to critique Grierson's technocratic logic of classification. The narrator suggests the following:

> More clues as to the nature of my grandfather's discipline
> were found on a slip of paper secreted in the film canisters.

After the shots of the camel, the film cuts to a close-up of a piece of paper entitled "Camera Negative Report Card," dated 6/6/45, with neat, legible printing listing six shots all under the heading "Day 17": "Lion", "Elephant slo-mo", "Fallen Elephant tries to get up", "Elephant gets up", "Camel Chewing" and "Insert Humps." Here is another piece of the film apparatus exposed—and if we read quickly enough, we can see that the shot list supports what we've been seeing. But questions arise: if this is a slip of paper the contemporary narrator has found, why would it be filmed with the same sepia tone as the grandfather's footage? The characteristics of different documents (paper and film) begin to collapse into one another.

Later in the film, we see that the contemporary filmmaker also uses these cards to chart the progress of his Holland diary, following in the family line, it seems. But here, too, the very neatness of the "documents" indicates that they are fictional constructions—not a log representing the process of filmmaking, but a later construction caught in the false, hermetic package of the fiction. All the shots listed on the grandfather's cards appear in *?O,Zoo!* (unless the film has a 1:1 shooting ratio, the report sheets must be reconstructions), and both the grandfather's and the filmmaker's cards list "S. Munger" as cameraman (explicable by continuity of family name, but improbable). Finally, later in the diary, we see the right-hand part of the grandfather's card from the first sequence, now dated 6/6/85, as a hand tapes a second card to it and writes "Day 17." This notation completes, in a sense, the missing left side of the grandfather's card (also Day 17). It would seem that even off-screen space can be recaptured by the hermetic bounds of the fiction-film frame.

Next, the long passage explaining the "making of a short film around the making of a fiction film" establishes *?O,Zoo!*'s link to Greenaway and Grierson:

> The footage was found in the winter. That spring, I went to the Netherlands to make a short film around the making of a fiction film. I met the director in a seminar in my native country in the fall before my grandfather's footage was found. This seminar, an annual tradition since 1939, is devoted to the documentation and categorization of all types of wildlife species ever captured on film. The seminar grew out of the same institution that employed my grandfather as a newsreel cameraman. I can still hear my grandfather's remarks about the founder of the institution, as he put it, "that old battle-axe."

This passage appears over shots of animals (a seal, peacocks, an ostrich), images which reinforce the grandfather's employment with the institution dedicated to wildlife photography. The phrase "documentation and categorization" alludes to Greenaway's obsession with classification and naming—that technocratic rage to impose order laid bare in Greenaway's films by the hyperbolic application of that rage. Though the allusion is no more than a nod to Greenaway's project, through recognizing their shared heritage in Grierson, Hoffman acknowledges the ideological implications underlying how documentary convention orders experience—and the subversive nature of any questioning of that ordering.

After the close-up of the ostrich and the narrator's statement "I can still hear my grandfather's remarks," the film cuts to a slow-motion shot of what seems to be the shadow of two gorillas. The gorilla is a Darwinian "founding father," and it turns out that the shadows of what appear to be two gorillas are in fact those of a single gorilla and the filmmaker. Once again, in the spirit of Greenaway, Hoffman slyly undercuts claims to cultural authority. On the soundtrack, we hear a mechanical whirring, then an old man's voice fighting through static and muted sound:

> That old battle-axe! What the hell does he know about this

country anyway? All he knows about [sound unclear here]
is whoring about in crammed-up pubs!

The narrator presents another piece of documentation, apparently a tape recording of the grandfather's voice (the voice explains the whirring as a tape recorder
rewinding), literalizing the idiom, "I can still hear him say ..." What the narrator
hears in his mind can be conjured for the film. The question "What does he know
about this country anyway?" refers to Grierson's status as a foreigner to Canada
and underlines one of the central ironies of the NFB: an institution designed "to
show Canada to Canadians" was founded by a Scotsman. The last line of the
"recording" is ambiguous, a false "rough edge" attesting to its status as "document."

The tape recording introduces a new element into the soundtrack besides
the narrator's voice. The next image, of a gorilla cage beside a spinning water
sprinkler, contains a "sync" sound effect of a jet water sprinkler playing underneath the narration:

> Though the director was from the same country as the old
> battle-axe, I couldn't see a connection. I couldn't see why
> he'd been invited to the seminar. Yet there seemed to be
> similarities between my grandfather's footage and the films
> the director presented at the seminar. I thought I would try
> to incorporate my grandfather's footage with the film I
> would take on location in Holland. As usual, I would keep
> a diary of the whole affair. [music begins]

The "sync" water-sprinkler sound (an allusion to another of Greenaway's obsessions, water) and the introduction of music flesh out the possible range of sound
at the narrator's disposal. The gradual and very subtle introduction of each sound
option in *?O,Zoo!* parallels the increasingly arbitrary rhetorical power of the narrator and the complexity of the fiction he weaves. The "authenticity" of the "personal" voice-over is first established and then used as a springboard for the introduction of more and more conventional rhetorical effects. All of this precedes the
announcement of the film's overarching form:

> As usual, I would keep a diary of the whole affair.

FAKING DEATH: THE ETHICS OF REPRESENTATION, FICTION, AND ACTUALITY
This short film around a fiction film has its own enigmas to be worked out in
its "narrative" progression. In the passage above, the narrator puzzles over the
connections between Greenaway and Grierson, between Greenaway and the

Documentary Seminar. On one ingenuous level, of course, the puzzlement is justified; Greenaway's films are indeed fictions, and furthermore, are absolutely antipathetic to Griersonian documentaries. In specific reference to the 1984 seminar, the puzzlement registered by the narrator translated to outrage on the part of many conference participants. The challenge that the anti-documentaries shown at the seminar presented to seminar participants, for whom the Grierson Documentary Seminar was typically a "tribute" to Grierson's official legacy, led to violent debates and charges that films like Greenaway's *The Falls* were senseless hoaxes. In *?O,Zoo!*, Hoffman seems to be quietly satirizing this debate.

Working out the relations between Greenaway and Grierson is one problem the narrator will tackle. The second is the resemblance he notes between his "grandfather's footage" and Greenaway's films. On the level of the fiction, the narrator says he will incorporate his grandfather's footage into the film he is "about to make" in Holland—the sequence we have worked through is, in a sense, a different film than the *?O,Zoo!* to come. On the most banal level, the narrator "discovers" that "the director" shares his grandfather's fascination with animals. More substantively, Hoffman seems to be announcing that his own exploration of the relations between Grierson and Greenaway will be affected precisely by taking a page from Greenaway's book. Here, the narrator introduces a hermetic fiction by pretending that his grandfather's footage is not his own.

These two levels interpenetrate to present two problems. First, for the viewer, the problem is reading *?O,Zoo!* between the levels of fiction and actuality, between the image and the voice-over. The second problem is Hoffman's. When he says that "as usual" he will keep a diary of the whole affair, Hoffman is situating the film within his own practice and preoccupations—not Greenaway's assured multiplication and excavation of fictions, but Hoffman's own tentative probings of the problems of representation. The "resolution" of these problems of reading and making appears as the film finally incorporates the two missing shots from the Day 17 shot card: "Elephant tries to get up," "Elephant gets up." Just after the diary section shows us the right half of the grandfather's shot report, the narrator tells a two-minute story over a black screen about his witnessing and filming an elephant having a heart attack at the Rotterdam Zoo. The passage is descriptive and emotional, centred around the filmmaker's crisis of conscience in deciding to film the death, and the accompanying responsibility and guilt. In the end, he decides "to put the film in the freezer. I decide not to develop it." Yet at the end of the film, after the credits (in a sense, after the end of the film), two extra shots, both twenty-eight seconds long, sepia-toned and silent, show an elephant struggling to get up and then an elephant getting up.

The effect of this framing of *?O,Zoo!* is double-edged. In one way, these last two shots expose the artifice of the voice-over. The events of the first shot (the elephant rocking back and forth, the attendants shoving bales of hay under the elephant) match the earlier voice-over, but in the second shot, the elephant gets up. The narrator lies twice. First, he developed the footage, and second, the events of the story are contradicted by the image. This decisive break in the fiction takes place by a radical separation of voice-over and image: the story is told over a black screen, the final images are silent. With this separation, the viewer can return to the film to reconstruct, in a sense, its non-meaning, and to question and revise the "authenticity" of the versions of events the film presents.

Working through these possibilities, of course, suggests that a thoroughgoing skepticism is called for in the viewer's relation to the film, and especially to the narrator's voice-over. For example, do the final images tell the whole story? Is there more elephant footage than is shown or listed? Is the order of the last two images correct? Yet thoroughgoing skepticism is not, it seems to me, the final effect of *?O,Zoo!* It is important to note here a crucial difference between Greenaway and Hoffman: Greenaway's oeuvre is obsessively interwoven with recurring images, themes, and characters, but his fictions are rigorously hermetic and unconcerned with the codes of realism. In *?O,Zoo!*, Hoffman exposes the hoax at the heart of his own work; moreover, the emotional resonance of the elephant's struggle is highly charged and excruciating to watch. One suspects that if the story of the elephant's death is a fiction, it is still a fiction filtered through Hoffman's sense of the crisis of representation.

The key to Hoffman's sense of his own intertextuality is this line in the voice-over: "I've come across this problem before." The statement refers to Hoffman's film made a year earlier, *Somewhere Between Jalostotitlan and Encarnacion*, where Hoffman, travelling by bus in Mexico, comes across a crowd of people around a dead Mexican boy just run over in the road. Hoffman puts away his camera and cannot film the scene. *Somewhere Between Jalostotitlan and Encarnacion* is structured around the absence of the visual representation of the event, which is instead described in written text "voice-over." Yet while making *?O,Zoo!*, Hoffman did begin to shoot the elephant's struggle, not knowing if the animal would live or die. The absence structuring *Somewhere Between* becomes a kind of contingent presence in *?O,Zoo!* Just as Hoffman gathers and organizes the images of *Somewhere Between* to hint at, refract, and rehearse the moment of hesitation at the heart of the film, so in *?O, Zoo!*, he organizes the film around the potential consequences of his decision to film the event—a kind of rehearsal of the various responses he felt as he filmed. The expressive urge behind Hoffman's work, always constrained by its tentative, questioning attention to and awareness of the process of filming, distills itself into the structure his films adopt: radically extended meditations on a single, almost ecstatic moment.

When Hoffman showed *Somewhere Between* at the 1984 Grierson Seminar,

he was taken to task by a veteran war correspondent, Don North, who wanted to
see the scene of the Mexican boy's death. Shelley Stamp, reporting on the conference, writes:

> [North] felt that the film would have been stronger with the
> addition of the death. What North missed, I think, was the
> very structure this absence provided, and Hoffman's
> implied critique of North's type of filmmaking.

The nature of Hoffman's critique is clearer in *?O,Zoo!* In the voice-over, the narrator rationalizes his decision to film the scene with a lame excuse: "Maybe the
television networks would buy the film and tell people that tragedy's in their neighbor-
hood." After the elephant "dies," he admits that his "idea of selling the film to the network now just seems an embarrassing thought, an irresponsible plan."

The "social utility" arguments of sensationalist news and documentary makers and institutions always carry a hint of the *National Enquirer* ("because people
want to know")–an epistephilia bordering on what Tom Gunning has called the
spectatorial mode of curiositas (38). But it is important not to interpret Hoffman's
tentative meditations on the problematic of representation as party to the oppos-
ing camp that censors represent under the flag of "responsibility to subject"–the
simplistic and squeamish argument that filming "takes advantage" of the subject.
Rather, Hoffman understands film's power to mediate between the consciousness
of the filmmaker and the viewer; his hesitations around the problem of representation reflect a personal ambivalence about the necessary link between his vision
and the viewer's. In an artist's statement for the Art Gallery of Ontario, Hoffman
writes:

> By means of the personal content of my films I seek to
> uncover subjective aspects of the way events were recorded.
> Focusing on the way that I, as a filmmaker, can and do
> influence both form and content allows room for the viewer
> to reflect upon ways in which meaning is constructed in
> film. Using the processes of reflection and revision, I seek
> to examine and express how we bring meaning to past and
> present lived experiences.

Although Hoffman here names the terms of his meditation on representation, he
does not make explicit the intensity of the tension between the filmmaker's
extraordinary control over images and the guilt this arouses, nor his own sense of
danger around his approach to the particular "lived experience" at the core of
these films—namely, bearing witness to death.[4]

4. The final images of the
elephant recall, in subject
and single long-take form,
that most astonishing primal
scene of death in early film:
Edison's *Electrocuting an
Elephant* (1903).

In the voice-over of the elephant story, Hoffman includes a sentence that clarifies this intensity of responsibility and danger:

> Concentrating on the image I had filmed as if my mind
> was the film and the permanent trace of the elephant's
> death was projected brightly inside. Somehow it's my
> responsibility now.

Hoffman makes explicit that central insight and concern of independent film practice and theory: film's status as a radical metaphor for consciousness and its relation to the world. Film's capacity to mediate the relation between consciousness ("as if my mind was the film") and events in the world arises from its indexical nature ("permanent trace"). This mediation carries the potential to represent death and suggests a radically powerful level of epistemological inquiry, carrying both an intimation of the ecstatic—outside space and time—and what Jean Epstein has called "a warning of something monstrous" at the heart of cinema (21). The "responsibility" Hoffman feels around this encounter with death is revealed by the word "projected." For if film is a radical metaphor for consciousness, we must understand the double-hinged nature of that metaphor as it swings between filmmaker and spectator. Hoffman's hesitations regarding filming, or developing, or showing his experience of death revolve around a terror of the urgent but reckless energy that representation burns into the filmmaker and the viewer.

If the filming of a moment of death is the central expressive theme of Hoffman's film, the moment's representation and deferral are never divorced from his recognition that the weight of film history and convention always interposes itself and structures the spectator's access to the image. The engagement of film history in *?O,Zoo!*, especially the Griersonian documentary tradition with its central claim to absolute truth, underlines the epistemological stakes behind Hoffman's questioning. Hoffman wants to bring the conventions and history of the construction of certainty to crisis, to clear a space for the spectator to approach, with Hoffman, the intensity of fascination and doubt inscribed in the image that appears literally as supplement, as coda, to the text of *?O,Zoo!* The point is not to escape mediation—this is not an Edenic pure image. Nor is it to restore certainty. Rather, Hoffman clears a space for consciousness to re-engage the world in "lived experience" via representation.

still: *?O,Zoo!*

WORKS CITED

Allan, Blaine.
"It's Not Finished Yet (Some Notes on Toronto Filmmaking)." *Toronto: A Play of History*. Toronto: Power Plant.
1987
83-92.

Burch, Noël.
"Film's Institutional Mode of Representation and the Soviet Response." *October 11* (Winter 1979)
77-96.

Della Penna, Paul, and Jim Shedden.
"The Falls." *Cineaction! 9* (July 1987)
20-24.

Elder, Kathryn.
"The Legacy of John Grierson." *Journal of Canadian Studies 21.4* (Winter 1986-87)
152-61.

Epstein, Jean.
"The Universe Head Over Heels." *October 3* (Spring 1977), Trans. Stuart Liebman.
21-25.

Grierson, John.
"The Creative Use of Sound." *Grierson on Documentary*. Ed. Forsyth Hardy. London: Faber, 1966.
157-63.

Gunning, Tom.
"An Aesthetic of Astonishment: Early Film and the (In)credulous Spectator." *Art & Text 34* (Spring 1989)
31-45.

Hoffman, Phil.
"Artists and their Work: Phil Hoffman." Toronto: Art Gallery of Ontario, 1985.
N. pag.

Morris, Peter.
"Rethinking Grierson: The Ideology of John Grierson." *Dialogue: Canadian and Quebec Cinema*. Eds. Pierre
Verroneau, Michael Dorland, and Seth Feldman. Montreal: Mediatexte/Cinémathèque Québécoise, 1987.
21-56.

Stamp, Shelley.
Program Notes for Somewhere Between … Toronto: Canadian Filmmakers Distribution Centre, 1984.

Winston, Brian.
Claiming the Real: The Documentary Film Revisited. London: BFI, 1995.

PASSING THROUGH

by Gary Popovich

still: *passing through/torn formations.*

It is from the Canadian tradition of the intuitive gathering of sounds and images that Canada's boldest works of film art have come. While the tradition is partially indebted to the documentary and realist conventions—their tireless reworking and, ultimately, sublimation into an aesthetic experience—it is a process that is distinctly different from scripted, pre-conceived image-structuring methods. One abandons literature and theatre and uses the microphone and camera to define the shape of experience. This legacy of Canadian cinema is situated between a European (most conspicuously, but by no means exclusively British and French) and American sensibility—the area "in between" the American technological imperative and a lament for what that suppresses. This is what Arthur Kroker calls the Canadian discourse on technology:

> … it is our fate by virtue of historical circumstance and geographical accident to be forever marginal to the "present-mindedness" of American culture (a society which, specializing as it does in the public ethic of "instrumental activism," does not enjoy the recriminations of historical remembrance); and to be incapable of being more than ambivalent on the cultural legacy of our European past. At work in the Canadian mind is, in fact, a great and dynamic polarity between technology and culture, between economy and landscape. (8)

It is in our films, predominantly from a group of filmmakers who are becoming known notoriously as the Escarpment School, that this discourse has been evolving its most fascinating and forceful configurations. I can think of few more powerful reflections on this discourse than Philip Hoffman's seventh film, *passing through /torn formations* (1988). In this film, Hoffman synthesizes a quasi-romantic European journey, home-movie-like segments, enigmatic family stories, poetic narration, and some of the most beautiful and harrowing images he has recorded to date. Through a fragmentary landscape of familial ties that criss-cross the continent of memory, Hoffman orders the generation and regeneration of images passed down, passed through a life's becoming. In the study of his own cultural legacy, this obsessive weaver of tales exposes the dark heirs that loom in camera.

passing through opens in darkness, while poet Christopher Dewdney recites a child's archeology. A young boy, oblivious to the others playing around him, becomes enraptured by the image of a rock whose layers come apart easily, freeing moths that "flutter up like pieces of ash caught in a dust devil." This transformation of darkness into the light of reflection, from darkness to speaking the image, from word to the mind-image evoked in a word, creates a spell where history is released, admitted and set free. In this equivalence between layers of stone and human generation, *passing through* discovers its own logic of layering.

The image is formed of the words which dream it.
Edmond Jabès

The next six minutes of the film comprise a silent, colour sequence (one of only three in this otherwise black-and-white film) where the camera hesitates, draws and redraws a scene in search of some way to record the filmmaker's in-stitutionalized grandmother (Babji) as she is being fed by her daughter. Moving from mother to grandmother, Hoffman draws a painful trajectory before inserting an intertitle ("To Babji") cut on the look of his grandmother to reaffirm to us that here the rock, the family, and the film are what hold and care for generations before they too flutter up like ashes. This release is also about letting go—dying.

What these ashes wanted, I felt sure, was not containment but participation. Not an enclosure of memory, but the world.
Mark Doty

In these first two disjunctions—sound without image, then image without sound—the film exposes the goals it sets for itself. *passing through* strives to return a fragmented history to a present-day unity and wholeness. The first coupling of image and sound in the film has the filmmaker's Canadian uncle Wally throwing his hand up in front of the lens in resistance to his nephew's attempts to capture his image. Wally has become a homeless drifter, a pool-shark with a taste for the bottle, and just as his demeanor has pushed him "outside" the family, so Hoffman, for the most part, refuses to show him, marking him as the limit of representation. Much of the labour of reconciliation clusters around this absent figure in a centripetal movement that comprises a series of messages, pleas, prayers and fictions, all attempting to join the body of the family in the body of the film.

Hoffman travels to the old country, bringing with him tapes and photos of his family in Canada; in Czechoslovakia, he collects sounds and images of his relatives, which he brings back to Canada. Hoffman's family has been severed, with one half remaining in the old world, and the other coming to Canada in an effort to escape Nazi persecution during WWII. But Babji's flight was incomplete: she carried within her a child conceived in the old world, a boil on her neck and a burgeoning virus that later turned into Parkinson's disease and purportedly caused mental disturbances in her son Wally. This inheritance from the old world is what Hoffman sets out to make whole again, using the technology of the new world.

The complexity of this dreamed reconstitution begins with a doubling of uncles—one in Canada, the other in Czechoslovakia—and is emphasized throughout the work, most notably in Wally's preoccupation with the corner mirror. The corner mirror is a looking glass that mirrors itself, and so provides not the usually reversed image of its onlooker, but a "true" picture. As Uncle Wally says, "It's the real you."

How often will I die, yet go on living?

The film's most challenging reconcilliation is that of Wally with his daughter Leesa whom he has not seen in years. Applying make-up in front of the corner mirror, Leesa tenderly describes what she sees into a tape recorder, a message for Wally, who is still emotionally unable to see his daughter. Breaking the ice of reflection, she comments on her gift: "I remember you, how you look, or how you looked, and a few people have said I look like you." Here the face becomes a chilling message, itself a reproduction, an image strained through genetics—the machine of the body—and the machines of hearing and seeing we call the cinema.

But Hoffman is not finished. He is not only interested in the father-daughter reconciliation, for this sequence unearths a host of images, as if inspired to generate its own reproductive force. Representation becomes resurrection. Over Leesa's face, in a return to colour, we advance with the camera over lilting waters toward the face of a rock wall, where we detect the outlines of Aboriginal petroglyphs etched into the stone. As we draw near, the surface of the film itself emits scratches of colour that break into further superimpositions that appear to emerge from the stone. We see cascading layers of home-movie images—the filmmaker perhaps, his siblings, other family members, Babji in her hospital bed— pouring out of the cut stone/film in an epiphany that magically joins the film's many threads in the eyes of its beholders.

Longing on a large scale is what makes history.
Don DeLillo

From the fissured video image of his mother translating messages sent from Czechoslovakia: "We hope that God will somehow make us get together again and we can talk some more." We then hear the family cheering, as if they have survived a mortal test of their being. Hoffman's journey ends on a train ride through Czech landscapes. There he recounts the tale of his Czech uncle, killed by his own son over a land dispute.

Life is lived forward but understood backward.
Soren Kierkegaard

The camera sweeps slowly past large rock fences that fragment the countryside, predominantly blue in colour—recalling the rocks of the epiphany sequence, the institutional blues of Babji's hospital room and Babji's craggy, blue-veined hands peacefully folded on her lap. The blue blood that surges through her body finds its mirrored image in the rock formations of her homeland, where her grandson now makes his pilgrimage. Here, in this dream landscape to which he awakes, he finds the final pieces of his project, a dreamer's reverie that draws together dispersed generations, recalled again in an image of the land.

Am I the sleep walker who does not tramp along the routes of life but who descends, always descends in quest of immemorial resting places?
Gaston Bachelard

While technology's path has often been a horizontal movement, a progression in which chronology, history and narrativity unfold as if in unbroken chains, here the intrusion of the poetic unlinks this endless procession of zeros and opens a view to the vertical, where being falls slowly out of time and into a configuration closer to the spirit of experience. Hoffman conjures another "I" whose being rests in the peace of imaginative reconstruction. Using the power of film, he generates his incantations and plunges us into meditations on our own generative powers. To make and unmake the past. To pass through.

This article was first printed in the *Liaison of Independent Filmmakers of Toronto (LIFT) Newsletter*, 1988.

Works Cited

Kroker, Arthur.
Technology and the Canadian Mind. Montreal: New World Perspectives, 1984.

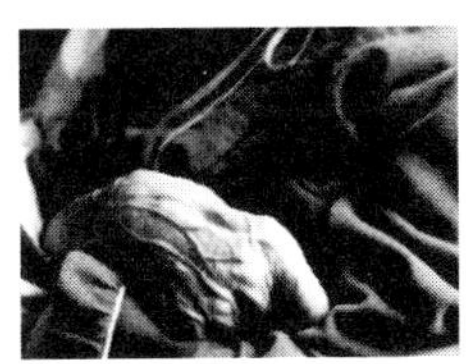

still: *passing through/torn formations.*

THE LANDSCAPE JOURNAL

by Ronald Heydon

Day One

Writing the first words, always something of a mystery. Might as well begin at the beginning. In *The End of Autobiography* Michael Sprinker traces the history of the word "autobiography" to the end of the eighteenth century. The Oxford dictionary credits Southey with the first usage in 1809, and the French Larousse attributes the French form to a derivation from the English. Prior to the eighteenth century, works that are today labeled autobiographies were known as confessions, memoirs, *journaux intimes*. As Sprinker describes it:

> Autobiography, the inquiry of the self into its own origin
> and history, is always circumscribed by the limiting condi-
> tions of writing, of the production of a text ...
> Autobiography must return perpetually to the elusive centre
> of selfhood buried in the unconscious, only to discover that
> it was already there when it began ... The origin and end
> of autobiography converge in the very act of writing ... for
> no autobiography can take place except within the bound-
> aries of a writing where concepts of subject, self and author
> collapse into the act of producing a text. (342)

Day Two

My first conscious encounter with landscape came in Saskatchewan, when I was nine or ten. On a bright, mid-summer day, I crossed the highway that encircled the city and entered the wheat fields. I walked for hours, gradually removing my clothes because of the heat. I remember the wheat scraping slightly my child's flesh. I remember seeing no one and nothing but wheat and golden sun for miles. People have been known to panic in such conditions. In such solitude (and in each direction the same view) one either feels incredible importance or insignificance. The feeling I had was communion.

In *The Interpretation of Ordinary Landscapes* (1979), D.W. Meinig writes that landscape is a technical term used by artists and earth scientists, architects and planners, geographers and historians. It is an ambiguous term, elusive. Landscape is, first of all, the impressions of our senses as well as the logic of our sciences. It is related to, but not identical with, environment. Landscape is defined by our vision, and interpreted by our minds.

In one of the books I recently read describing the frontier landscape of western Canada (was it *New and Naked Land* by Ronald Rees?), the author referred to early survey expeditions undertaken to determine if the prairies were habitable. The Plains Indians had roamed there for centuries and one of the surveyors (1857) wrote in his journal that "Apart from various trails, the Indians left the prairie unmarked."

The land, which was at first ignored (by earlier expeditions) and then explored and appropriated, was later treated as a commodity. It was surveyed, sectioned off and given away in parceled bits to incoming Europeans.

"Apart from various trails, the Indians left the prairie unmarked." Does the landscape remember? Can we talk of land and memory?

Day Three
Heard trumpeter Lester Bowie's jazz interpretation of *It's Howdy Doody Time.* Great title for an autobiography! Went to a party at Steve's (from sound class) last weekend. Most of the MA students were there. I started asking others about "referential productivity" (from one of Bill Nichols' articles) but no one had a clue. Rick Hancox has given me a video copy of the Philip Hoffman films to view for a class presentation on the 10th of November. Now I must find a friend with a VCR.

photo: Man on rock face by Keith Spencer.

Day Four

The closer I look at "autobiography," the more infinite it appears. There are four hundred years of it! Rick has set up the agenda so that I'm to defend the notion of autobiography in film. Does it need defense? Do the others understand? Does documentary only promote a cause? Expose malfunction? Couldn't all this be applied to self? What about autobiographical documentary as therapy?

Day Five

In an interview, Hoffman says his experience taught him the value of the film-making process as much as the finished work. He gathers "pieces of evidence"—films, videotapes, audio recordings, written diaries—that are reworked to create a meaningful understanding of past events. It's only while editing that patterns emerge. But this process of reflection and revision is extended to the viewer, who is asked to witness both events and their reconstruction. This "experimental" work allows an ambiguity that permits spectators to bring in remembrances from their own lives.

I view *On the Pond* (1978), his first film. Family album photos are juxtaposed with images of a young boy playing a solitary hockey game, on the pond. Still photos of hockey teams appear in succession as the boy becomes a teenager. Like my older brother, it appears the filmmaker lived his youth as part of a team. In the teen's bedroom, a slow pan takes us from a projector and record player, the instruments of reproduction, to a bookshelf, a row of hockey trophies, and finally to the boy in bed, looking over a hockey scrapbook.

It's the trophies that trigger my own personal flashbacks. Already the associations begin. I am from a family immersed in sports, a family of professionals. My older sister is a gym instructor and has played on Canadian volleyball teams for years. My older brother played every sport, won many trophies and now coaches football. My younger brother settles into karate and badminton (he was with Ontario's Champions last year). Even my mother has trophies from her younger, basketball years. "Star" they used to call her. I look at the wall next to my desk at the picture of my father, taken just before his marriage. He played basketball for the Canadian team at the 1936 summer Olympics in Berlin. (I look for him walking with the teams whenever I see images from the Riefenstahl film, but have never yet found him.) His team came in second after the Americans. In the photo, he is seated at a desk, wearing his Olympic leather jacket, pen in hand, about to sign some register or other. There are many trophies in my parents' home, but none of them bear my name. I never won any. Obliged, like all the children, to play every sport (I could swim and skate before I could read), my own boy's landscape was outside the team.

Day Six

Autobiography is a cultural act, where language acts as a focusing glass. Eakin quotes Spengemann, who insists that the autobiographer brings together the personal experiences of the writer with the shared values of a culture. He discerns a core belief in "individual identity" which he conceives of as "an integrated, continuing personality which transcends the limitations and irregularities of time and space and unites all of one's contradictory experiences into an identifiable whole" (qtd. in Eakin, 73). Do all cultures compress essential values and convictions in human models? Is "self-conception" a problem in most cultures? Autobiography comes into its own at the end of the eighteenth century "in conjunction with the rise of individuality as the dominant ideal of personality" (Eakin, 74). This in itself is a complex issue—that we all possess unique selves, continuous identities that develop over the course of a lifetime. Eakin calls this belief in individuality an anti-model sort of model:

> In the opening lines of his Confessions, Rousseau captures the paradox at the heart of the notion of embracing individuality as a model, for he claims for his identity an absolute value of singularity. "I am like no one in the whole world," he writes, while enjoining others to confess the uniqueness of their own selfhood with an equal candor. "I have displayed myself as I was." His uniqueness, in other words, is exemplary, a model for others to follow. We must recognize accordingly that the very generality of such a model engenders problems of self-definition that every autobiographer and critic must face anew: what do we think our experience is really like, and how do we conceptualize the experiencing self? (74)

Day Seven

"Oh, you write? You keep a journal?" a school chum asks. "Yes, and hand-written too. Not in the computer," I am quick to add. I'm old-fashioned. I like the texture of the page, the written word. Sure it's "time consuming," but so is watching television. Handwriting is like a snapshot: it conveys mood through style. My writing is sometimes harried, sometimes slow and methodical; sometimes in black ink from my father's fountain pen, sometimes in spur-of-the-moment ball point.

"Oh, you write? Are you so important?" I have been asked in the past, for I have kept a journal since leaving Saskatchewan. But journal writing is so much more than this. It has little to do with fame, importance, "posterity." The journal is a work place. Asked by CBC's *Brave New Waves* to join a panel on journal writing, my initial response was yes, of course. Asked to read from my journal I quickly changed my mind. "But why not?" asks the organizer. "It's my own personal working-out of private dilemmas," I answer, "not always for another's eyes, let alone ears!" Then I write a piece in the journal, a "working out" of the dilemma of a public text. I decide I could present this piece on the CBC (though probably they'll want something more revealing). Katz, in the Art Gallery of Ontario catalogue on autobiographical film, says that a journal brings one face to face with the meaning of one's personal existence—there, before one's eyes, and collected in one's own handwriting. A journal helps to put one's life in focus. Can I present this? I consult my agenda and see that I have an art history presentation the very next day—my most ambitious project and the one for which I'm least prepared. I decide I can't do both so I cancel the radio show. Missed opportunity? Story of my life.

"Oh, you write?" Remembering that time in New York, summer of '92, just after Raymond Carver passed away. There was an obituary in the New York Times that I quickly copied out before my taxi arrived to take me to the Port Authority terminal. The friend who had showed it to me, not realizing I had already copied it by hand, said he would photocopy it and mail it to me. "It's OK, I already have it," I told him. "You wrote it out?" he nearly gasped, as if I'd wasted so much energy. Of course his vehement reaction might seem relevant if the obituary had been a full page of text, but it was just the following:

> I don't know why people write stories.
> Raymond Carver said he wrote them
> because he was drunk a lot, and his kids
> were driving him crazy, and a short story
> was all he had concentration for.
> Sometimes, he said, he wrote them in a parked car.

Day Eight

Should a camera record death? There is no narrator in Hoffman's *Somewhere Between Jalostotitlan and Encarnacion* (1984), but there is a narrative in the form of intertitles that resemble Japanese haiku poetry. This story takes place in Mexico, where Hoffman chances across a dead Mexican youth surrounded by children. It begins:

> Looking through the lens at passing events
> I recall what once was and consider what might be.

We never see the dead youth, but read via intertitles that the filmmaker has put his camera down. While the intertitles tell the story of this encounter, the "walking" camera enters a village landscape, follows a textured wall overlaid with religious icons and paintings, and then a street procession (are we back in Ontario or still in Mexico?). A lone saxophone wails as if recounting the sad, difficult emotions. The hand-held camera pulls the spectator into the scene:

> The little girl with big eyes waits by her dead brother.

I am suddenly in a different scene. I am eighteen-years old and hitching around Europe. I am somewhere between Modena and Florence, seated in a medium-sized truck with a young Italian of about my age, who also prefers the back roads to the autoroute. He speaks no English, while I manage just a smattering of Italian and French. With much hand gesturing and laughter he tells me that not only does he have a girlfriend, but that she is pregnant (la luna, la colline, capische?). Just ahead of us on the narrow road, an older man on a bicycle. We try to drive around him but the man turns left (doesn't he hear the truck?) and we drive right over top of him. We sit there, immobile and white. There is not a sound. I get out of the truck and see children running from a neighboring farm. The man is dead. The young Italian can't face him, he stands and weeps. I hold him and watch the children's silent faces that look at us as if we were murderers. "It was an accident," I want to say, but don't even know the words. I thought I would never forget the look on those young faces, but I did forget until Hoffman's film brought them back. I understand his ethical dilemma at filming death. What amazes me is his ability to make a thing of beauty from his coming to terms with it.

Day Nine

"Maybe I'm just more observational than the average person," I say to myself, trying to find some context for the constant cruising, the way I engage others on the street. I don't just look at people as I ride by on the bike, but rather provoke a response. Maybe I'm spending too much time alone.

I did get to see a Dutch documentary film entitled *The Ditvoorst Diaries.* Back in the early 70s, Ditvoorst, the filmmaker, had been compared to Godard. Not long after his last film, *Witte Waan (White Madness),* he returned to the town of his birth and drowned himself, exactly like a character in his first film *Paranoia.* It was a strange film to see on a Sunday afternoon, and we were only six people in the whole cinema. Much of the text for the film was taken directly from his diaries.

An incredible snowstorm the first of November. The following day the tree branches are laden with snow in the bright, early-morning sun. Orange and black balloons remain tied to a tree in the neighbor's yard. A little snowman now stands by the sidewalk, next to a discarded jack-o'-lantern.

Our human landscape is our unwitting autobiography, reflecting our tastes, our values, our aspirations, and even our fears in tangible, visible form … The cultural record we have "written in the landscape" is liable to be more truthful that most autobiographies because we are less self-conscious about how we describe ourselves … There are no secrets in the landscape.
D.W. Meinig, *The Interpretation of Ordinary Landscapes*

Day Ten
The idea "to defend" Hoffman's methodology leads to other questions: what is documentary film anyway? Can it be experimental? Can something become so personal it's no longer documentary? Who decides these things? Most docs unwrap issues: poverty, racism, child abuse, hunger. These are worthy topics, so why in my communications MA have I steered away from TV news and opted for documentary film, sound, art and identity? Art demands becoming more of who you really are. Not just the exposing of an issue, some "master narrative," but allowing local concerns, personal issues, to surface. And if some of that's labeled "experimental" —well, I'll deal with labels later. What was it Cocteau said while adapting George Auric's music to one of his early films? Something about scrambling the pages and using the notion of chance, which might reveal another way of interpreting the material. In that tension, some new aspect might arise. What is learning, if not a sense of discovery?

Discussing film music and image, Claudia Gorbman calls the relationship between music-image and music-narrative "mutual implication." Could any music accompany a film? Of course!

Whatever music is applied to a film segment will do something—will have an effect—just as any two words will produce a meaning different from each used separately. Kracauer's reactions to a drunken movie-house pianist from his youth, whose inattention to the screen resulted in pleasingly unorthodox audiovisual combinations, recall the Surrealist's delight in the fortuitous encounters between two unlikely entities. Jean Cocteau actually scored some of his films on the principle of what he called "accidental synchronization." He took George Auric's music, carefully written for particular scenes in the film, and applied them to different scenes entirely. Whether the relation between sound and picture is deliberate or not (surrealist word-games versus traditional poetic activity, the drunken pianist vs. a score by John Williams), their collaboration will generate meaning. Image, sound effects, dialogue and music-track are virtually inseparable during the viewing experience; they form a combinatoire of expression.
Claudia Gorbman, *Unheard Melodies: Narrative Film Music*

Why can't learning be like the viewing experience? It was Jim Lane, in 1993, who equated the ideology of "the personal as political" with autobiographical documentaries. He said they moved between life and representation, and were as much about the genre itself as the people who made them.

Even Eakin equates the writing of autobiography (the "art of self-invention") with culture, in the sense that no writing, no matter how private, exists in isolation. It is made up of shared words.

Day Eleven

Hoffman's early interests related to photography and place. His pictures are the establishing shots of his life. The landscape sequences in *passing through/torn formations* (1988) were places he traveled in his youth. The remembering of that time, he says, is essential to his work. "Only now I must deal with those moments of discovery using the camera." *The Road Ended at the Beach* (1983) was the result of several years of hitching back and forth across the country, not only experimenting with image making, but also struggling with the conventions of documentary. One reviewer wrote that Hoffman uses failure (in that film) to make his strongest points about the convergence and intermingling of anticipation and event. He was apparently spurred on by Kerouac's life "on the road."

I remember the jazz essay I wrote, the one based on Pierre Bourdieu's *The Aristocracy of Culture*, in which he expounded on taste ("manifested preferences") and the way, according to "educational capital," cultural products were consumed. I was trying to relate all this to the jazz fan: "The Construction of a Jazz Fan in the Post-Bop Era of the 1950s" or: "Jazz is a Language/Culture is a Game." Ambitious kid! Trying to adapt Bourdieu to the Beats. More interested in the music and those tapes of Kerouac's poetry.

… tortured by sidewalks—starved for sex and companionship—open to anything—ready to introduce a new world with a shrug.
Jack Kerouac, *The Beat Generation*

Miles Davis, leaning against the piano, fingering his trumpet with a cigarette hand—working—making raw iron sound like wood—speaking in long sentences like Marcel Proust.
Kerouac, *The History of Bop*

Day Twelve

I go to Vanier Library in search of the Katz book on film and autobiography. I notice that it has been checked out until the end of November. At the front desk, I ask the fellow if he can let me see who has the book, as it may be someone in my class. "We can't do that!" he says. "It's against our rules." "Well, just look the

other way," I say: "It's happened before." He types in the number of the book, and
then my ID, then nonchalantly shows me the screen. "Seeing is believing," he
smiles. "The book is checked out … to you!" All the books I have are entitled
autobiography anyway. And I have so many. But this is the height of absurdity,
running after books I already have. Must slow down.

Day Thirteen

I prefer to write at sunrise. It's quiet and I can greet my ideas, reflections, impressions (the state of mind to write this) like an old friend. I think that if I wrote at
night, I would sound desperate. In the morning I reconstruct and face another day.

Day Fourteen

"Art is not a mirror but a hammer," John Grierson wrote in the early 1930s,
though it is his definition of documentary as "the creative treatment of actuality"
that is most often quoted. In *Representing Reality* (1991), Bill Nichols discusses the
evolution of documentary, how it organizes the materials presented to us and how
the interaction of filmic codes produce meanings. Nichols suggests that contemporary filmmakers have lost their voice (i.e., replaced it with mere observation and
unquestioned empiricism). He sets out to fashion his historical overview in order
to advise filmmakers on how to make documentaries that will more closely corre-
spond to a contemporary understanding of "our" (whose?) position in the world;
in this way, effective political/formal strategies for describing and challenging that
position can emerge. Nichols' concern is how to understand images of the world
as speech about the world, and how to place that speech within formal, experien-
tial and historical contexts.

Now let's face facts: the number of filmmakers who actually work this way
can probably be counted on one hand. And though Nichols gives an excellent
summary of the four types of documentary film (only four?)—expository, observational, interactive and self-reflexive (32-33)—I can't seem to place Philip Hoffman
anywhere, save the self-reflexive, and then only up to a point. Nichols defines the

photos: (left) Hoffman; (right) Babji.

self-reflexive as a strategy (right away a problem) where the representation of the historical world becomes the topic of cinematic mediation (69).

It's odd that Nichols skims over the expository, voice-of-God mode (34-38), since his article exemplifies this approach. All his arguments lead to the self-reflexive mode as the only one worth pursuing. So why are television news and most documentaries still caught in the expository mode?

Day Fifteen

Today I only feel like quoting.

The aim is to depict the place as some sort of historical palimpsest and/or the corollary of this, an exposition of a state of mind.

Patrick Keiller, *The Poetic Experience of Townscape and Landscape*

It seems, then, that making moving pictures of spaces and places involves the same sort of consideration as any other picture making—perspective, framing, pro-portion, left and right, and so on—even when the camera is moving, and especially when it is not. The virtues of this approach can be seen in those of Vermeer's paintings where there always seems to be more shown of the corner of the room than there actually is. In other words, the picture of the corner of the room is so good that we can infer the rest of the room from it.

Keiller, *The Poetic Experience of Townscape and Landscape*

The deeper I delve the more complex it becomes. What was it Diane Arbus said, "A photograph is a secret about a secret. The more it tells you, the less you know" (qtd. in Sprinker, 321).

Day Sixteen

Fellini passed away last week. Big state funeral on the news. I notice, on a record jacket I have of selected music from his films, some quotes from *Fellini on Fellini*. "I am my own still life." "I am a film." "Everything and nothing in my work is autobiography."

Last week I gave my class presentation on autobiography and documentary film. As if I wasn't nervous enough, Phil Hoffman was also present. He was very relaxed though, and afterwards, we had a good talk. But trying to cogently present the complicated theories surrounding autobiography was another matter. I started skipping paragraphs, darting across the page, scanning for the essential, *un*sutur-ing. I felt I was watching the paper crumble before my eyes.

After *passing through/torn formations*, most of the class left on break and I stayed to speak with Hoffman. I told him the story (which suddenly jarred in my memory during his film) of my own grandfather. Originally from a tiny hamlet of a place in England called Hook Norton, he emigrated to Canada with his family and never returned. I never knew his wife, my grandmother. She was a French woman, and died shortly after giving birth to their sixth child. My grandfather raised his six children alone. When I was hitching around Europe as an eighteen-year-old I decided to visit Hook Norton, which is just north of London, though the only Heydons there were on the gravestones. I took a few black-and-white photos, staying for a few days, and spoke with the oldest woman of the village, who remembered my ancestors. I even copied out the record of christenings at the church going back over two-hundred years. The next year, back in Canada, I visited my grandfather, who still lived in Windsor with two of his unmarried daughters. I showed him the photos—silly, Instamatic pictures—and told him of my adventures there. My grandfather was a big man, and watched me with steady eyes as I spoke. I spent three or four days there and then left on a Sunday evening for Toronto. The next morning I received the telephone call from my aunt: "Come back. Your grandfather passed away last night in his sleep."

There were a few students who also listened to the story, and one of them suggested that it was my fault that he died! "You probably triggered something in memories long buried." Phil found it interesting, but only said, "Looks like you've got enough there to make a film yourself."

Day Seventeen

Hoffman made *?O,Zoo! (The Making of a Fiction Film)* (1986) ostensibly to document Greenaway's making of *A Zed and Two Noughts*. Hoffman's film, however, is concerned with the conditions of how it was made—as Nichols suggests is the purpose of self-reflexive documentary. *?O,Zoo!* connects Canadian film history with references to Grierson ("that old battleaxe") and to a personal, diaristic travel experience. Landscapes vary from a small square in a Dutch city, to a static shot of one of Greenaway's outdoor locations, to lion cages in the Rotterdam zoo. As in Hoffman's Mexican film a death occurs, only this time it is an elephant that is dying. The question of filming this death is the same, however. The screen is left blank as the narrator describes the event. How to categorize a film that pokes fun at conventions while seriously searching for new forms and asking us to create these forms with him? The spectator is part of his ethical dilemma. The filmmaker's dilemma is also ours.

Day Eighteen

Some years ago, while preparing a demo tape of a radio broadcast (which turned out well, as I was hired immediately at CKUT), I included several quotes from an autobiographer who has influenced me greatly. Peter Handke's *The Weight of the*

World (1984) is a text made of reflections, observations, self-inventions.

Washing a shirt in the washbasin when all is still and the heart is heavy.

Someone has written me a letter in which he apologizes for not having phoned me instead.

A television talk-show host laughs aloud at something, quite spontaneously—but all the same he forces himself to laugh into the microphone.

A little while ago (evening) for the first time in ever so long—while standing at the kitchen sink eating grapes and spitting the seeds into my hand—I man aged to think of a future.

Independent film and video artists, Renov (1989) tells us, are asking themselves questions about the representation of their own subjectivity, in which history and subjectivity become mutually defining categories. Renov calls this "embroiling of subject in history" the new autobiography.

Day Nineteen
"It is a warm grey afternoon in August. You are in the country, in a deserted quarry of light-grey devonian limestone in southern Ontario. A powdery luminescence oscillates between rock and sky … "
I can see through Chris Dewdney's words, through the text, the poem, through the words on the page. I am a spectator. I am also a reader. I am the viewer in the dark, before a black screen, listening to these words, the introduction to *passing through/torn formations*. And I am glad Hoffman left the screen black. Some things are better left unshown, where the landscape of imagination and memory can more easily reside.
Hoffman describes the peopled landscape as "an inevitable collision between the old and new worlds, like two great landscapes colliding, erupting … Some people in my family just got caught at the epicentre."

Day Twenty
There are many family voices in *passing through/torn formations*, as well as a relentless movement of overlapping images. Sometimes we see the sameimage/ scene from different angles. This restatement of imagery (never exactly the same) Hoffman compares to oral history (which changes through the retelling), or to the literary method of Gertrude Stein.
It was Stein who said, back in 1934, that to understand modern painting, one

had to fly over the plains of the mid-West.

With the many changes in the dominant systems of communication that affect our culture as a whole, will film and video replace writing as our chief means of recording, informing and entertaining? Is there a cinematic equivalent for written autobiography and, after four hundred years, is it close to extinction? Should I be angry with Philip Hoffman? Is writing to be formally displaced? Elizabeth Bruss writes in *Eye for I: Making and Unmaking Autobiography in Film* (1980): "The unity of subjectivity and subject matter ... seems to be shattered by film; the autobiographical self decomposes, schisms, into almost mutually exclusive elements of the person filmed (entirely visible, recorded and projected) and the person filming (entirely hidden; behind the camera eye)" (297). What is there in language to explain its peculiar fitness for autobiographical expression? Can the autobiographical "I" survive the move from text to film?

Again I am faced with Descartes, as Bruss begins her search. The more radical his doubts (in the *Meditations*), she suggests, the more certain the being of the doubter—Descartes never considered whether the "doubter" might not be the product rather than the producer of the doubt (298).

She offers three parameters to autobiography: 1) truth value (autobiography is consistent with other evidence; it is sincere); 2) act value (autobiography is a personal performance); and 3) identity value (the logically distinct roles of author, narrator and protagonist are conjoined) (299-300).

Like the sentence I have been composing, language allows the same individual who plays the role of speaker to serve as his own referent—the speaking subject and the subject of the sentence are the same and this conflation is crucial to autobiography. In film, Bruss notes that " ... the autobiographical self begins to seem less like an independent being and more like an abstract 'position' that appears when a number of key conventions converge—and vanishes when those conventional supports are removed" (301). Film, in other words, offers a new variable: the choice between "staging the truth" or recording it directly. Can we call a film sincere, she asks? Can a film shot (apart from vocal accompaniment) express doubt? (303)

But all film is manipulation, I want to cry out at her! And hasn't Hoffman overcome this very thing?

I look at *Kitchener-Berlin* (1990), Hoffman's latest film. I am immersed in family history—landscape, memory, time—and I go for a long bike ride afterwards to ponder. I think of my other grandfather, who came to Canada from the Ukraine many years ago. He came to our house one day and dumped my grandmother at our front door. "Here," he said to my mother in Ukrainian (he never did learn English), "Take your mother. She's sick. She can't work anymore." Or at least, that's the version my mother tells, not in anger, but in the hopes I'll understand.

"It's their way." Three weeks later, my grandmother was dead. I know it had something to do with cancer, but what I remembered most (as a young child) is that she died in my bed. I had to sleep in my sister's room. Why do I think of this grandfather who couldn't even talk to me, who could only say "hello" (in English) and pat my head?

I go out for a drink. Filled with books, papers and ideas. I stop at a singles bar in the Plateau where there are many people, voices, music, smoke, shouting and laughter. But tonight, there's no one here I know. Standing alone, watching others casually cruise and flirt, I remember my teen years on the prairies.

> Tonight, in the sky
> Even the stars
> Seem to whisper
> To one another.
> Oraga Haru Issa, *The Year of my Life*

Day Twenty-one

Last day. One final glance to that Bruss article. In studying, we don't just read the things we want to hear.

"It is doubtful," she remarks, "that the effects of shooting, editing and staging are capable of expressing what we conventionally call 'personality' to the degree that language can" (306). To distinguish the point of view of the first-person narrator in film from that of literature, "Mieke Bal has recently proposed a separate category, a 'focalizer' as distinct from 'narrator,' to make the different qualities of these vantage points more clear" (306).

Bruss argues " … there is a total absence of 'identity-value' in film. In speaking, 'I' merge easily, almost inextricably, with another 'I' whose character and adventures I am claiming as my own" (307). But as Bruss points out, in film there is an impassable barrier between the person seeing and the person seen, because the film spectator is always out of the frame. A merging of subjects would require the viewer to be in two places at once (307). Viewing films could relate to our sense of privacy, anonymity—viewing, yet feeling unseen. Bruss quotes Cavell: "We do not so much look at the world as look out at it, from behind the self" (317).

As Hoffman himself has noted, "when photography was invented, painting changed; but photography never replaced landscape painting. If avant-garde film is dying in its struggle to survive, let's celebrate its death and make it into something else" (1978). Perhaps film could offer a new way of experiencing ourselves. Bruss concludes:

> Film simply shares—or better, articulates—the dilemmas of
> an entire culture now irrevocably committed to complex

technologies and intricate social interdependencies. To
make the means of film human without falling back on out-
worn humanism, to achieve more fluid modes of collaboration and diversity rather then the standardized expression,
to establish practices in which "I" may no longer exist in
the same way but nonetheless cannot escape my own participation—these concerns are not unique to film but among
the most fundamental problems that confront "the age of
mechanical reproduction" as a whole. (320)

Works Cited

Bruss, Elizabeth.
"Eye for I: Making and Unmaking Autobiography in Film." *Autobiography: Essays Theoretical and Critical.* Ed.
James Olney. New Jersey: Princeton UP, 1980.
296-320.

Eakin, Paul John.
Fictions in Autobiography. New Jersey: Princeton UP, 1985.

Gorbman, Claudia.
Unheard Melodies—Narrative Film Music. Indiana University Press, 1987.

Handke, Peter.
The Weight of the World. Trans. Ralph Manheim. New York: Farrar, Strauss and Giroux, 1984.

Hoffman, Philip.
Artist's Statement. *Autobiography.* Ed. John Stuart Katz. Toronto: Art Gallery of Ontario, 1978.

Lane, Jim.
"Notes on Theory and the Autobiographical Documentary Film in America." *Wide Angle* 15-3 (July 1993).
21-36.

Meinig, D.W.
The Interpretation of Ordinary Landscapes: *Geographical Essays.* London: Oxford UP, 1979.

Nichols, Bill.
Representing Reality: Issues and Concepts in Documentary Film. Bloomington: Indiana UP, 1991.

Renov, Michael.
"The Subject in History—The New Autobiography in Film and Video." *Afterimage* 17-1 (1989).
4–7.

Sprinker, Michael.
"Fictions of the Self: The End of Autobiography." *Autobiography: Essays Theoretical and Critical.* Ed. James
Olney. New Jersey: Princeton UP, 1980.

NOTES ON RIVER

by Philip Hoffman

The Saugeen River was named Sauking, "where it all flows out," by the Ojibwa in the early 1800s. It runs into Lake Huron. The place where I know it is twenty miles south of Owen Sound, Ontario, near Williamsford, where I spent lots of time in my youth exploring. Over the past dozen years I've returned there to film and collected these moments in a fifteen minute meditation called simply, *river*. In 1977 I arrived with a wind-up Bolex and one roll of 16mm colour film. In 1981 with a half-inch, reel-to-reel, black-and-white video portapak. In 1984, indoors now, I used a rear screen set up to record the original 16mm footage on video. And finally, in 1989, I went for the first time beneath the surface of the water, the camera loaded with hi-con printer stock.

All the video images were transferred to film in the version that's now in distribution, though I sometimes still screen the piece as a film/video installation—once even outside, in a forest, on the snow.

On the way to the river to shoot the underwater section in 1989, I made a quick call to my parents, who live near the Saugeen, to let them know I was on the way up. My mother told me that my uncle had been found dead that day. He shot himself by the river (a different river) near our home town. She told me not to tell anyone because his immediate family wanted to say it was a heart attack. I got into the car with Garrick and Tim, my friends who were helping me with the filming, and we drove up. Churning inside.

I know that the death had something to do with what we filmed that day, and how I edited the section. I used the filming and editing as a way to mourn for him whom I cared for, who never had the chance to be heard.

In this last section of the river, underwater, I gave up the camera. I told Garrick—"just start the camera and let the current take us." I stood in the boat wondering about the death and watching. Giving up my hold on the camera.

KITCHENER-BERLIN: OR HOW ONE BECOMES TWO (OR NONE)

by Steve Reinke

I know it's a hollow rhetorical ploy, a cliché even, an excuse for a certain kind of sloppiness, unpreparedness, but I mean it sincerely: I have given up on the essay I meant to write. Instead I submit these pathetic notes in the form of a letter asking for forgiveness. By now I should be used to my failure as a critic. I continually back away from planned essays, taking refuge in the literary: the aphorism, the satiric manifesto, the autobiographical anecdote. But this retreat is more disappointing than most. When I watched *Kitchener-Berlin* (1990) again (I hadn't seen it in many years), I was struck by its rightness, its perfection. It seemed to me exemplary. Trebly exemplary: to (or as) the work of Hoffman, to Canadian cinema, and to experimental film. The film surely merits close textual analyses from a variety of approaches. Moreover, it seemed to me that these analyses would constitute a more general discussion of experimental film as an endeavor.

APOLOGY

Sure, art is long and life is short, but I am not troubled by this condition. What bothers me is that art is complex and I am simple, though conflicted: stupid. Art makes dullards of us all. Writing about it is a clumsy thing, doomed always to miss what is most significant and instead gloss the petty. Criticism becomes an act of contrition, an extended apology. I am sorry, and sorry that this is the case.

FILM CONTRA VIDEO

Experimental video is centred around the voice: an individual talking, rhetorically deploying a particular subjectivity in relation to a certain construction of consciousness. Video is willfully interior: its relation to the world is never direct, but processed through a particular subjectivity. Video is thus doubly mediated; there is no direct perception, no immediate apprehension of the world. One cannot speak of phenomenology in relation to video without undue strain. Experimental film

stills: *Kitchener-Berlin*. Photo courtesy of Kitchener Public Library. "Rescuing the Bust of the Kaiser from Victoria Park Lake," Kitchener 1916.

has a completely different relation to voice and the world. There is no such thing as a "personal" film. The voice in film always aspires to be the voice-of-God. Film is singly mediated, self-consciously authored by authors who retreat behind subjectivity to become merely thinking, perceiving bodies. Interiority is impossible, the world itself impinges too strongly. Experimental video proceeds through a process of talking to one's self as if one had a self; experimental film through a process of swallowing or incorporating the world into a self that is no longer human, but an author, a hollow signature attempting to structure perception.

DELEUZE

This season it's all about Deleuze's cinema books. I keep reading these books because his distinction between the time-image and movement-image seems a fertile launching point for a discussion of experimental film. But the only films people seem to discuss are Hitchcock's (when Žižek via Lacan should have silenced them all, at least long enough so these hacks could take a break and think a little bit harder). I asked Laura Marks why Deleuze is so rarely applied to artists' film and video. (She is one of the few academics who has used Deleuzian ideas to discuss experimental work.) She replied that, because artists like Hoffman are applying Deleuze's insights directly, (that is, literally enacting or embodying the ideas in their work rather than merely referring to or discussing them), the need for commentators to apply (reapply) a Deleuzian perspective is not so pressing, and perhaps even redundant. This is probably true, but still I am not satisfied, and regret I am not able to supply such an analysis at this time. But here is what I have learned from Deleuze: there is a kind of vertiginous ecstasy in being always on the verge of coherency, in endlessly deferring sense with the hope that one approaches something previously unfathomable.

DREAM

I dreamt last night that I came across a book called *Kitchener-Berlin* and it was a really big book—lots of words, hardly any pictures, a few diagrams—something between an encyclopedia and an autobiography. It contained all the information about the images in the film, where they came from and what they mean. This dream is partly a response to my hermeneutic anxiety—a feeling that I can't write about the film without a greater level of mastery, specifically the ability to form a reading based on an extensive knowledge of what is depicted in individual shots. So while I continue to remain firm that *Kitchener-Berlin* does not call for that kind of interpretation (that is, will not constructively yield to a directly hermeneutical approach), perhaps the film's dream book does (and would). Perhaps this dream book is a bible situated between the artist and the film and ready, in its encyclopedic detail, to tell us everything. We would study the book endlessly in order to derive increasingly accurate interpretations of the film. And the film itself—the hermetic, incorruptible art object—would sink into the background, as pure and coyly mysterious as the Mona Lisa.

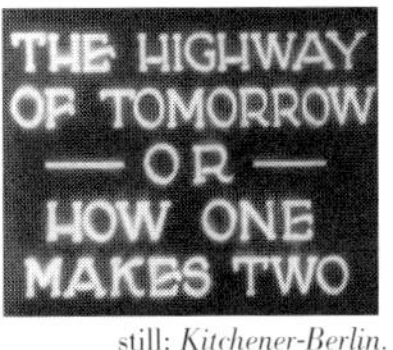

still: *Kitchener-Berlin*.

CIRCUITOUS QUESTS: PASSING THROUGH PHILIP HOFFMAN'S FAMILY CYCLE

by Peter Harcourt

I entertain the thesis that "avant-garde" in Canada is an instance of misprision and that the notion of experimental documentary may prove more productive in a Canadian context.

Michael Dorland[1]

1. International Experimental Film Congress, 33

There is a moment in Philip Hoffman's *passing through/torn formations* (1988) when we see a young boy entering a culvert. At a later moment, we see him coming out again. Who is this character? What is he looking for? How does he relate to the young girl we see at other moments in the film, sometimes in a field with cows?

As the film evolves, we might be able to infer that the girl is Andrea, a niece of the filmmaker, and that she is standing in for Sue, the filmmaker's mother, for the re-enactment of a story concerning Sue's childhood in Czechoslovakia, when she one day went looking for some cows. But who is the boy? *passing through* is the most probing film of Hoffman's Family Cycle films.[2] It is the most intricately concerned with a sense of quest. As a Canadian of European extraction, Hoffman is trying to understand the world in which he lives.

2. The Cycle includes all films made between 1978 and 1990. (see Hoffman list of works.)

Philip Hoffman belongs to the third generation of Canadian experimental filmmakers. He is part of what is now referred to as the Escarpment School. As Mike Hoolboom has explained:

> The Escarpment School is a loosely knit group of filmmak-
> ers that includes the likes of Rick Hancox, Carl Brown,
> Gary Popovich, Marian McMahon, Steve Sanguedolce,
> Philip Hoffman and Richard Kerr. Born and raised along
> the craggy slopes of the Canadian Shield, their work typi-
> cally conjoins memory and landscape in a home movie/doc-
> umentary-based production that is at once personal, poetic
> and reflexive. (43-44)

The notion of home movie is important. Like his friend, Richard Kerr, Hoffman often employs the diary as impetus for more extended inquiries.

As much a photograph album as a diary, *On the Pond* (1978) was an auspicious beginning. Already Hoffman's family is everywhere; already he is concerned with the past; and already Hoffman combines family photographs with dramatic re-enactments, this time using a cousin, Bradley Noel, as stand-in for himself as a boy.

The structure of the film is simple, the effect immediate. While photographs fill the screen, we hear the ooing and awing of Phil's family remembering past times. There are shots of Phil's cousins and sisters, one of whom, Franny, speaks the desire of the film. "I wanna go back," she exclaims, as we see a photograph of two girls pirouetting on the ice beside Phil with a hockey stick. The wish to go back provides the thrust for all these films, as if by examining where he has been, Hoffman might better understand who he has become.

Already in this student film, Hoffman the filmmaker senses the limitations of Phil, the boy. An aspiring jock performing push-ups on the ice, going fishing, playing hockey, even if it is just passing the puck around with Princess, the family dog—while still a young man, Hoffman already recognizes that the projector of these values and the soundtrack of this life are exhausted. When the boy Phil goes out onto the pond (actually Lake McCullough) to push the puck around with Princess and a friend as if for one last time, the projector and record-player are left flapping away in his basement room. The story they have registered has come to an end.

If the life explored in *On the Pond* is over by the time filmmaking began, the same is true of *The Road Ended at the Beach* (1983). Incorporating some "road journals" that Hoffman shot while still at Sheridan College, the film achieves a complex structure for what seems a simple piece. The older footage, shot both on Super-8 and on 16mm colour reversal, refers to previous trips, travelling west. But now, again with his friend Jim McMurry and also with Richard Kerr, the journey is east to Newfoundland. A tension is established between the journeys west—the footage of the past—and the journey east, the footage of the present. The point of view also moves from external to internal. Hoffman has explained the structure of the film:

> The first part is the external trip. It's getting on the road and moving forward. There's more of a linear plot there. Then there's a dissolve into a red screen. Now I look inside the van. The film becomes more psychological and emotional. That's when it starts jumping around, which gives me the go-ahead to be non-linear because I'm dealing with the emotional things that are happening on the trip. In the third part, it goes to blue, which are the realizations. It begins with me looking at close-ups of film on the light-box."[3]

3. Unless otherwise noted, citations from Philip Hoffman are from a personal interview conducted on 27 June 2000.

The idea of "realizations" needs to be explained, but first we might examine how the film jumps around. Leaping forward in space and then back again, the film fudges its own sense of direction. We see Dan with his wood-carving before we know who he is; we have a flash-back of Jim in his studio in Ann Arbor, unrecognizable as he manages molten metal; Robert Frank, an icon of the independent American spirit, appears and then appears again. Geography is scrambled as the destination becomes unclear. The structure thus enacts, kinaesthetically, the confusions in Hoffman's mind. *The Road Ended at the Beach* becomes, in Michael Dorland's apt phrase, a "documentary of consciousness" (153). Hoffman wanted to make a road movie in the tradition of Jack Kerouac. "I expected adventure," his commentary explains, "But somehow the road had died since the first trip west with Jim."

The film engages us, however, not only through its structure but also through the random characters we encounter on the trip. A hitch-hiker is picked up who once appeared in a Robert Frank film; Mark, an accomplished trumpeter, jams with Jim in Ottawa; Conrad Dubé, initially a polio victim, has bicycled several times around the world—a man who, as Jim explains (drawing upon Aboriginal legend), has perhaps been "touched by God"; and Rup Chand, a Tibetan friend of Jim's, establishes with an Urdu diary appropriate spiritual expectations at the beginning of the film.

The encounter with Robert Frank could have been a destination, but is actually a non-event. Like *On The Pond*, *The Road Ended at the Beach* becomes an exorcism of received ideas about male buddy-ism and adolescent adventure.

Although Jim's dog is named (dogs are an important part of buddy bonding), Phil's sister Philomene, who is present on one of the previous journeys, remains unidentified!

After we hear Jim declaiming, in front of an "Export A" billboard, "I wanna live, I wanna find some place better," the film does achieve a kind of nirvana. The "realizations" that Hoffman referred to entail a recognition that such inherited quests must now discover a different kind of harmony.

The beach the road ends at is Burgeo, on the south coast of Newfoundland, about two-hundred kilometres east of Port aux Basques. The camera holds on the waterfront for an extended period, almost undetectable jump-cuts foreshortening time as dogs and children gambol back and forth with no direction and no perceivable goal. An island is visible in the distance and, along with a nonsense verse sung off-screen by a young girl, we hear the sounds of surf. Because we also heard these sounds at the beginning of the film, these sonic references to nature bring this filmic odyssey acoustically to a close. The quest is over, the scrambled journey at an end. The beach represents the surrendering of desire, a sense of peacefulness before inevitably moving on. Once again, Hoffman the filmmaker prepares the way for Phil the character to mature and expand.

Since the 1970s, when experimental film began to find a tiny place in academe and occasional sources of financing through government agencies, the practice may have lost its innovative edge. In a polemical piece published in the *Millennium Film Journal* in 1987, Fred Camper complained that the institutionalization of experimental film has produced schools of supposedly avant-garde practice, but with none of the genuine creativity that had marked the works of (say) Maya Deren or Stan Brakhage in the past. "By the start of the institutional period," he contends, "the fundamental techniques and values of avant-garde filmmaking have already been established, and what once was a movement now becomes a genre" (120-121).

Lamentations for originary moments in film–viewing experiences are legion. Experiences are never as vibrant as they were in the days when we were young! Furthermore, in his insistence on internal coherence and on individual creativity standing out against the conformity of mass society, Camper is romantically modernist and relentlessly American. With the passing of time, however, the notion of "genre" can be seen in a different light. As Janine Marchessault has suggested:

> If modernism was characterized by the drive towards origin
> and purity, then the post-modernist practices of a new gen-
> eration of filmmakers emphasize heterogeneity of materials:
> a reconciliation of forms at once profoundly cynical and
> politically hopeful. (*International Experimental Film Congress* 115)

Marchessault goes on to suggest that the films of this generation "take on the difficult task of making sense through the fragment" and she concludes that "the struggle to create meaning out of chaos, to express a different conception of history and experience is one that, in Canada, continues to be strongly inspired by our documentary tradition" (115).

Traditionally using a wind-up Bolex and thus a minimum of synchronous sound, often keeping separate the elements of sound and image, the filmmakers of the Escarpment School are dedicated to a fresh, simultaneous exploration of the relation between film viewers and film works, and between self and world. If the diary format dominates, with the narration generally in the first-person singular, the films also retain a documentary integrity in relation to the historical world.

The Road Ended at the Beach was followed by *Somewhere Between Jalostotitlan and Encarnacion* (1984). On the surface a slight film and supposedly a documentary, it is extremely evocative and, on examination, may be more complex than it appears. Apparently shot in Mexico, *Somewhere Between* conveys a sense of suspension, a waiting in the face of an alterity that Hoffman has no heart to penetrate. Although we see Mexican musicians in the film, the sounds of Mike Callich's saxophone come from another space. Mexican footage is abandoned to silence, conveying the sense of nightmare or dream. Unlike the Coca-Cola sign that hangs over a village intersection, Hoffman feels he has no right to be in this forbidding place. Private events occur that ought not to be invaded.

The crucial privacy concerns a dead boy in the streets, whom Hoffman decides not to film. Intertitles inspired by haiku serve as narrative markers, telling the story we are not allowed to see. However, we do witness images of a religious procession and of Christian icons appropriate for the solemnity of death. Meanwhile, the solo saxophone continues along its apparently uncaring, improvisational path.

The structure of *Somewhere Between* is entirely contrapuntal. The three filmic elements of image, sound, and language (here exclusively in the form of intertitles) are all kept separate, coming together serendipitously from time to time as when, for a moment, the acoustic rhythms of the saxophone seem in synch with the visual rhythms of a Mexican drummer. Although the film conveys the feeling of an impenetrable territory, a space of suspension between two worlds, "the bardo state in Buddhist terms," as Hoffman once explained, (*Inside the Pleasure Dome* 142) attentive viewers may observe that much of the film was shot elsewhere. The religious procession, the Feast of Fatima, was filmed in Toronto. The band we see and the radiant girl at the end of the film, seemingly the dead boy's sister, were actually filmed in Colorado—at a conference in honour of Jack Kerouac!

While partly the result of low-budget exigencies, this geographical cheating suggests universality. The film is placed in Mexico, perhaps initially still in hom-

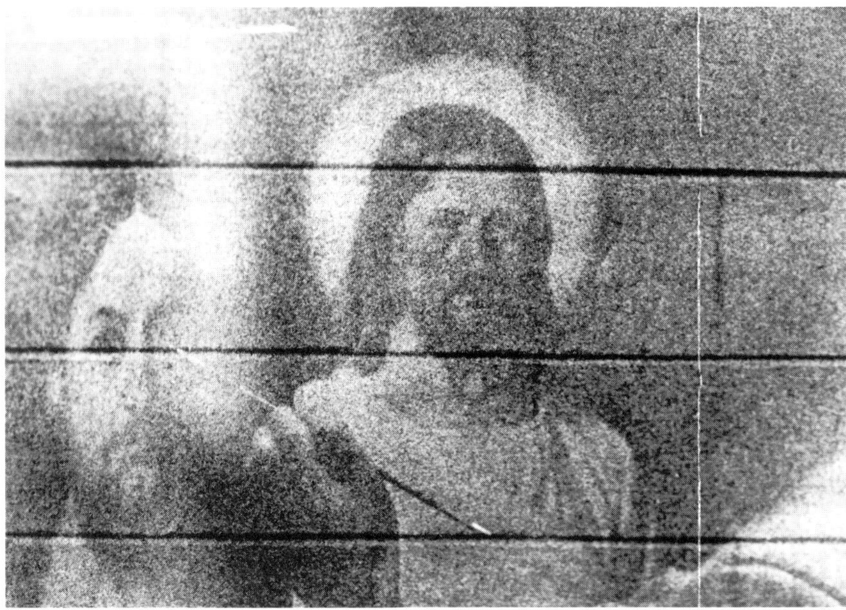

age to Kerouac and Cassady, as in *The Road Ended at the Beach*, but death occurs everywhere. Religious processions celebrate the mysteries of existence, and young girls gaze out at us—whether Dan's lovely daughter in Sable River, Nova Scotia, during a key moment in *The Road Ended at the Beach*, or a nameless child on her rock shell, supposedly the sister of the dead boy in the streets of Mexico but actually a stranger from Boulder, Colorado.

> The little girl
> With big eyes
> Waits by her dead brother
>
> Big trucks spit black smoke
> Clouds hung
> The boy's spirit left through its blue.

So conclude the final bits of printed commentary in Hoffman's *Somewhere Between Jalostotitlan and Encarnacion*, anchoring it in a specific place that, in actuality, we have scarcely seen. If, as in *The Road Ended at the Beach*, the roads of the Beats are now closed to Hoffman's generation, perhaps so too is Mexico as a site for mystic contemplation. Except by sly ruse. For if we think about it, was there ever, in reality, a dead boy in the streets?

For Philip Hoffman, going home has generally entailed a going away. The three major works of his Family Cycle all explore an elsewhere. In their very different ways, both *?O.Zoo! (The Making of a Fiction Film)* (1986) and *Kitchener-Berlin* (1990) explore the paternal inheritance, while *passing through/torn formations* (1988) explores the maternal one. All three of them touch upon fracturing and disease. Let us look at the two male films together.

?O,Zoo! doesn't appear to be a family film. Demonstrably, it is the most public film that Hoffman has ever made. It is certainly the wittiest, the most self-reflexive, the most deliberately theoretical. As Blaine Allan has written:

> *?O,Zoo! (The Making of a Fiction Film)* is ostensibly about the making of Peter Greenaway's feature film, *A Zed & Two Noughts*, the production of which Phil Hoffman was invited to the Netherlands to observe. However, Hoffman's film actually concerns the terms and conditions under which it was itself made. In part, the film translates actuality and memory into invention and fiction in which the symbolic father is cast as a real ancestor. Hoffman rewrites the Canadian documentary tradition into a family memory and romance. (90-91)

Indeed, the fiction film that *?O,Zoo!* supposedly observes is as much Hoffman's as Greenaway's. For *?O,Zoo!* is a fiction—a fiction about family and a fiction about film. Although the film is narrated as if in the first person, Hoffman withholds his own voice. He also invokes a host of imaginary father figures.

To begin with, there is the fictional grandfather, the newsreel cameraman, who made films supposedly for some federal film agency—an oblique reference to the National Film Board. The "old battle-axe" referred to is obviously John Grierson—the father of documentary and godfather of Canadian film. There is also the fleeting presence, evidently innocently included, of the source footage for *Watching for the Queen* (1973), a film by David Rimmer, one of the "father figures" of the first generation of Canadian experimental film.[4] Next there is a fuzzy shot of the Pope as seen on TV and even a decapitated statue of Christ in a Rotterdam square. Finally, there is the presence of Peter Greenaway, with his huge production facilities for the fabrication of his fanciful universe.

Purporting to be a documentary, offering us "truth" in the way that documen-

4. At the time of filming, Hoffman had not yet seen David Rimmer's film.

tary is assumed to do, *?O,Zoo!* actually lies about its own practice. It constantly invites us to look carefully at discrepancies between images and sounds. In one scene, we witness swans swimming in a pond while their absence is described.

Furthermore, the film playfully parallels Greenaway's. Like *A Zed & Two Noughts*, Hoffman's short examines the relationship between earth and world, between nature and civilization's efforts to tame it, whether through confinement in zoos or through photographic representations.[5] If Greenaway's film involves dismemberment, Hoffman's shows decapitation. If there are two brothers in *A Zed & Two Noughts*, there are two boys in *?O,Zoo!* If Michael Nyman's musical score is a witty part of Greenaway's film, so Tucker Zimmerman's pulsational minimalism is a witty part of Hoffman's film. As Hoffman has explained:

> It may be my story but there's a lot borrowed from
> Greenaway. Even my voice-over is like a Greenaway ruse.
> It's playful and there's humour in it—the kids playing with
> the shoes and getting shooed away by the parents. It has
> that play with language.

If the death of a boy in *Somewhere Between* was too private to film, so the death of an elephant in *?O,Zoo!* prompts the same kind of discretion. Except that in this film, the death is definitely a lie. Not only might we have noticed on one of the camera report sheets the scribble, "Elephant gets up," but by the end of the film—after the closing titles—we do indeed witness a resurrection!

Only in relation to Hoffman's other work can *?O,Zoo!* appear as a family film; yet without some recognition of family, the concluding shot of an old man with a camera in his hand walking side by side with a young boy wouldn't make much sense. The boy isn't Phil, but it could be; and as always in Hoffman's films, they are both, supposedly, relatives.

An immensely playful film rich in observational detail, *?O,Zoo!* moves us by its intimacy, yet challenges our assumptions about the nature of filmic truth. Hoffman acknowledges that the film "is less the diary of personal experience than an exploration of the ways in which we create fiction to make meaning of lived experience" (*Toronto: A Play of History* 157). As an "experimental documentary," it is an extraordinary achievement.

Less satisfactory, it seems to me, is Hoffman's *Kitchener-Berlin*. As a family film, it is certainly less accessible. Comprising footage shot by his paternal Uncle John, the images are less anchored in an observable reality, and Hoffman seems absent from his own film. Mapping such a work is difficult. Abstract in conception, the film is more concerned with ideas than people. "The film is about technology and its rise, which is the machine world," Hoffman has explained. Perhaps desiring to retreat from the insistent family preoccupations of *passing through/torn*

5. By way of Bruce Elder, Dennis Lee, and Martin Heidegger. See R. Bruce Elder's "Forms of Cinema, Models of Self: Jack Chambers' The Hart of London" in *Take Two: A Tribute to Film in Canada*, 264-274.

formations, in *Kitchener-Berlin* the "here" is contrasted with the "there," activities with buildings; however, in both the new world and the old, a restless camera mounted on a steadicam floats about, collapsing discernible differences.

Although the steadicam is itself an example of technology, Hoffman employed it for metaphysical reasons. "There's an obvious kind of spiritual feel to it, because you're floating in a world where the sky and ground are equivalent," he writes (Inside the Pleasure Dome 145). But this assertion may not make sense. To what extent can "the body of film itself, its flesh and voice," as Bruce Elder once insisted, achieve film's "liberating potential"? (International Experimental Film Congress 45) Although films may aspire to the condition of transcendence, I would argue that if the stylistic tropes of cinema can suggest eternity, they cannot depict it. For instance, about *?O,Zoo!* Blaine Allan has written:

> A scene shot with a static camera captures the sight of Greenaway's camera crew in liquid motion as they track laterally across the screen. The dolly and tracks are concealed below the frame line and the figures float across space, appearing as disjoined from the earth as actors against a painted or projected backdrop. (91)

Here the connotation of weightlessness is arguably more evocative within an observable filmic space than when earth and sky are collapsed, as throughout *Kitchener-Berlin.* Furthermore, with the male display of slaughtered animals earlier in the film and the family scenes of enforced Christmas kissing towards the end, *Kitchener-Berlin* seems too reminiscent of Jack Chambers' *The Hart of London* (1970), but without the personal voice that so tentatively concludes Chambers' "transcendent" film.

As part of its patrimony, in *Kitchener-Berlin*, images of aggressive male activities recur. The cannons of war shoot missiles away from the earth; miners drill at its entrails beneath. The Pope makes an appearance, again on television, blessing Aboriginals; a magnificent cathedral in Cologne appears to be "penetrated" by a huge, orange crane.

At the centre of the film is an apparent newsreel item about a dirigible flight from England to Canada. As elderly twins are supposedly involved in filming the flight, the item repeats Hoffman's concern with splitting and doubling. *Kitchener-Berlin* is also in two parts, the second part more impersonal than the first. As Hoffman has explained:

> The second part of the film moves towards the surreal. I
> tried to make the second half of the film without thinking.
> So with the sunflowers out of focus and the cave, it
> becomes like a Brakhage psychic-type film, and especially
> at that time I was touched by Brakhage.

Hoffman has also suggested that "the way the images arrive is a surprise. They

still: *passing through/torn formations.*

don't seem to connect and, formally, they're hard to follow."[6] Many viewers would agree. Although its visceral appeal is palpable, *Kitchener-Berlin* is difficult to grasp conceptually. The references are too arbitrary. Like the ongoing *river* project (1979-89), *Kitchener-Berlin* perhaps works best at a precognitive level—as a film of surfaces, psychedelic superimpositions and kinaesthetic effects. It marks a retreat from the examination of the specificities of Hoffman's family inheritance, as represented by *passing through/torn formations*, and moves through abstractions toward some kind of closure to this family cycle. There is also, perhaps, a sense of fatigue.

6. This "newsreel" footage is itself a ruse, contrived by Dent Harrison, the creator and actor of the sequence. He doubled himself by superimpositions to create his twin brother.

After the achievement of *passing through/torn formations*, a sense of fatigue would be understandable. If *?O,Zoo!* is Hoffman's most public film, *passing through* is his most private. At the same time, through the choreography of its images and through the guiding presence of Hoffman's questing voice, it is the most fully realized of the Family Cycle.

The film begins with the voice of Christopher Dewdney. While the screen remains dark, he speaks about a boy freeing a dead moth from its fossilization within a piece of layered stone, thereby establishing the geological dimension of the film. The story also establishes a specificity of space. Dewdney explains, "You feel sure that you could recognize these clouds with their limestone texture out of random cloud photographs from all over the world."

passing through is dedicated to Babji, Phil's grandmother. She is, of course, the mother of Sue, Phil's mother, but also of Wally, the disturbed uncle who is the unseen victim/hero of the film. A tale told with love, *passing through/torn formations* is full of shadows. Speaking Polish on Czechoslovakian soil that had once been part of the Austro-Hungarian Empire, the Kaczmarzyk family has been afflicted by fragmentation as well as sickness. Europe has been ravaged by two world wars and families are scattered in the pursuit of emigration.

After the Dewdney poem at the opening, there is a silent scene of Babji in a nursing home, being cared for by Sue. The silence is eerie, as is the blue wash of colour. Although we can see the women talking, we cannot hear what they are saying. While the camera cuts away to register curtains on a window and flowers on a table, we get a sense of the perishability of life—a perishability reinforced by the end-of-roll flare that keeps recurring on the screen, suggesting by association the end of Babji's life.

The simplest way of unpacking this film might be to deal with two sustaining moments: (a) Wally's instability, his need for a corner mirror, and his accordion; and (b) Sue's recurring depressions and the scene of the missing cows. Both moments embrace healing.

The mirror was devised by Wally in his schizophrenic panic as an attempt to deal with his split personality—to see himself as others see him, in double reflection. Like the mirror, Wally's accordion is also an image of splitting and doubling, since the left hand deals with the bass and the right hand with the melody. Performance is part of healing, of putting the two sides together. As Hoffman's commentary explains, " … while Polish polka turns to Irish jig, turns to German march, and then a note repeats itself, again and again," the scattering of self and of national cultures is contained by music. "The music was a vacant place to return to," Hoffman recites. "Over and over. His playing gave him passage."

Born during sickness, Wally is the victim of historical and personal events. There had been the influenza epidemic at the time of Babji's birth, as there had been a boil on Babji's neck at the time of Wally's. "He is to me," Hoffman has clarified, "the epicentre of the pain of the family." Wally exists at "the point where the old world and the new world collide" (*Inside the Pleasure Dome* 146). Like the cyclist in *The Road Ended at the Beach*, Wally too has perhaps been "touched by God."

The scene of the missing cows addresses the healing powers of memory, both for Phil's mother, whose story it is, and for young Andrea in Czechoslovakia, who helped Phil recreate it. Sue has often been subject to severe depressions, a situation referred to as far back as *On The Pond*. Part of her healing, Hoffman's film implies, involves the recovery of memory through the sharing of stories, central to which is the story of the cows.

The story is both told and recreated—once again blurring past and present, fact and fiction, images and words. For instance, Sue is often framed at the lower right-hand corner of the screen, translating from Hoffman's Polish interviews, and the family references are both specific and general. Family members from Canada and relatives from Czechoslovakia are not easy to identify because their identities continually shift and slide. These characters are transferable throughout the film; for instance, you see an image or images of a certain person with an accompanying voice-over. Later on, different voices are attached to the image of the person earlier seen. The technique is a way of avoiding the conventional approach to character construction, whereby the character's identity gets pinned down and there's less work for the audience.

Throughout *passing through*, the camera constantly pans over the gnarled trunks of old trees and along stone fences, the images sometimes superimposed over photographs of family, sometimes on their own. Not only do the fences echo the opening image of the fossilized rock, but as Gary Popovich suggests elsewhere in this volume, the "blue blood that surges through her [Babji's] body finds its mirrored image in the craggy rock formations of her homeland, where her grandson now makes his pilgrimage" (59).

Are these stone fences barriers against easy entry into the past, into the otherness of a relinquished world? Or are they structures of containment—enduring punctuations of human spaces that have evolved over time? If metaphorically the walls are barriers, with the passing of time they have also become culturally created geological formations. They are part of the natural world that, with our addiction to the practicalities of wire fencing, has been lost in North America.

Like the moth emerging from stone in Dewdney's poem, the present emerges from the past. While there is damage—the formations may be torn—there is also life. As Tucker Zimmerman can transform Wally's accordion riffs into the impulsional portamenti that animate this film, so an equilibrium can be found within this world of veined hands and craggy fields.

After the final shots of the stone fences that demarcate the fields of present-day Slovakia, over black leader we hear Marian McMahon reading from her memoir, *A Circuitous Quest*: "Early one morning, when I was eight years old, I skipped a flat stone across the surface of Lake Kashagawigamog." Momentarily, weight has been defied. A stone has been made to float. Balance has been achieved—and with it, a sense of wonder.

Hoffman's Family Cycle films consist entirely of quest stories. They follow the circuitous movement of away and return. The early journeys of *On The Pond* and *The Road Ended at the Beach* are a questing after self; the later ones—*Somewhere Between*, *?O,Zoo!* and *passing through/torn formations*—register a confrontation with alterity. Perhaps it is the absence of a personal confrontation that renders *Kitchener-Berlin*, to my mind, a less satisfactory achievement.

In Hoffman's work, the quest can be seen as a personalized enactment of everyone's journey through life. The quest embodies a search for more individual goals, not all of them attainable. Although the past may be explored, it cannot be claimed. If you do manage to go back, as Franny wanted to do in *On the Pond*, you cannot stay there. As Janine Marchessault has declared, "Memories are immutable cells that can be rearranged but never made to speak" (28).

Hence, except for the "realizations" of the closing shot, the quest in *The Road Ended at the Beach* is a "failure." When the Beats were in their prime throughout the 1950s, politically the world was opening up. By the 1980s, it was closing down. "The Beats were the fathers I took on the trip," Hoffman has explained, "but their roads are closed now" (International Experimental Film Congress 116). Besides which the Beats' quest was probably too American, too drug-induced, and perhaps, finally, too homoerotic to serve as a controlling model for a young buck from southern Ontario. Hoffman has had to retreat from such classic allegorical journeys to enable him to move forward in his own life and work.

Similarly, the films of the Escarpment School signal a retreat from modernism. Although Bruce Elder, with his musical commitment to Wagnerian repetition and redundancy, still strives to achieve works of high modernism in a postmodern age, the filmmakers of the Escarpment School espouse more modest goals. Their quests are less concerned with self in relation to metaphysical transcendence than with self in relation to the social world.

The important point, then, about the boy exploring the culvert in *passing through/torn formations* is not who he is or what he might find or even what his relationship is (if any) to Hoffman's family: the important point is the fact that he is looking. He embodies the curiosity of a new generation, attentive to discovering his own voice within the landscape available to him and to making his own peace with the world.

So once again, we return to documentary. Through the confrontation of self with alterity, with the fractured otherness of the world in which he lives, Hoffman seeks to make sense of his historical world. And yet, at his best—supremely in *passing through/torn formations*, with its movement through disease, derangement and death toward moments of epiphany—this confrontation does achieve a spiritual dimension. Drawing upon a theological term adduced by Dennis Lee when writing about Al Purdy, we might refer to a mysterium tremendum—a holy otherness. "An appropriate response to the tremendum," Lee elucidates, "is awe, joy, terror, gratitude"—exactly the emotions we may feel while experiencing Hoffman's most achieved films (141).

The experimental cinema of Philip Hoffman embodies some of the finest attributes of the work of his generation. Like his colleagues, Richard Kerr, Gary Popovich, and Mike Hoolboom (among others), through the diary format Hoffman achieves a cinematic poetry that is as distinguished as any experimental films today. In a world in which theatrical film has become a big brass band, the filmmakers of the Escarpment School content themselves with chamber films—with trios or string quartets, sometimes made for instruments with only two or three strings!

Bart Testa once suggested that these films become, finally, "voyages of discovery that shift interest onto formal questions of how meaning is disclosed and expressed" (92). This self-reflective play throughout Hoffman's work constitutes a large part of its value. If experimental filmmaking is now really "a tradition which new filmmakers have to face," as Fred Camper has insisted (35), Philip Hoffman has faced it with courage and originality. The circuitous quests undertaken by his Family Cycle films enshrine his lasting value as an important Canadian artist working in film.

Works Cited

I would like to thank Barbara Goslawski and Alan McNairn of the Canadian Filmmakers Distribution Centre in Toronto for re-screening Hoffman's films for me; Mike Hoolboom for having invited me to write this article and for his most helpful suggestions; and, of course, Phil Hoffman himself, both for his trust and for his films.

Allan, Blaine.
"It's not finished yet (Some Notes on Toronto Filmmaking)." *Toronto: A Play of History*. Ed. Louise Dompierre et. al. Toronto: The Power Plant, 1987.
90-91.

Camper, Fred.
"The End of Avant-Garde Film." *Millennium Film Journal 16/17* (Fall/Winter 1986/87).
99-124.

Dorland, Michael.
"The Void is Not So Bleak: Rhetoric and Structure in Canadian Experimental Film." *Canadian Journal of Political and Social Theory 14*, No. 1-3 (Montreal, 1990).
148-159.

Hoffman, Philip.
"A Play of History." *Toronto: A Play of History*.
100-101.

Hoffman, Philip.
"Philip Hoffman: Pictures of Home." *Inside the Pleasure Dome: Fringe Film in Canada*. Ed. Mike Hoolboom. Toronto: Gutter Press, 1997.
138-147.

Hoolboom, Mike.
"A History of the Canadian Avant-Garde in Film." *The Visual Aspect: Recent Canadian Experimental Films*. Éditions des Archives du Film Experimental d'Avignon, 1991.
43-44.

International Experimental Film Congress. Toronto: Art Gallery of Ontario, 1989.

Lee, Dennis.
Body Music. Toronto: Anansi, 1998.

Marchessault, Janine.
Lift Newsletter. November 1988, Toronto.
28.

Povovich, Gary.
"passing through/torn formations, by Philip Hoffman." *LIFT Newsletter*, 1988.
26-28.

Testa, Bart.
Spirit in a Landscape. Toronto: Art Gallery of Ontario, 1989.

PICTURES OF HOME: HOFFMAN IN THE 80s, AN INTERVIEW

by Mike Hoolboom

Mike Hoolboom: Any early experiences with pictures you can remember?

Philip Hoffman: The first one I can think of was my grandmother, Babji, who used to shoot from the hip, without looking through the viewfinder. These low-angle shots always turned out and made us look as big as John Wayne. That was the perfect size when we were little. I didn't think of it until years later when I realized I was shooting like that sometimes, using the body to find the picture. I had a box camera for years but didn't get into photography until I met Richard Kerr. He was a couple of years older than me and was going out with my sister. We set up a darkroom in my basement and figured out how to work it ourselves. I was writing poetry, but never showed it to anyone. The photography was different. It was a language I could use to talk to people because I didn't have words. I was shooting a lot of family stuff—moments of everyday life. I played hockey and tried the accordion unsuccessfully because there were always rules. I was made to play scales, which gave me an ear for rhythm, but killed the play in it. Kitchener was a very business-oriented city; you had to look around to feed your interests. I managed to find small pockets where I could work, and those were private places, caves. That's where I did the writing and the photography. I went into business in my first year of university, which was just remote control—everyone in the Hoffman family went into business. But after one year, that was enough, and I took English literature and some film courses, still trying to decide what to do. To support myself I was working in a factory making boxes and figuring out all week what I'd do at the weekend farm house. I would go up with friends and get blasted and shoot these crazy skits on super-8. There was a rift between what the poet desired and what I thought was desired of me: to be a good citizen of Kitchener-Waterloo. It's just driven into you there.

still: *Opening Series 2.*

HOOLBOOM: Were you expected to work at Hoffman's Meats?

HOFFMAN: My grandfather expected me to. I was Philip the Third, you know. [laughs] I was kind of the heir. My father always wanted to be something else, but he had to work in the factory. His father was one of those staunch Germans, so he never got a chance to do what he wanted. He was quite open to letting me go, giving me the chance he never had. When he was selling the business he asked if I wanted in, and I told him no. Then I decided to go to film school. I tried York and Queen's, which dropped me because of my business marks. Then I called up the chairperson at Sheridan College, and I was so welcomed that it seemed like the place to go. Richard had been there a year already.

HOOLBOOM: That's where you made *On the Pond* (9 min., b/w, 1978)?

HOFFMAN: Yes. It was a personal documentary because it makes sense to begin with something you know. It wasn't so different from the kinds of writing and photography I'd done up to that point, which dealt directly with people around me. *On the Pond* began with a slide show. I was fairly quiet in the family. I had three sisters who were a couple of years older than me—triplets. They garnered lots of attention. But this was my birthday, so I knew I had the full attention of the family. I miked the whole room and showed slides. I constructed another slide show for the film and cut the comments down from a couple of hours to a few minutes. The slides showed moments with the family. There's one picture taken from behind my mother. My dad's looking off in the distance as if he's discovering some new world. We were out in the bush, where we would go for walks. In the film you hear voices saying, "Oh, do you remember when we went out on that walk?" And then to my mother, "Oh, that's when you were feeling lousy." Except it's not "feeling lousy." There's an incredible amount of trauma which is being dismissed, and the photo shows the shadow of her sickness. You can hear the way her memory is being taken away, how her voice is being levelled. We were taking "good care" of her pain. And then someone says, "Oh look, there's Phil and he's smiling," because I'm smiling in the corner of the picture. So, what's taken up isn't my mother's problems, but the face I made for them. The smile has to do with pleasing her, hoping to make things better. So everything's there in that photograph. It was shot from the hip, unposed, and it was exciting going through these photos for clues to a past I'd slept through. I think childhood is so traumatic we sleep through most of it.

HOOLBOOM: Was the whole film going to be photographs?

HOFFMAN: No, I wanted to make a kind of docudrama. I got my cousin to play me as a little boy, getting up early, skating out on the ice, stickhandling with the dog. Then the social space enters in the soundtrack, breaking his solitude—you hear the coach yelling and other voices while the boy does push-ups alone on the ice.

HOOLBOOM: The film moves between these two arenas—between hockey and the family—as if you have to choose one or the other, or that hockey was a way to leave home.

HOFFMAN: That's what happened in my life—the year I made *On the Pond* I quit hockey. I was playing for the college team, and we had an exhibition game at Kent State, where there was a big demonstration. The university was trying to

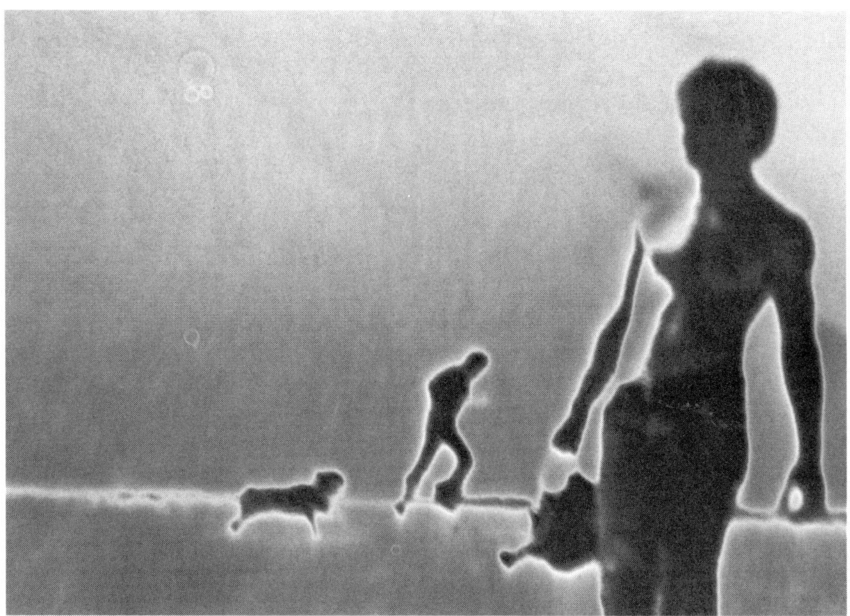

build a gym on the ground where the students had been gunned down. There were cops on horseback trying to gas the demonstrators, and I grabbed a camera and filmed it. That was the point where I left hockey. It was becoming apparent that hockey players weren't the people I wanted to spend time with. The competition was so draining. So I simply transferred the energy I was putting toward sports into filmmaking.

I finished *On the Pond* in a very heavy Marxist time, and some people were taking a lot of knocks for making films about their own experiences. "Personal" filmmaking was considered self-indulgent. But now things have come 'round again. Now you can't just run out and point a camera at someone. Personal work wasn't thought of as political back then, but to my mind it's the most political.

HOOLBOOM: How did *The Road Ended at the Beach* (33 min., 1983) start?
HOFFMAN: Before I went to Sheridan I used to go on trips through Canada. I'd work the first part of the summer, then travel for the last month and go back to school. In those days, in my late teens, I carried a super-8 camera with me just to shoot stuff, not thinking or knowing anything about making films. While I was at Sheridan, I continued travelling and collecting footage and called it Road Journals—it was an ongoing sketch pad. After school ended, I planned a trip with some cameras and sound gear, and this became the central trip the others would weave in and out of. Jim McMurray and I started in Ann Arbor because that's where the van was, then drove north to Kitchener to pick up Richard Kerr. Then we headed east and visited Robert Frank in Cape Breton. And Danny, a friend who'd gone to school with us, wanted to make films, but got dragged down with his life in Nova Scotia. You see this idyllic setting with the dogs playing in the water, and then he says, "Well I have to work in the fish plant—you have to do that if you want to live out here."

still: *The Road Ended at the Beach. Photo* by Richard Kerr.

The trip was staged—we'd travelled together in the past—and we were trying to remake what we'd already done, to recapture that feeling. But that didn't work at all. I'd known Richard for ten years. It would have been different if we'd gone five years earlier, because then we were in the maturity of our relation. The same with Jim. All that comes through in the film. This isn't *Highway 61* or *Roadkill*, because the romance is gone. We're travelling through a cold Canadian summer and not meeting any "girls." [laughs] It's a different kind of journey. By the late 70s the road film was dead. And these three guys can't really talk with each other. We're all waiting on an experience that isn't coming and no one's sure why. It has a lot to do with how men relate to each other, dealing with outer realities, getting the job done. Filmmaker Mark Rappapport said that it's a record of the time: when Kerouac travelled, things were opening up, but by 1980 everyone was hunkering down for Reagan, everything was closing up. Everyone on this trip is alone and isolated: Frank's retreated to Mabou, the guys on the road are caught in dead-end jobs, and nobody's relating to each other in the van.

HOOLBOOM: *Road Ended* pictures a series of imagined homes to which the film attempts to return. Some of these homes are from past trips, or past times spent with folks in the van, and these are presented against a backdrop of 50s Beat writing, especially Kerouac's *On The Road.*

HOFFMAN: Well, that's the myth right there—it's confronted by drawing these different decades together in the editing. The Beats were the fathers I took on the trip, but their roads are closed now. I was attracted to the possibility of spirituality that Kerouac held out through his Zen practice, even though he died an alcoholic far from the lotus tree. But it was one of the first expressions of Eastern culture I'd encountered. It wasn't the drugs or parties, but those simple moments of description of what's there in front of him.

Hoolboom: Kerouac's trying to live in the moment, to conjure the present through his writing, and finally to make life that moment.

Hoffman: Kerouac was writing while he was on the move, but when you're filming the camera gets in the way. Personal relations become performance when a camera is there. Have you ever seen that old Neil Cassady film when he's on camera? It doesn't work. The mythology isn't there. The camera says, "I'm immortalizing you." The present moment can't be returned; the camera takes it apart. But you can go off alone with the camera and create energy—like the last scene where I'm dancing on the beach. That kind of thing expresses the Kerouac ideal of pure energy in movement. As far as Robert Frank goes, even though nobody was making photographs like him in the 50s, he was still taking the moment and stealing it from someone. I've always had trouble taking pictures of people I don't know. He had a social reason—he was trying to show America's spiritual bankruptcy. I was making a personal film. That's why the photography in *Road Ended* is so careful, so unlike a road movie. There's no barging into strange places and waving cameras around. That was done in cinéma vérité in the 60s, and I have problems with that.

Hoolboom: How did *Somewhere Between Jalostotitlan and Encarnacion* (6 min., 1984) begin?

Hoffman: There was a reunion of Beat poets in Boulder at "Jack Kerouac's School of Disembodied Poets," at least that's what Ginsberg called it. I drove down with my sister and a friend. Robert Frank was there, and I wanted to ask him if I could use one of his photographs in *Road Ended*. But every time I tried to talk to him something would happen, some guy would walk up, "Are you really Robert Frank?" Finally, I bumped into him by accident, smashed right into him, and he was his normal humble self. He remembered our dog. So that was fine. I wanted to go to Boulder before going down to Mexico, where I had this romantic notion of shooting very simple events—I had been reading haiku. The Bolex is a camera powered by a spring that you wind up and it runs for twenty-eight seconds. I wanted to use the length of its wind as my frame for these haiku shots. The Bolex was perfect because it's light and doesn't need batteries, and I'd worked with it so often I knew when the shot would end. I used its so-called limitation to my own advantage as a structuring principle. I went with ten minutes of film. I'd met Adriana Peña on one of my *Road Ended* trips and was going down to see her. She was taking me around, and I became involved with her family. It was a bit strange. She was showing her family the man she was maybe going to marry, and then I realized that this was perhaps not such a good idea. [laughs]

Hoolboom: Can you explain what a haiku is?

Hoffman: Haiku is a three-line poem with a five-seven-five beat structure. It usually describes everyday events. The three images, or lines, go together to form a new expression—Eisenstein used haiku as an inspiration for his ideas about montage. So I shot things for twenty-eight seconds, each shot the same length, and in the midst of this shooting found myself on a bus between Jalostotitlan and Encarnacion. The bus stopped, and a woman came screaming across a field. Her little boy had been run over. I watched from inside the bus with the camera in my hand, trying to decide whether to film or not. And that's what the film becomes. When I got back to Toronto, I decided to try and make a film about that moment without the image.

Hoolboom: Why didn't you film it?

Hoffman: Gut reaction. I can intellectualize it now. I could say: I didn't want
the camera to get in the way of the experience, or I wasn't ready, or it would have
made a lot of people uncomfortable, or I didn't want to be like some reporter
"getting" the scene. In the editing I inserted intertitles, which talk about the boy
on the road in a bastardized kind of haiku. It has to do with my own working
through death. I've been taught that death isn't part of life—it happens on television, or in life as a theatrical event at the funeral parlour with make-up and
masks. The title *Somewhere Between Jalostotitlan and Encarnacion* suggests, for
me, the passage from death to birth—the bardo state in Buddhist terms. Between
these two places is the death of a boy. Jalostotitlan has, in its centre, an ornate
graveyard that we passed by on our way to the death. Encarnacion suggests
"incarnation," an embodiment in flesh. Visually the film is bookended with shots
in black and white. The death is rendered metaphorically in colour superimposition before the film returns to black and white for the last shot, which shows the
passing water of a river, the rebirth.

I was working on the film in my basement apartment when I heard a religious
parade pass by. I went out and filmed it, not sure of how I'd use it or which film it
was going into. I count on this kind of coincidence to make my work. I was experimenting with multiple layers of pictures—shooting a roll of blue brick wall, then
winding the camera back and letting chance have its way. The work I'd done up to
that point had been more representational and used static camerawork, even in
my Mexico shooting. My ideas of documentary had been quite traditional, but
what I'd learned in *Road Ended* was that there's always something outside the
frame, and that's what *Somewhere Between* is about.

Bart Testa was the first person to offer this work some public attention. He pro-
grammed the Grierson Documentary Seminar in 1984, calling it "Systems in
Collapse." The seminar doesn't happen anymore, but back then it was important
in my theoretical development as a filmmaker. There were people making television documentaries and others making experimental work, so there were very
heated debates. Bart's programming was critical, and he said he wouldn't do the
seminar unless he could show *The Falls* by Greenaway. He also invited *Road
Ended* and *Somewhere Between*. There were people complaining they only had
$100,000 to make a film, while I was showing *Somewhere Between*, which was
shot on three rolls of film. So Bart was making a point by inviting me. At the seminar, my work was paired up with a guy named Don North, a news correspondent
who'd made a number of films about Vietnam. There was one bloody massacre
after another, and he said that was the stuff they didn't cut. Then my program
came on, which also dealt with death but never showed it. Because television and
violent movies have conditioned us to see pictures of death in a certain way, when
we see it for real it's just the same. My film argued that you could deal with
another side of death or that the possibility of mourning lies in the unseen.

Hoolboom: There's something very Catholic in this refusal. Death is granted
a power because of its secrecy; there's an awe and mystery that its revelation could
only trivialize.

Hoffman: Not showing death wasn't because of fear, but respect. I didn't
want to barge into its territory, to try to exploit it for my own work. It was a cere-

mony that didn't belong to me. I was honoured to be in its presence but, at the same time, it wasn't mine. So after the seminar North approached me and said, "Phil, I really enjoyed the discussion, but you know when you were in the editing room, didn't you just wish you had the footage?" Some things don't change.

I think Peter Greenaway connected with the independent filmmaker in me—the idea of making work with what you have available. He was really moved by *Road Ended*. He talked about the poetry in the images. I asked if it might be possible to see one of his film shoots and he said sure and wrote me a reference letter. The only way I could arrange financing was through an apprentice program, but he's not into "learning from the father." He felt my work would develop on its own. In his letter he said I needed opportunities to make work and that I should get funding to make a film about anything I wanted and that I didn't need to use a script. That was the other thing—I was working without a script, just collecting images over a long period of time and making sense of them in the editing. So in the summer of 1985, I got $3,500 to go to Rotterdam and spend two or three months gathering pictures. I had about forty minutes of film. I worked the same way as in the past, shooting about thirty seconds a day, whenever the light and my inclinations met. I shot on and off location while Greenaway was making *A Zed and Two Noughts* in the Rotterdam zoo.

?O,Zoo! begins with images the narrator says are made by his grandfather, who was a newsreel cameraman—it's a Greenaway-type ruse. Then it shifts into the making of the film around *A Zed and Two Noughts*. The diary starts with the trip to Holland and fairly mundane images—of animals, a huge, wooden apple in the park, a headless statue—while the narrator speaks of what happens before and after the shot, with what's outside the frame. Then the screen goes black and the narrator speaks:

> From a distance I heard the scream of a beast. Moving closer to the source of the sound, I saw that an elephant had fallen down and was struggling to get up. Outside the enclosure, I noticed that a group of people had gathered to watch and inside some elephants and zoo workers had surrounded the fallen animal, trying to give it encouragement as it rocked its huge body in the sand. As I watched, I tossed over and over in my mind whether to film the scene or not. I've come across this problem before. Like the crowd that had gathered, I was feeling helpless; I wanted to assist the beast and filming would make me feel that I was doing something constructive. Maybe the television network would buy the film and show people that tragedy is right at their doorstep.
>
> I took out the tripod, set up the camera and looked through the viewfinder. The compressed image caused by the telephoto lens intensified the sounds coming from the huge rolling body. I pull the trigger, listen to the spring

slowly unwind, and watch the elephant's painful rhythm. I
wind the camera tight and press the trigger for another burst
of twenty-eight seconds. Now the zoo keeper is shoving
bales of hay under the elephant as the others surround it.
This only gets the elephant more aroused. The heat is
intense and in its excitement the elephant plunges back into
the sand and with one last scream, stretches out its body …
and then it stops moving. The attendant says that the elephant has had a heart attack. My throat is parched, and
sweat pours off my body; I watch the dust settle. I go looking for a drink, pushing through the crowd, fixed on the
image I'd filmed; as if my mind was the film and the permanent trace of the elephant's death was projected brightly
inside. Somehow it's my responsibility now. I wonder why I
took the film. There seems no reason to develop the negative; my idea of selling the film to the network seems just an
embarrassing thought, an irresponsible plan. I decide to put
the film in the freezer. I decide not to develop it.

This is another example of the unconscious speaking. I wrote the story after the
event happened, then realized it was directly connected to one of the first deaths
I experienced. After my grandfather died, my uncle asked me to go to the funeral

still: *passing through/torn
formations.*

home and take pictures of him in the casket. I showed up and didn't know what I was doing there. I'd been making photographs for years and didn't want to document him in this fake place. But I took the pictures and put the film in the freezer for eight years. In a way, the film was a way to act this out, to return to my grandfather. It keeps coming back in my films, so whether I've laid him to rest or not …

Hoolboom: How does *passing through/torn formations* (43 min., 1988) relate to your previous work?

Hoffman: In terms of my film work, *On the Pond* relates to my boyhood and family. *Road Ended* deals with travelling and friends and adolescence. *Somewhere Between* and *?O,Zoo!* deal with fathers and a documentary tradition brought down by fathers from which I'm trying to make something of my own. *passing through/torn formations* is the first film to deal with my mother's side of the family—it's filled with passion and chaos. The previous work features a locked-down camera in confined spaces. But *passing through* begins with a camera floating through a nursing home, hovering over my mother as she feeds my grandmother Babji. I couldn't show death in my previous work, but here I had a very close connection. I loved my grandmother very much; she was the first to tell me that dreams were important, so her decline had to be dealt with directly. The film unravels from her; she's the matriarch. But it doesn't begin there. It starts with a Chris Dewdney poem called "The Quarry." A boy opens a rock which has a moth inside, destined for fossilization, and as he opens it, the moth flies out "like dust from a dust devil." The moth that's being freed is the uncovering of family history, making it an open, interactive system. My purpose in making the film was to try to return my uncle to the family. He's a street person who's been cast out because his mental instability and violence caused a lot of grief. Idealistically, I felt that I would make a film with him and make an interjection into a family history that never moves, where things aren't spoken.

Hoolboom: You remarked earlier that while making *?O,Zoo!* you'd assumed some of the form of Greenaway's work—that this was part of your diary approach. In *passing through* I felt you'd assumed or mimed your uncle's demeanour—the film is rife with splits, multiple exposures, simultaneous address, broken subjects, departures, wars, and arguments.

Hoffman: One of the stories my uncle told me was about his accordion. His father made him practice every day because he was going to be a great musician. But the instrument isn't balanced. You play the melody with your right hand and the bass line with your left, so you have to split your mind in two. He felt that's what led to his "manic depressive" or "schizophrenic" behaviour. I have a different take on it. I think he had a great capacity as an artist but wasn't allowed to express it except through the accordion. His parents had come to Canada from Czechoslovakia—at that time, the Austro-Hungarian Empire—and were already in their forties when he was born. He wound up in the pool halls listening to Elvis Presley and playing jazz accordion, but they couldn't accept that, and this rift grew into a psychosis. He thought it was bad to split your mind. But in order to watch the film you have to split, you have to think in a non-linear way. Because many stories are being told at the same time, the viewer has to choose how to move through it. The form relates not only to his ideas about the accordion but to the way he is, as if I were him.

HOOLBOOM: The film also tries to heal some of these splits, and the central image of this integration is a corner mirror your uncle builds.

HOFFMAN: He made it because he'd heard someone talk about left/right-brain differences. He felt that when you shave in front of a mirror you're actually seeing yourself as a reflection—you don't see yourself as others do. He felt that all the years he'd been shaving helped split him apart, and he could solve this with the corner mirror: two mirrors which reflect into each other. He had to relearn how to shave because the reflection was the reverse of what he'd grown used to. He felt that ritual would exorcise his demons and heal him. He did the same thing in prison, when he rewired an electric organ so all the low notes started at the right and left ends of the keyboard: they were symmetrical and moved to a central note in the middle. Of course, he was the only person who could play that organ. [laughs] He was trying to unlearn conventions of the past, the way he'd conditioned himself to live. That moment of creation and transformation is the moment of freeing the moth from the rock. It's the moment where the image comes to the paper when you're making a photograph. It's magical because you're totally in the present watching what's becoming. That's what I got from him, that living instant, but on the other hand there were other things attached to him that became too difficult. He was like the elephant in *?O,Zoo!*, or the dead boy in *Somewhere Between*—the image that couldn't be looked at because he would be judged. So he's hardly shown.

My brother Phillip died at birth. My uncle Wally wasn't much older than me, so he became the brother I never had. Wally was born during the Second World War, while my grandmother was in great anguish over her brothers and sisters. While she was pregnant she grew a huge boil on her neck, and I use this as a metaphor in the film—as a poison coming to the surface. My grandmother was hearing stories about her brother's wife being raped by Russians and Nazis as they went through the country. After the war, my grandmother, mother, and Wally went back to visit. I guess Wally was about five. There were still blood-stained walls and ruins, and Wally got sick. No one went again until I did in 1984. That's the trip I show in the film, where I asked my grandmother's sister to tell me what happened with Uncle Janyk, who was shot by his brother. There was an argument over land. The son had built a house on land which had been promised to him but the father refused to sell it to him. He wanted to own his son. So the son killed the father. All these stories are strewn through the film, which has been deliberately made so you can't follow it like a Roots chronology.

I should say something about Marian McMahon's involvement with the film. With my life. We've been together a long time now, and she's changed the way I look at things, and I thought it was important to have her present in the film. The film ends with her voice making a very simple statement: "When I was eight years old, I skipped a flat stone six times across the smooth surface of Lake Kashagawigamog." This recalls the Dewdney poem at the beginning of the film, which is also spoken in darkness. Her speaking returns the film to Canada, or to a pre-Canadian continent, because Kashagawigamog is a Native word. So even though all these ethnic migrations are going on, both ends of the film deal with a time before the Europeans came. Dewdney's poem refers to geological time, and Marian's to a time belonging to the Natives. The kind of relentless uncovering that the film attempts is something I learned from her. I had been working with "personal" film, so these interests attracted each other, but she showed me a way to go further. She's a companion in this uncovering of our own histories. She taught me that our past is living in our present, in our bodies, and that it's worth the dig. If you don't uncover the past, you freeze up. There's pain involved in both states, but the continued uncovering is alive—it feeds a living cinema.

HOOLBOOM: How did *river* (15 min., 1978-89) begin?

HOFFMAN: It started off as a shooting exercise when I was studying film at Sheridan. The idea was simply to make a film that would be edited in-camera. So I went to the Saugeen River with a Bolex and a Rex Fader that allowed me to dissolve from one shot to the next. Richard Kerr steered the boat. The Saugeen goes through Lake McCullough, where my parents have a cottage, and we'd go up there in the summer. I would fish for trout or just drift down the river. I wanted to come back now that I'd decided to work with images instead of fishing poles. To see what was there. I shot parts of the boat, and the water and the light, looked at it and put it away. Three years later I got hold of a black-and-white video port-a-pack, an old Sony half-inch, open-reel deck. I wanted to drift down the river and let the camera run. The microphone was on the bottom of the boat, which amplified the sound in a weird way—it picked up anything the boat hit. This time I went down the river without anyone paddling; the boat just followed the current while I stood up holding the camera. What ensued was the chaos of the trip. The sound is important because every little nudge and scratch is very loud, which contrasts with an idyllic floating-down-the-river scene. To my surprise, when I first showed it, people found this section quite humorous—the person's struggle in the boat, a confrontation of "romance" with chaos. That became the second section. Then I duped the in-camera edit onto video with a looping soundtrack—instead of seeing the dissolves fade to black, you see the screen it's being filmed off, which deconstructs the romance of the first scene. That was the third section, and each plays sequentially, one after another, moving on like the river. The last scene is shot underwater. I went with a couple of guys who were helping me because they had underwater housing for the Bolex. On the way up, I phoned my mother to tell her I was coming and she said, "Your uncle was found dead by a river; we think he shot himself." Pretty gruesome. It really coloured my thinking about the river, deciding what to shoot in this last scene. It's all filmed underwater with a high-contrast stock, and unlike the other sections, which flow smoothly, it's fast, almost Brakhage-like. In the editing I worked on the death-rebirth motif. Three times the camera moves up into the light, and the film ends with light. Buddhists believe that the Bardo state is the moment where the spirit dissolves into the universe, and it's commonly represented as light. I felt I needed to mark the death of my uncle because of the way it happened, the way it came to me. The only guides I've had in my filmmaking are these so-called coincidences.

HOOLBOOM: I remember when you started working on *Kitchener-Berlin* (34 min., 1990), you said that you'd spent so long working on your mother's side of the family that you wanted to turn to your father—to tell his story.

HOFFMAN: I related my visual nature to my father's side, the silence and image-oriented expression that were a part of my earliest experiments with photography. I used home movies that my uncle shot (my father's brother). There's no story, just home-movie moments mixed with photographs of Kitchener back when it used to be called Berlin. These are joined with newsreels from the other Berlin during wartime. Then the film revisits both sites in the present, using a Steadicam camera. It floats over surfaces, looking as if it can move without gravity, gliding in space.

HOOLBOOM: Why the Steadicam?

HOFFMAN: There's an obvious kind of spiritual feel to it, because you're floating in a world where the sky and ground are equivalent. It's something we can't do with our bodies, except through technology. So it's a metaphor for the spirit released. I wanted to contrast that with the low technologies—the home movies which take a familiar form and subject. The Steadicam provides a solitary and other-worldly stance, an emptiness and separation from anything it shows. There's something that separates the people sitting in front of these old buildings, that separates the remnants of German history from the present, and the camera signals this. This relates to masculinity. The Steadicam is part of the technology that can take us to far away places or destroy the world. I wanted to show different aspects of technology through the century, using the Steadicam to create a feeling of introspective space where one can look back and account for what's happened.

HOOLBOOM: Juxtaposed with images of the past, the Steadicam is filled with a sense of returning. Because its movement isn't attached to a body or person, and its movement is so uniform, it's as if the ghost of technology had ventured back to visit what it had occasioned, to look over all that's been constructed in its wake.

HOFFMAN: Yes, that's the journey. The Steadicam floats over continents, adding layers until there are three, four, five images over top each other. They show an old Austrian church, Berlin's bombing, an orange crane that looks like some technological beast, the Pope shaking hands with Native peoples, and machineries of the city. It builds to a point where the camera moves toward the sky, and then it breaks, overloaded, and the film dips into another strata. I went to the National Film Archives in Ottawa, looking for images of Kitchener during the war. An archivist named Trap Stevens said, "You should look at this old film—it's quirky." He pulled it out, and I was really moved by it. It touched something in me. The film was made by Dent Harrison, a British immigrant who came to Canada in the early part of the century. He arrived penniless and went into the bakery business, where he figured out how to cook a lot of bread at once by using rotating ovens. He made enough money to travel and own a movie camera. He made what I think is the first, Canadian, surrealist film. It pictured a dirigible flight from England to Canada, which I saw as technology coming to North America. I'd already related Kitchener to its German roots in Berlin and suggested how the philosophical bent of these new technologies related to the rise of fascism—how humans tried to become machines.

At first, I couldn't legitimize using Harrison's footage since it didn't have to do with Germany, but I realized I was neither German nor English, and that the English presence had been very strong in Kitchener. Harrison crosses the Atlantic in a dirigible and on a boat, and speaks of himself and a double making this travel. He's split himself in two in order to shoot the trip from two different perspec-

tives. Later, he begins to edit his film and he uses a superimposition of himself, so you see him and his double in the same space. After that, when he's asleep, his double moves out of his body. Then a subtitle reads: "Have you people seen all that I have in my dreams?" Then my film breaks into another section, which is more meditative, where the technology digs up the earth, using National Film Board footage of miners interspersed with stuff I shot of a more ethereal nature. There are more home movies and wheat fields and footage I shot in a cave, all defying meaning. The way the images arrive is a surprise—they don't seem to connect and, formally, they're hard to follow.

In the first section, you expect certain patterns to recur, while the second section tries to deal with images in a way that's less filled with "meanings"; it moves into a flow of dreams. After screenings of the film some people have spoken about unremembered images from their past. That's an area I'm working with in my new films. Among the images of the underground, the last picture shows a red dress— the little girl slips into the emulsion—which says to me, "Stay tuned. We'll see what comes out." The whole film is a rendering of what I see as my male, Germanic side. The first section is a walk through physical realities connected to the effects of technology, the male hand, so it includes the war and the Pope and the co-opting of Native cultures, all glimpsed through an ethereal camera. The second section is an inward journey. It's that simple. This shift is signalled by Harrison's old home movie, which begins in a very analytical and documentary fashion and then slides into a dream reality of doubles. The voyage over the Atlantic is linear, but once he's home, things begin to unravel. That's the inward journey.

Hoolboom: After finishing *Kitchener-Berlin*, you gathered up all of your work and named it as a cycle. This series of films progresses through the familial and the formal, through a number of documentary styles that seem finally bent on shaking off narrative or any traditionally understood sequencing of events.

Hoffman: It has to do with transformation. When I named this work as a finished cycle, I had to start again, and was as lost as I'd been at the beginning of my making. That's where I am now. Rick Hancox said the last films I've done all look very different. I feel that recently I've gone through a lot of changes very fast, and that's not always easy. You do it with your work, and then there's your life. So to imagine work in a cycle is useful. Finishing closed a way of working with the past, of dealing with the uncovering of family history. I'll always be able to return to that, but now it's time to make something else.

I went back to shooting super-8 without a plan or film in mind. This started in Banff, where the first films I ever shot—some of the super-8 footage in *Road Ended*—had been made. I returned in 1989 and new ideas came up. Two ways of shooting developed. One came out of the haiku of *Somewhere Between*, shooting events of everyday life in a static frame, but this time in super-8. The other way was a single-frame zoom. Maybe I'm contriving this new cycle, but it's a path to follow in the midst of all this chaos. The single-frame shooting will find its way into *Chimera* (15 min., 1996), while the haiku project is called *Opening Series*. The idea is to make twelve short films, using three shots for every film. They'll all be silent and wordless except for the title *Opening Series* (1992, ongoing project), which is a reference to Olson's "open form" and free association. It can't be pinned down as a static work of art or exhibited as my new film because it's always changing. These twelve films range from a few seconds to three minutes, and each has a picture on the cover of its box. I've been making paintings and xeroxing them and putting them on the covers; these serve as the titles. To decide on the order of the films, you look at the pictures and choose. So the film has many possibilities of flow. Every screening is different because it's connected to the person who picks the drawings, or sometimes the audience decides the order collectively. I was working on the paintings at the same time I was editing the films, so there's an organic connection between the two. I keep track of the different screenings and what I get out of them, the relationships between the films. They're images shot around the world. One begins with a wave cutting the screen diagonally and cuts to a bird sitting in remnants of old Egypt. The bird flies off and then there's a half-second shot of the falcon god. Images in other films have more formal connections. And then there are more "personal" pictures, images of home …

Hoolboom: Will you put this film in distribution?

Hoffman: Maybe after a while, but I want to stay with it at this point just to see how it's working, because it all happens in connection with the people who make the choices. I need to see whether that works. I have a lot of fear in pinning down the films. I don't have a drive to repeat what I've already learned.

IN/BETWEEN SPACES

by Darrell Varga

Every story is a travel story—a spatial practice. For this reason, spatial practices concern everyday tactics.
Michel de Certeau, *The Practice of Everyday Life*

I think childhood is so traumatic we sleep through most of it.
Philip Hoffman, *Inside the Pleasure Dome*

The play of light and dark in Philip Hoffman's *river* (1978-79) arises from the tension between film and video, water and land, silence and sound, nature and culture, in an invocation to awake from the trauma of personal history. These tensions are not simple dualisms, but dialectical processes enmeshed in the experiences of space and time suggested in my opening quotations. *river* opens with a series of images shot on film from a small boat drifting down the Saugeen River, the sequence suggesting tranquility even as the calm flow is unsettled by the absence of sound.[1] We are presented with the frame as signifier of absence rather than window onto the world. The subsequent sequence realizes this landscape surface in the altogether different texture of black-and-white video, but now our relationship to this framed space is overdetermined by the presence of sound. While the technology of reproduction shifts from tactile and mechanical photography to its electronic counterpart, there is no longer human intervention in the steering of the boat, which now drifts according to the river's current. The boat's surface amplifies the sound waves as it floats over the water's surface in a movement of becoming simultaneously free and confined. The microphone rests on the boat seat recording the bump and grind of collisions with tree branches jutting out from the river's edge. The sound is both jarring in its amplification and hollow in artificiality. Likewise, the images are at once tranquil and interlaced with sudden reframing movements.

The camera frames the liquid surface, which in turn reflects the clouds floating in the sky above, at once an opaque sheen and permeable depth always mediated by the touch of photo-mechanical process. This easy contrast suggesting

1. I am indebted to the published description of the making of this and other of Hoffman's films in: Hoolboom, *Inside the Pleasure Dome*.

human intervention within nature is complicated by the subsequent scene in which the first segment is rephotographed. Here, the edges of the frame are evident, and the space on-screen where the dissolve sutures together transitions from one shot to another is effaced. Instead, we see the white screen onto which this rephotographing process is projected. This deferral of meaning is further destabilized in the final segment, a return to the river to film underwater. In this sequence, silent images move quickly between lightness and dark in an onward flow through the liquid surface and across the textures of sand, rock, and light, marking a reterritorialization of our relationship to this space in front of the camera. Movement no longer confined within the boat merges with the object of the image, the water as both surface and depth, recalling Gilles Deleuze's commentary on Jean Vigo's *L'Atalante* (1934):

> On land, movement always takes place from one point to
> another, always between two points, while on water the
> point is always between two movements: it thus marks the
> conversion or the inversion of movement, as in the
> hydraulic relationship of a dive and a counter-dive, which
> is found in the movement of the camera itself ... Finally, a
> clairvoyant function is developed in water, in opposition to
> earthly vision: it is in the water that the loved one who has
> disappeared is revealed, as if perception enjoyed a scope
> and interaction, a truth which it did not have on land.
> (*Cinema 1* 79)

In drawing out the relationship between Deleuze's thinking and Philip Hoffman's film practice, it is important to recall that for Deleuze, philosophy is not theoretical abstraction but is vital conceptual practice, a kind of "assemblage" in which the engagement with cinema reveals the practice of thought outside the confines of Cartesian dualism. Hoffman's filmmaking practice similarly depends upon the immediacy of intuitive and physical response. For Deleuze, cinema is a primary determinant of our understanding of space and time, and must be met outside of the constraining technical-interpretive methods of psychoanalysis.[2] Like the hollow sound of the boat bumping into the shore in *river*, Hoffman's films grind up against normative conventions of documentary and genre categorization. They offer a reconfiguration of indexical presence emerging against assumptions of fixedness formed by the borders of the frame, of order, finality, Truth. They can be understood, following Deleuze's fluid metaphors, as experimental process:

> ... no longer measured except in terms of the decoded and
> deterritorialized flows that ... [are caused] to circulate

2. Gilles Deleuze, *Cinema 2: The Time-Image*. Translated by Hugh Tomlinson and Robert Galeta. Minneapolis: University of Minnesota Press, 1989. The concept of "assemblage" comes from the translator's introduction, page xv, while Deleuze's relationship between philosophy and cinema is best articulated in his conclusion (280).

beneath a signifier reduced to silence … embracing all that
flows and counterflows, the gushings of mercy and pity
knowing nothing of means and aims. (*Anti-Oedipus* 370)

By disrupting the ordered measure of images toward a coherent teleology, cinematic experimentation serves a necessary critical function. But its function is not simply as corrective to the positivist tendency of realist narrative and critical discourse; instead, it is the creation of an alternative space in-between that which is simply given and the idea of art as transformative and in which the act of seeing cannot be made co-extensive with believing.

That which is within the frame is never fully known and always points to absences beyond the border; it is this space that is both celebrated and mourned as simultaneous site of possibility and nothingness. While the commonplace understanding of space, of the landscape around us and within our movie frames, is as something that is simply a location for action and in itself simply given and neutral, space must be better understood as something that is socially produced and that can only be understood through our systems of cultural encoding. Hoffman's image-making, as exemplary of experimental practice, does not offer an unmediated window onto the world. Deleuze describes the importance of contemporary cinema as engaging a new mode of thought in three ways:

> ... the obliteration of a whole or of a totalization of images,
> in favour of an outside which is inserted between them; the
> erasure of the internal monologue as whole of the film, in
> favour of free indirect discourse and vision; the erasure of
> the unity of [hu]man and the world, in favour of a break
> which now leaves us with only a belief in this world.
> (*Cinema 2* 187)

What cinema offers, when it breaks free from the relentlessness of the culture industry and systems of measure, is an image of thought outside of the commodified and spatialized containment of difference.

Hoffman's films engage this thought-movement by confounding easy distinctions between documentary and experimentation. These films exist in the spaces in-between film forms, in-between image and text, place and space, the body and its absence, photography, history and memory. As Blaine Allan indicates for several films, including *Kitchener-Berlin* (1990):

> The slash and the hyphen in the titles suggest both a sever-
> ance from the past and connections to it, an ambivalence
> that is especially poignant for the descendants of the area's

German settlers. The history of the area underpins the film,
but refuses to bind it or restrict it from free association.
(Program Notes: New Works Showcase, Part III)

The landscape that is the surface texture of Hoffman's films is overlaid with a discourse of territorialism, of personal and political struggles over the domain of space. Prior to World War I, the Canadian town of Kitchener was called Berlin. The juxtaposition of war images with home-town in peacetime elicits a desire to uncover and transform the complicit relation between the name, the regimentation of territory, the onslaught of time, and technologies of mass destruction. This process is not nostalgia for a pre-war law of the father; throughout these films, and especially in the later *Sweep* (1995, co-directed with Sami van Ingen), there is a realization that the binding of a place to a name is an effacement of earlier cultures. The film's title evokes this brutal gesture of erasure—the legacy of colonization under which a discourse of Canadian space must begin.

The performative hyphen of *Kitchener-Berlin* both links and keeps apart these spaces, and it is here that personal history is uncovered through film images that play against the borders of static photography, the moving image, memory and forgetfulness, and through the creative process of immersion engaged by the multiplicity of overlapping images. The personal is complicit with instrumentalized destruction, whereby the silence institutionalized by the change of the town's name is given voice through cinematographic technology, itself enmeshed in the brutality that is the history of the twentieth century. Hoffman explains how this unresolved contradiction is present in his use of the Steadicam for present-day images acting as both free-floating spirit and masculine aggression:

> … you're floating in a world where the sky and the ground are equivalent. It's something we can't do with our bodies, except through technology. So it's a metaphor for the spirit released. I wanted to contrast that with the low technologies—the home movies which take a familiar form and subject. The Steadicam provides a solitary and other-worldly stance, an emptiness and separation from anything it shows. There's something that separates the people sitting in front of these old buildings, that separates the remnants of German history from the present, and the camera signals this. This relates to masculinity. The Steadicam is part of the technology that can take us to far-away places or destroy the world. I wanted to show different aspects of technology through the century, using the Steadicam to create a feeling of introspective space where one can look back and account for what's happened. (145)

This process of movement is not a re-writing of history but an evocation of its absences, following Walter Benjamin's demand that we "brush history against the grain" (256-257). The relation to Benjamin is not incidental; his writings are filled with references to the shock effect of images and experiences that flare briefly and then disappear, but which, if recognized, fundamentally transform spatial and temporal understanding. Hoffman's archeological process is a Benjaminian translation of the past and casting forward into an unnameable future. There is no synthesis of this dialectic; instead, it is an offering that includes the necessary absences of forgetting and misconception haunting the reconfiguration of memory, an offering that realizes Hoffman's assertion that "the possibility of mourning lies in the unseen" (142).[3] To think critically about Berlin is to look into the disaster of history and, in this case, to recognize the silent complicity in such acts as the erasure of the name Berlin from a place now called Kitchener. The art process that takes memory as canvas requires the failure of recognition (which is not the same as the absences of official history), in order to suspend instrumentalization and engage thought, as Deleuze describes:

> When we cannot remember, sensory-motor extension remains suspended, and the actual image, the present optical perception, does not link up with either a motor image or a recollection-image which would re-establish contact. It rather enters into relation with genuinely virtual elements, feelings of déjà vu or past 'in general' … [as in dream and fantasy]. In short, it is not the recollection-image or attentive recognition which gives us the proper equivalent of the optical-sound image, it is rather the disturbances of memory and the failures of recognition. (*Cinema 2* 54)

Hoffman's use of silence and the abrupt stasis of still photography disrupts the flow of movement as teleology of action and reaction, and acknowledges the unsayable: a mourning that cannot be reduced to the awkward gestures of language, but instead emerges in chance relations.

The overlap of image and experience in the opening segment of *Kitchener-Berlin* confounds the instrumentality of space. Under the simultaneously hypnotic and menacing drone of church bells mixed with intermittent construction machinery sounds, images of nighttime bombing in Berlin are juxtaposed with home-movie footage in Kitchener. The first image we see is of children opening Christmas presents, suggesting, however innocently, the commodification of home space, while the following war images indicate the brutal contestation for the control of nation-state territory—the bloodbath over who gets to name this space as "home." Intercut are still photographs of public spaces in the earlier days of

3. The comment refers to the decision not to photograph the body of a dead boy encountered during the filming in Mexico of *Somewhere Between Jalostotitlan and Encarnacion* (1984) and prefigures the need to reconcile the tragedy of loss that underpins *Destroying Angel* (1998).

Kitchener, and prominent among these are snapshots marking a "successful" hunting expedition, in which we see a row of deer carcasses inverted to bleed dry. Violence looms even in so-called peacetime. Our attention is drawn to both the violence which underpins homosociality and the way photography similarly frames, confines, and captures the subject while signifying absences beyond (and within) itself.

The photographs are ordered in temporal reverse (images of Kitchener appear first, and then those from when the town was called Berlin), while the film images move chronologically. A young boy steps forward to look into the camera and into a future he cannot see, except in fragments of the past. These images overlap the flow of present-era Steadicam shots, which suggest a wandering and free-floating quality while also drawing attention to the relentlessness of Western notions of progress. Frequently, we see the camera operator's shadow floating through the collage, a reflexive presence engaging a link between past and present, between Kitchener and Berlin. But the shadow darkens the image, making it indistinct and the past irrecoverable.

Circulating through Hoffman's films are documents from a past that can never be wholly known, while the overlaid present has already begun to fade. Out of what Bruce Elder, in his description of a tendency to investigate the nature of the photographic image in Canadian experimental film, calls this "double-sided nature of the concept of representation"(253) in which presence is always bound to absence, Hoffman's film practice brushes assumptions of photographic indexicality against the grain. Our relationship to these temporal and spatial domains is determined by structures of power out of which emerges the photographic trace. The towering trees of the Canadian forest circulate beneath images of imposing European cathedrals. Tourists gaze upward while their bodies legitimize the commodity-conquest of space. Simultaneously, Aboriginal peoples gaze into the camera as the Pope moves through the crowd, his image reproduced from television, the relentless flicker of video transferred to film reminding us of the invasiveness of systems of power even as the seductiveness of the image evades naming it as such. In the overlap of these images, the dialectical process of negation forces a recognition of absence without reconciliation.

The notion of cause and effect, of a teleology of history, is blasted apart and recognition is forced in the space of absence. There is no longer a totalizing unity in which thought is contained and experience is managed. Deleuze describes the importance of montage in the contemporary film as engaging the new by evading a causal association of images:

> What counts is on the contrary the interstice between
> images, between two images: a spacing which means that

> each image is plucked from the void and falls back into it
> … Given one image, another image has to be chosen which
> will induce an interstice between the two. This is not an
> operation of association, but of differentiation, as mathe-
> maticians say, or of disappearance, as physicists say: given
> one potential, another one has to be chosen, not any what-
> ever, but in such a way that a difference of potential is
> established between the two, which will be productive of a
> third or of something new. (*Cinema 2* 179)

For Deleuze, the cinema frame once allowed a stable system of measure in which disparate elements were brought together, but the contemporary screen is one of chance and simultaneity. Like Robert Rauschenberg's overloaded frames of experience and detritus, contemporary cinema arises out of a social and historical context in which faith in grand narratives has dissolved. Where we may see something new, it is in the unfixed, unstable terrain of the in-between.

The final section of *Kitchener-Berlin* is titled "Veiled Flight," evoking the recurring tension of simultaneous movement and the obstruction of vision. The final image of the film is of an unfocused figure bathed in washed-out red, a home-movie image superimposed over cave walls and appearing at first glance as an irregular beam of light. That which was given in memory and history has dissolved into waves of colour and a deferral of narrative mastery. This image follows a sequence in which the camera moves into a darkened cave where candles and a flashlight illuminate wall carvings, photographs, and other static images. Some of these images are similar to those found in primary school history texts, such as drawings of dinosaurs and early explorers, but from which the concluding dissolve of light sets us free. If we are bound in chains within this Plato's Cave, they are chains of our own making, images of power and discipline cast onto the earth.

This cave, in a town called Maastricht on the Dutch-Belgian border, is a quarry for the local community, and while material is extracted, local people bring images inside to affix to the walls. This space of found objects in turn reflects the collection of material with which the film itself is composed, and likewise reflects Hoffman's cinematic practice of free-moving immersion in the everyday. Following the collage of technocracy in the film's first half, this section can be understood as an inward journey, but it is a journey likewise bound up with the social process of mediation and materiality. The section begins with an inverted rural landscape and hydro-electric structure. The camera arcs downward and the hydro tower penetrates into the earth. Superimposed over this movement is archival footage of an old man awakening from his dream of technological progress (the trans-Atlantic Zeppelin flight of the middle prologue discussed below) to gaze into the disaster of history. What follows is a montage of underground mining footage cut with home-movie images of Christmas gift-giving, a horse-riding competition, and footage from the making of an Imax film that stages Aboriginal communal life. In this film within the film, we again see the image of animals dead from the hunt, staged for the surveillance eye of the looming, authoritarian camera.

Hoffman has called these complex image-collages "polyphonic recitations" (Cantrill's Filmnotes 41), evoking a contrapuntal multiplicity in the telling of stories through the entanglement of personal memory and history. It is interesting that the term privileges sound within this complex layering of images, perhaps to suggest an ephemeral musicality to the visuals in order to circumvent the instrumentalized relation between word and image common to conventional film reception. Likewise, the collage evokes another kind of absence. If the images from old home movies are obscured by the fading of the film surface and the scratches from many passes through the family projector, they speak as well of the impossibility of figuring the family as united by the law of the father—even as the film is explicitly described as marking the paternal side of the Hoffman family, its patterns of dispersion and settlement (41). The film does not present a simplistic nostalgia for a prelapsarian age, for it is a movement caught up in the blinding gust of the present combined with a masculinist desire to both know father and get out of his house.

The middle "Prologue" of *Kitchener-Berlin* is in fact a masculinist journey/progress narrative. It is composed entirely of edited material from an archival film called *The Highway of Tomorrow* or, *How One Makes Two*, made in the 1930s by a Canadian businessman named Dent Harrison. Hoffman describes being moved by the inventiveness of this film, which depicts a dirigible flight across the Atlantic and in which Harrison photographically creates a double of himself to facilitate photography from both the inside and the outside of the ship. Harrison then falls into a dream in which we see the double moving out of his body, as the final title card asks "Have you people seen all that I have in my dreams?"[4] The question raised by this quirky film is complex; while serving as a document of flight, it freely embraces non-realist representational strategies, as if to signal that the dream of mobility is co-extensive with an alternative imaginary. The film is neither newsreel nor museum piece, and the opening title announces Harrison's membership in the "Amateur Cinema League: The Worldwide Organization of Amateur Movie Makers." As if to signify legitimacy through this internationalism, the title appears over a circulating globe similar to the opening of commercial newsreels. Yet "amateur" indicates a break from commercial or "professional" image-making, and the use of the title here signals an affinity with experimental practices in the true spirit of the term: an energy and practice of discovery unconstrained by commerciality.[5]

Experimental practitioners are likewise accustomed to having their work

4. The film is from the Dent Harrison Collection of the National Archives of Canada in Ottawa. See description in *Inside the Pleasure Dome* (146).

5. Philip Hoffman, personal interview, August, 2000.

derided as "amateur" by some elements of the mainstream. Harrison's film is a story about travel and technological achievement, engaging Deleuze's understanding of movement as the central concern of pre-WWII cinema, a reflection of technocratic will-to-mastery combined with a belief in the possibility of unity:

> The mobile camera is like a general equivalent of all the
> means of locomotion that it shows or that it makes use of-
> aeroplane, car, boat, bicycle, foot, metro ... In other words,
> the essence of the cinematographic movement-image lies in
> extracting from vehicles or moving bodies the movement
> which is their common substance, or extracting from move-
> ments the mobility which is their essence. (*Cinema 1* 23)

Hoffman uses this footage to embrace the everyday and the idiosyncratic personal experience of time and space, but he also asks whether Harrison's dream recognizes the collapse of order that is the consequence of our uses of technology, as reflected in Hoffman's earlier comments on the use of the Steadicam.

Travel is a recurring motif in Hoffman's films. His first, *On the Pond* (1978), is a reflection on childhood memory and how photography provides traces of the past while framing absences impossible to recover. His next, *The Road Ended at the Beach* (1983), presents the failure to enact Kerouac's *On the Road* in the unfreedom of the Reagan-Thatcher-Mulroney era, as Hoffman has explained:

> We're all waiting on an experience that isn't coming and no
> one's sure why. It has a lot to do with how men relate to
> each other, dealing with outer realities, getting the job done
> ... The guys on the road are caught in dead-end jobs, and
> nobody's relating to each other in the van ... The Beats
> were the fathers I took on the trip, but their roads are
> closed now. (Hoffman 141)

One thread of their destination is a meeting with Beat-era photographer Robert Frank to ask about the spirit of those times and the nature of his images. Instead, they end up talking about Frank's life beside the ocean and lend a hand with the renovations to his cabin. Frank admits to an earlier innocence in the Beats, which allowed a sense of freedom, but then bluntly states that Kerouac is dead. Memories of other journeys intercede. The travellers encounter a man who has been continuously cycling since 1953 and has spanned the world numerous times with only the baggage he can carry on his bike. In contrast, the van these friends are driving in is cercarial and subject to frequent breakdowns. Yet the film persists with the question of what it means to travel, to document, and to exist within homosocial structures of power.[6] Spontaneity and the poetry of free movement

6. The place of desire in the relationship between homosociality, homosexuality, and homophobia is explored in Eve Kosofsky Sedgwick's *Between Men: English Literature and Male Homosocial Desire* (New York: Columbia University Press, 1985).

emerge when Hoffman is alone with the camera dancing on rocks at the water's edge. Here the images swirl, making tactile the visual plane in a celebration of looking unencumbered by obligations of language and social discourse. Yet the film refuses an easy privileging of this moment; while it offers pleasure and intensity, it exists within the borders of the social.

Sweep (1995) sifts through the imperialist legacy of travel. It is a journey north to the remote Ontario town of Kapuskasing and then to Fort George, a destination for Robert Flaherty, who was the great-grandfather of Sami van Ingen, Hoffman's collaborator. As the author of a foundational film in the history of documentary, *Nanook of the North* (1922), the spectre of Flaherty is collaborative, like it or not. But where that cinematic father journeyed north with the belief that the cinema can unproblematically capture and thus museumize northern people, Hoffman's desire is to shake off this legacy of colonialism, as he describes the problematic homosocial context of the film: "Two men, on the road AGAIN, sifting through past worlds where there is everywhere, dusty remnants of the 'great white father'. Colliding head on with the passing present we see him living in us."[7] Past and present, fathers and sons: again, desire exists in-between these limits. This gap is filled with invocations of the everyday, in the gestures of home movies (another kind of hyphen), drawing us to the brink of representation and then dissolving in an overlap of experience.

The camera gazes at the spaces in-between image and text, photography and memory, body and place. The surface texture of the film, like the land north of Lake Superior, is overdetermined by the discourse of territorialism, the cultural divisions of space and place framed and divided amid the ruins of history. An irritating buzz overlays parts of the soundtrack, signifying the hydro-electric development that has irreparably disrupted life in the north, while at the same time extending a modicum of material benefits. The filmmakers understand themselves as embodying this southern technocracy, and choose to turn the camera onto their own presence and process of looking. Here, they work against the tendency, present since the days of Flaherty and in his more recent imitators, to objectify Aboriginal peoples within an unnameable (and thus exploitable) landscape.

The colonial project requires the landscape to be empty and unnamed in order to legitimize the narrative of discovery, conquest, and exploitation. *Sweep's* counter-narrative displaces that prescriptive and exclusionary project of imagining community, in which difference is displaced by the construction of unity under the banner of tradition. In this way, my use of the concept of in-between spaces intersects with Homi Bhabha's use of that term to describe the intersection of theory and practice. For Bhabha, the hybrid subject position within colonialism, where the act of production is overdetermined by the spectre of the West, at the

7. Philip Hoffman, *Sweep* catalogue description, Canadian Filmmakers Distribution Centre. <http://www.cfmdc.org>.

same time subverts these hegemonic and binary assumptions. As Bhabha states:

> Counter-narratives of the nation that continually evoke and
> erase its totalizing boundaries—both actual and conceptu-
> al—disturb those ideological manoeuvres through which
> 'imagined communities' are given essentialist identities. For
> the political unity of the nation consists in a continual dis-
> placement of the anxiety of the irredeemably plural modern
> space. (149)

Sweep opens with a silent, archival film of white explorers interacting with the indigenous Cree people. They are on the deck of a ship posing for a photo when the white men begin to playfully fight with each other. The image fades to black, but this spectre of homosocial aggression continues to hang over the landscape as the camera pans in a sweeping gesture of our technological view. The final passage of the film weaves together images of the landscape with that of a cultivated flower garden, memories of family and childhood experiences, the looming hydro-electric structures, and the archival footage of the Cree, in front of which stand the filmmakers in silhouette. This intertwining of history and structures of settlement, of looking and landscapes suggests how all of these spaces are produced within a given cultural context and how they overlap and change in the process of engagement.

In-between framed space are the desires and betrayals of the body—caught in the photograph's decisive moment and in the relentlessness of time. *Destroying Angel* (1998, co-directed with Wayne Salazar) is, on the one hand, a mourning for the death of Hoffman's life partner and collaborator, Marian McMahon, while also being a celebration of Wayne's gay marriage. In an early scene, Wayne and Marian are cooking dinner while Hoffman, from behind the camera, implores: "Come on you guys, act." The photographer-subject power relationship is inverted as Marian asks Phil to explain how he would "act." The dialogue merges this gap of presence and absence while revealing the performative nature of representation and confounding the possibility of verisimilitude—that which is true is transformed in this process of seeing, remembering, and making into film. These are intensely personal images, which raise questions over the representation of self. The scene follows Wayne's introductory narration, which reflects on his childhood travels through the American mid-West with his insurance-salesman father, and foregrounds the role of memory in Phil and Marian's work. Wayne's reflection is triggered by the spatial similarity of Phil and Marian's home to those farms he visited during childhood. Childhood is embraced as a place of wonder, but this process of memory simultaneously brings forth an archeology of tyranny. The convergence of space through the figurations of memory allows the emergence here of both art and mourning, following de Certeau:

> Memory derives its interventionary force from its very
> capacity to be altered—unmoored, mobile, lacking any fixed
> position. Its permanent mark is that it is formed (and forms
> its "capital") by arising from the other (a circumstance) and
> by losing it (it is no more than a memory). There is a dou-
> ble alteration, both of memory, which works when some-
> thing affects it, and its object, which is remembered only
> when it has disappeared … Far from being the reliquary or
> trash can of the past, it sustains itself by believing in the
> existence of possibilities and by vigilantly awaiting them,
> constantly on the watch for their appearance. (86)

What de Certeau asserts for memory follows his understanding of space as a network of transformative possibilities that emerge in movement rather than in the
fixedness of property, and evokes the treatment of space and travel throughout
Hoffman's films.

What is necessary for Wayne is a movement of reconciliation, which requires
confronting and moving away from his father. The camera holds on a close-up of
his face against a black background, as we hear (but do not see) him read a letter
to his father, in which he expresses his anger for childhood physical and emotional abuse while understanding that in spite of this pain, there remains love
between them. The close-up at first appears to be a still image, but the subject
blinks a few times and his presence is felt. The purpose of Wayne's letter is to gain
control over his life, to set himself free from the constraints of family by controlling the terms of contact. Here, Wayne tells his father he has AIDS. Earlier shots
expose the array of pills he consumes each day. A later scene, again in the
kitchen, has Wayne explaining to Marian the purpose of the various medications,
while a series of quick cuts of close-ups relates the everyday pleasures of cooking
and sharing food. The subject of disease is integrated into the everyday, and formally Hoffman is, in his words, "cooking with the camera."[8] These ritual gestures
recur throughout Hoffman's films, as if what can no longer be found in the fixed
assertion of language or the disciplinary boundaries of space exists in the margins,
in the fluidity of the everyday. The conversation between Wayne and Marian
reflects upon the need to exercise individual control in confrontation with disease.
It is the flipside to the more formal ritual of Wayne's gay marriage which, while
celebrating and affirming love, is also a public demand for social recognition and
legitimacy in the face of homophobic patriarchy.

The father, in a moving speech during the wedding reception, celebrates
Wayne's marriage while at the same time reasserting his own sense of authority,

8. Philip Hoffman, personal
interview. August, 2000.

even if only to himself. Wayne's father claims that he has learned to be "liberal-minded," while earlier the film has detailed the tyranny of control hanging over his relationship with Wayne. These gaps are not reconciled in a negation of the past; rather, they acknowledge the coexistence of contradictions—the context for self-discovery and social transformation. The father's speech and its inclusion in this film is a means of passage out from under the difficult memories of childhood. This movement is, unfortunately, met by the painful news of Marian's fatal cancer, a tyranny of the body, which is caught like Walter Benjamin's angel of history:

> A Klee painting named *Angelus Novus* shows an angel look-
> ing as though he is about to move away from something he
> is fixedly contemplating. His eyes are staring, his mouth is
> open, his wings are spread. This is how one pictures the
> angel of history. His face is turned toward the past. Where
> we perceive a chain of events, he sees one single catastro-
> phe which keeps piling wreckage upon wreckage and hurls
> it in front of his feet. The angel would like to stay, awaken
> the dead, and make whole what has been smashed. But a
> storm is blowing from paradise; it has got caught in his
> wings with such violence that the angel can no longer close
> them. This storm irresistibly propels him into the future to
> which his back is turned, while the pile of debris before
> him grows skyward. This storm is what we call progress.
> (257)

As tragic as Marian's death is, the film does not sentimentalize or mystify. Her death is instead put in the context of life as a process that necessarily includes struggle and suffering beyond individual control. The film's title, *Destroying Angel*, recalls Theodor Adorno's comment that Klee's angel is caught up in the destructiveness of the present:

> The Angelus Novus, the angel of the machine … The
> machine angel's enigmatic eyes force the onlooker to try to
> decide whether he is announcing the culmination of disas-
> ter or salvation hidden within it. But, as Walter Benjamin,
> who owned the drawing, said, he is the angel who does not
> give, but takes. (194)

I have made earlier references to Hoffman's use of images "caught up in the blinding gust of the present" to express what is a central concern of his work, so well encapsulated in Benjamin's meditation on Klee's angel: the impossibility of totality and reconciliation in any movement into the future.

Like the history of territorialism that constrains the potential for freedom in travel, memory harbours suffering, and its presence can unwrap the protective veil of forgetfulness. *Destroying Angel* concludes with Wayne reading from Marian's journal. In this entry, Marian works through the possibility that her desire to retrieve painful memories has triggered illness:

> How can we reclaim memories without them becoming burdensome? I travelled to a forgotten past in order to understand a fragmented present. What I retrieved was a pent-up history of abuse and violence that I sometimes, usually afterwards, thought best left hidden. What I am beginning to understand is that insight does not come suddenly but rather slowly and repetitively.

As we hear Marian's thoughts and accept her absence, we see still images of her walking along the edge of a body of water. The photograph grows larger as it moves through a tunnel-like black frame toward the camera (recalling the background black void of Wayne's close-up, cited earlier). Her body and the landscape are frozen by technologies of looking, transforming earlier images of the shore and the water in motion, forever shifting in form and direction even if understood only through the fixed perspective of the frame. These questions of the space of nature and the place of mourning are forever contained within the structures of the living.

still: *Destroying Angel.*

Works Cited

Adorno, Theodor, in Ernst Bloch et al.
Aesthetics and Politics. Trans. and Ed. Ronald Taylor. London: NLB, 1977.

Allan, Blaine.
"Thought-Riddled Nature." *Program Notes: New Works Showcase, Part III*. Kingston, Ontario: Princess Court Cinema, February-March 1990.
n. pag.

"An Interview with Philip Hoffman on his film, passing through/torn formations." *Cantrill's Filmnotes*, September 1989.
59-60.

Benjamin, Walter.
"Theses on the Philosophy of History." *Illuminations*, Edited by Hannah Arendt, translated by Harry Zohn. New York: Schocken Books, 1968.
253-267.

Bhabha, Homi K.
The Location of Culture. London and New York: Routledge, 1994.

de Certeau, Michel.
The Practice of Everyday Life. Trans. Steven Rendall. Berkeley: University of California Press, 1984.

Deleuze, Gilles.
Cinema 1: The Movement-Image. Trans. Hugh Tomlinson and Barbara Habberjam. Minneapolis: University of Minnesota Press, 1986.

Cinema 2: The Time-Image. Trans. Hugh Tomlinson and Robert Galeta. Minneapolis: University of Minnesota Press, 1989.

Deleuze, Gilles and Guattari, Félix.
Anti-Oedipus: Capitalism and Schizophrenia. Trans. Robert Hurley, Mark Seem, Helen R. Lane. Minneapolis: University of Minnesota Press, 1983.

Elder, R. Bruce.
"Image: Representation and Object—The Photographic Image in Canadian Avant-Garde Film." *Take Two: A Tribute to Film in Canada*. Ed. Seth Feldman. Toronto: Irwin Publishing, 1984.
246-263.

Hoffman, Philip.
"Pictures of Home." *Inside the Pleasure Dome: Fringe Film in Canada*. Ed. Mike Hoolboom. Toronto: Pages-Gutter Press, 1997.
138-147.

THE WORKMANSHIP OF RISK:
THE RE-EMERGENCE OF HANDCRAFT IN POSTMODERN ART

by Polly Ullrich

1. Pierre Cabanné. *Dialogues with Marcel Duchamp*.

2. David Pye, quoted in Tanya Harrod's *"Paradise Postponed."*

3. Joseph Beuys, quoted in Peter Burger's *The Decline of Modernism*. University Park, PA: Pennsylvania State UP, 1992.

Pierre Cabanné: "What is the cerebral genesis of the 'Large Glass?'"
Marcel Duchamp: "I don't know. These things are often technical."
Cabanné: "It's odd that you, who are taken for a purely cerebral painter, have always been preoccupied with technical problems."
Duchamp: "Yes. You know, a painter is always a sort of craftsman."[1]

Craftsmanship is "a word to start an argument with."
British crafts theorist David Pye[2]

Art is shaping.
Joseph Beuys[3]

A generation after the advent of conceptual and electronic art, handcrafts—long bound by tradition—have re-emerged as radical and fresh practices. Paul Shimmel, North American curator for the most recent Sao Paulo Bienniale, has identified "a concentration of decoration and craft as the new common ground" for the next generation of young artists (Leffingwell 39). Lisa Phillips, curator of the 1997 Whitney Biennial, has also identified increased "attention to handmade things and elaborate processes" as a noticeable characteristic of some of the newest art (Kaufman 12). Laura Hoptman, an assistant curator at the Museum of Modern Art in New York, who included works by the painters Elizabeth Peyton, John Currin and Luc Tuymans in a recent show, calls their hand-built surfaces "radical" because of their "unashamed" celebration of the act of painting itself and their lack of postmodern ironic cynicism.[4] Even the stuffy National Portrait Gallery in London last year reported a record number of entries (689) to its portrait competition for artists under the age of forty.

4. Author's interview with Laura Hoptman, fall 1997.

Much of the disembodied "avant-garde" conceptual art made now no longer seems as fresh as it once did—perhaps because it relies too heavily on conventions devised twenty-five years ago. Indeed, one of the original practitioners of "dema

terialized" art, Mel Bochner, has now embraced heavily handworked abstract painting. Other artists who once worked in an "old-fashioned" conceptual, deconstructive mode, such as Richard Prince, have followed suit. "Most of the forms that artistic 'rebellion' has taken in the last twenty-five years have become academic," Bochner has said. "Ironically, painting is now a lot less predictable" (qtd. in Meyer 142).

Today, embracing handwork does not necessarily mean abandoning Conceptualism. Bochner, for example, uses his paintings to address philosophical issues as dense as any he worked on in the '60s, primarily by recording—via brushstrokes made by hand—the mental processes that go into making art. And Courtenay Smith, curator of last year's *Post-Pop, Post-Pictures* show at the David and Alfred Smart Museum in Chicago, points out that while younger artists such as Michelle Grabner, John Pomera and David Szfranski produce shimmering, compact surfaces, their work still speaks to conceptual and postmodern themes, and is not a regressive revisiting of Modernist purity and formalism.[5]

How can the handcrafts in art be "radical"? In some circles, the terms seem mutually exclusive. Actually, the synthesis of hand facture and postmodernism has roots in the nineteenth century with the invention of photography, when it became clear that mimesis was no longer the primary function of art. The emphasis on artworks as special, handmade, precious objects conveying a peculiar, individual power, rather than as attempts to replicate reality, began to take hold. The handcraftedness of fine-art objects, downplayed since the Renaissance in an effort

5. Author's interview with Courtenay Smith, fall 1997.

to distance them from less prestigious handcrafted objects such as pottery or textiles, gained new respect. Now, with the postmodern blending and leveling of categories, art and craft have edged closer toward an acknowledged, and not shameful, union. But more than that, the increasing status of handcraftsmanship—and the issues surrounding it in art—subverts some basic philosophical and aesthetic tenets in the West. Handcrafts, with their relation to the body and the physical senses, counteract the drive toward technology and dematerialization in our culture. The traditional identification of handcrafts with minorities and women also allows these processes to reveal alternative voices. Critic Barry Schwabsky commented that the African-American artist Robert Colescott's paintings in the United States pavilion at the 1997 Venice Biennale were "a reminder that what seems most traditional can be most subversive" (23).

What does it mean to be using hand processes to make art in this postmodern age of the simulacrum? The recent renaissance of handwork can be identified with a wide variety of sources. The following is an attempt to draw on some of these sources to clarify the place of the hand in contemporary art.

The Hand and Art as Sensuous Idea

A sixteenth-century duel, recounted in the memoirs of the Renaissance sculptor Baccio Bandinelli, was fought between Bandinelli's cousin and the Vidame of Chartres because of some particularly rancorous fighting words from the Vidame. The Vidame claimed that Florentine nobles who had taken up painting and sculpture were actually practising the "manual arts" (Mainzer 186). This, of course, was an insult not to be ignored during the Renaissance. Artists were struggling then to separate themselves from hand-oriented crafts such as glass-making or pottery and to ally themselves with poets, architects, and musicians into a new, more refined, intellectual and prestigious category called "fine art." Historically, sculptors and painters had been classified as artisans and craftspeople—not "artists"— and they therefore suffered from an association with manual labor, a prejudice going back to ancient Greece.

During the Middle Ages, sculptors belonged to guilds that included stone masons and bricklayers, while painters belonged to guilds for gilders and saddlers. Eventually, craft guilds became powerful political forces—powerful enough to challenge the grip monarchs had thus far held over such activities. It was no accident that the advent in the seventeenth century of artists' academies, which drew artists away from membership in guilds, was heavily sponsored by monarchs and those in royal courts who saw an opportunity to break the power of the guilds. This separation—between painters and sculptors and the other craft workers—definitively severed fine art from craft, and also led to a separation of intellect and hand (or body), a break that was a result of politics rather than aesthetics.

The duality between craft (the hand/body) and art (the mind) came to a head in philosophical and aesthetic debates during the Enlightenment in the eighteenth century. The foundation of this dualism—the Cartesian split between the mind and the material world (where the act of thinking, rather than feeling or sensing, assures us of our existence)—still reaches into our postmodern culture. The dominance of brainwork over handwork is reflected today in art and cultural theory that privilege language over images and objects. "I often talk about postmodernism as precisely the fulfillment of certain Enlightenment agendas," University of Chicago art historian Barbara Maria Stafford has said. Nevertheless, she adds, there is a human need to be "anchored in something that isn't merely simulated, degraded or cerebral ... The body is our locus ... for experiencing the world. So we have to at some fundamental level revalue it again, and say that it is aesthetically spiritual and that it is mental, just as the mind is corporealized and spiritualized" (qtd. in *Sculpture* 13-14). The privileging of the human hand in art-making calls into question Western dualism: what cultural theorist Homi Bhabha calls "binary boundaries," the domination of either/or polarities in defining the world around us (251). However, the search to reintegrate the hand, the body, and the physical senses in art does not mean a retreat into an essentialism or universalization. The hand, as a sign of the individual, is potentially the ultimate purveyor of idiosyncrasy, personal identity, and spiritual power. Probably for that reason, prehistoric artists covered cave walls with hundreds of hand images.

The synthesis of the hand and the mind as a way of life has a long history in craft art. The potter Marguerite Wildenhain, for example, writes:

> This intimate correlation of the quick perception of the eye
> with the inner concept of the heart and mind, and the sen-
> sitive training of the hand, this immediate reaction of all
> the capacities of a human being, will always be the aim of
> any training of a craftsman and artist. It is only the potency
> of these combined abilities that will give the artist the
> power to convey what he feels in his own personal way. (133)

Contemporary craft theory of the hand also has deep roots in Asian art. Japanese aesthetician and writer Shoetsu Yanagi, whose classic *The Unknown Craftsman* influenced several generations of Western craft artists, calls the question of the survival of handcrafts ...

> ... not simply technological or economic, but, basically, a
> spiritual question ... It seems to me that there is something
> so basic, so natural in the hand that the urge to utilize its

> power will always make itself felt … The chief characteristic
> of handcrafts is that they maintain by their very nature a
> direct link with the human heart, so that the work always
> partakes of a human quality. (107-108)

Yanagi helped popularize the 400-year-old Japanese tea ceremony in the West, an aesthetic outgrowth of Zen Buddhism. The Way of Tea counters Western dualistic notions of beauty and ugliness, asymmetry and symmetry. According to the Japanese custom, the best art shows austerity, humility, depth, simplicity, restraint, intuition, and even imperfection—qualities that are the very opposite of many Greek ideals.

Trying to find the way out of the problem of dualism (beautiful/ugly, mind/hand, art/life, consciousness/world) has been a persistent thread underlying twentieth-century Western philosophy and aesthetics. Two writers—French philosopher Maurice Merleau-Ponty and crafts theorist David Pye—have made perhaps the most striking contributions by interpreting the work of art—and its making—as a seamless fusion of the sensual and the intellectual. This radically moves the artwork beyond pure idea or mere intentional act.

Merleau-Ponty, a phenomenologist, countered a dualistic philosophical tradition beginning with Plato by suggesting that human consciousness and perception are fundamentally connected to the world; there is no "inner realm" that opposes, dominates, and organizes an otherwise impenetrable and meaningless "outside" world of matter (including the body). This "theory of embodiment" argues that human perception, rather than being cerebral and transcendental, is incarnated through, and inseparable from, the body and its senses. Humans perceive the world, then, from a position of reciprocity, not domination: when one touches, one is touched in return. Since art is about perception, this interconnection has striking ramifications. While works of art have semantic qualities, "formal configurations which refer, in some sense, beyond themselves," they are also more than their linguistic structures (Crowther 48).[6] Art tries to engage "our whole being"—not just cognitively, but by constructing a sensual reality as we might encounter it in perception itself, through the marks, the erasures, and the physical processes left by the artist's hand in the work. Artworks reflect our own insertion in the world —a blend of transcendental meaning and physical presence—and are "individuals, that is, beings in which the expression is indistinguishable from the thing expressed" (44).

The craft world has always intermixed process, material and meaning. The meaning of a traditional ceramic vessel, for example, is deciphered in the complex of associations about it—its clay (and the historical lineage that the use of the clay reflects), its method of making (and the historical alliance with artists who developed the method over thousands of years), as well as its function (the meaning of the pot is completed only when it is used). This last, of course, was recognized by that great saboteur of art categories Marcel Duchamp, who, although he detested sensual painting, handcrafted his masterwork *The Bride Stripped Bare by Her Bachelors, Even* over a seven-year period.[7] Duchamp insisted on calling himself a "craftsman," and maintained that bad craftsmanship in an artwork should never be allowed to detract from the purity of its idea. Like a craft artist, Duchamp combined meaning with use, linking the audience (or user) with the essential meaning of the art: "I consider, in effect, that if someone, any genius, were living in the heart of Africa and doing extraordinary paintings everyday, without anyone's seeing him, he wouldn't exist," Duchamp told the writer Pierre Cabanné. "The artist exists only if he is known … because, in brief, it's a product of two poles—there's the pole of the one who makes the work, and the pole of the one who looks at it. I give the latter as much importance as the one who makes it … A work is made of the admiration we bring to it" (Cabanné 69).

The British architect, designer and craftsman David Pye, who casts a skeptical eye on the moralizing and sentimental aspects of the craft world, also subverts dualism in art theory by identifying a core idea that has—until recent times at least—always been valued both in fine and craft art. Pye, a woodworker, never liked the phrase "done by hand," saying that it is uselessly restrictive and inexact. "What does 'handmade' mean?" Pye asks. "No tools?" What about a hand loom, or a potter's wheel? He likes to point out that the use of machine processes did not begin with the Industrial Revolution, adding that the water-driven hammer is an ancient tool. Pye's core value, an essential component in the process of making, is what he calls the "workmanship of risk." The workmanship of risk

> … means simply workmanship using any kind of technique
> or apparatus in which the quality of the result is not prede-
> termined, but depends on the judgement, dexterity, and
> care which the maker exercises as he works … The quality
> of the result is continually at risk during the process of
> making. (20)

Pye contrasts this with the "workmanship of certainty," which is found in quantity production and automation. Speed is usually the incentive behind the workmanship of certainty, and the quality of the product predetermined and predictable. Pye maintains that the workmanship of risk means that the "risk" must be real: "Can the worker spoil the job at any moment?" (61-62)

Why is the workmanship of risk valuable in art objects? The workmanship of certainty can also yield high quality. Only through the workmanship of risk, however, is it possible to reveal the sense of life and moment-by-moment human decision that are recorded in the process of making. The workmanship of risk may

7. Robert Motherwell was the first to call Duchamp "the great saboteur" in his introduction to Cabanné's book. *Dialogues with Marcel Duchamp.*

produce subtlety, richness, and variety in a work's formal elements, qualities that deepen upon inspection. Pye writes: "A thing properly designed and made continually reveals new complexes of newly perceived formal elements the nearer you get to it" (61). These slight improvisations and irregularities, with contrast and tension between them, from the smallest visible scale on up, are what vitalize and individualize art.

Although Pye dislikes the term "handmade," the qualities he finds most important in art making are almost always associated with the hand: individuality; variety; facility; close, tactile familiarity with a material; and an emphasis on an intimate visual range in experiencing an artwork. To perceive what Pye calls "diversity" requires the observer to move in close—within hand's reach—and to employ much more than a narrow, Cartesian cerebral capacity.

The Hand and the Problem of the "Real"

Art that is grounded in materials-based handwork holds a special dialogue with a postmodern culture, which negates a firm foundation as a basis for constructing reality. When Belgian artist Luc Tuymans describes his paintings as "authentic falsifications," an apparent oxymoron, he articulates the syncretic position of artists who make handmade postmodern art. Tuymans' pale brushmarks construct aloof, barely legible, abstracted images of troubling subjects, as in his elegant, understated, late-1980s paintings of concentration camps. These pared-down, psychically bland works—which Tuymans calls "unimages"—force the viewer to complete their meanings (Hoptman). But Tuymans' evanescent paintings—like the work of a number of younger and mid-career artists—pointedly remain physical objects that accomodate and reflect their conditional, ever-mutating postmodern environment. Their status as objects is gained through their handmade qualities.

This work elaborates on contemporary art theory inaugurated by Walter Benjamin, who wrote that technology, with its speed and its endless ability to multiply and reproduce, has transformed art irrevocably. Mechanically appropriated images, while undermining traditional assumptions about originality in art (what is real or authentic?), circumvent a direct, physical give-and-take with the art object, for the maker and viewer alike. Even more broadly, deconstructive theories coming out of a French philosophical context and taken up by the art world have challenged the very idea of unequivocal, or grounded, perception itself and have described a dematerialized "everyday surface of life." Finding meaning either in oneself or in the world depends not on a single perceptual standpoint and a bedrock of certain meaning, but on deciphering an unstable, ever-changing network of relations surrounding it (Crowther 5).

While Tuymans' paintings seem to echo the fleeting style of contemporary

electronic culture, his concentrated hand facture pulls his art into the physical
world. Significantly, Tuymans began his art career in film, and carefully culls his
images from books, newspapers and snapshots. But the work is obstinately somewhere, of a place. Laura Hoptman calls this a "significantly changed attitude
among new painters," an integration of the conceptual with a serious, passionate
and unironic love for the physical act of painting. "This work is about preparing
to stun you with the painting," she says.[8] Tuymans has called his work so "concentrated" that he compares it to "another type of arousal" (qtd. in Hoptman). While
the images may be pulled from standard media sources, these artworks are not
merely "representations of representations." Rather, they unabashedly seduce the
viewer into a visual engagement with the material qualities of the art, and as such
hold a radical, and rooted, position in the variable play of meaning.

The combination of a fleeting, transient, postmodern sensibility with the flat-
out gorgeousness of handworked material is also apparent in the work of some
mid-career artists such as Lari Pittman's baroque, flamboyantly decorated paintings, for example, or Phillip Taaffe's Islamic patternings, which involve numerous
hand processes that include constructing templates, sanding, painting, hand-ink-
ing and collaging. Taaffe describes his art-making as "a search for the ruthless
thing," noting, "what I want to make is something very physical and very percep-
tually demanding" at the same time (122). The Smart Museum's *Post-Pop, Post-
Pictures* featured work that is "highly conceptual and also a seductive object,"
according to curator Courtenay Smith.[9] In the show, John Pomara's heavily
worked enamel, Varathane varnish, and ink diptychs with images that echo the

8. Author's interview with
Hoptman.

9. Author's interview with
Courtenay Smith, fall 1997.

electronic blurs on television; Michelle Grabner's painstakingly hand-replicated household patterns painted with enamel on plywood; and David Szafranski's legal pads minutely and densely covered with tiny prints and hand drawings all expressed edgy postmodern themes while still calling attention to how carefully the pieces were made. This intentional positioning of the artwork in the material world does not deny the complexity—and diffusion of standpoints—in constructing meaning in postmodern culture. But the mediation of meaning through the human hand and body can rehumanize art and provide a powerful embodied reference point—a "real" map—within a provisional experience that has been "analyzed away in a mere play of relations" in much currently fashionable theory (Crowther 17).

THE HAND AND THE CONVERGENCE OF SPACE, TIME AND THE SENSES

Early conceptual art evolved from what was called the "priority of the idea" in art-making, a sense that the idea for the work comes first, and therefore is the most essential part of art. In the early 1970s, Mel Bochner's masking tape and text artworks, for example, were not just straightforward vehicles for communicating ideas, but were actually visual investigations into—and critiques of—ideas as institutions. Bochner, however, had already begun to lose faith by the mid-1970s, noting that there is no primacy to any aspect of experience. What, for example, about ideas that develop while making art? Bochner's transition to intensely hand-worked, sensuous abstract painting allowed him to continue his investigations into watching how the mind works. "For me, painting, because it is in and of the material world, offers an access to the processes of the mind, to the indecisions and uncertainties philosophy can't cope with," he notes (qtd. in Stuckey 19). His distaste for "literalist" or "declarative" art—"painting is not merely a statement; it is also a question"—allows Bochner to emphasize process in art-making, along with the complexity, ambiguity and doubt that are part of it. In his early work, Bochner explored the intersection of space and language (or ideas) through visual riddles. Now, by recording a "narrative of revisions" through his brush strokes, Bochner's paintings intersect space (or the visual) with time. "In painting, I want to encode time as it evolves" (qtd. in Meyer 101).

The compression of time into an artwork through hand processes turns up in contemporary sculpture as well. Tom Friedman and Gary Justis both use meticulous handwork to produce their conceptually oriented pieces. Friedman's obsessively hand-processed everyday materials—a self-portrait carved out of an aspirin, a piece of bubble gum stretched twenty feet from floor to ceiling, or 30,000 toothpicks glued into a starburst form—skewer Modernist conventions of solemnity and scale. Justis' elegant, hand-made machines echo a Duchampian mixture of mechanics and mythology. There is no one-liner quality to these works; the sculptures of both artists take time—both to make and to experience. Justis hammers home the message with his sculptures, so to speak: they sometimes contain small gongs that chime in repetitive cycles, lulling the viewer into a meditative wait—with an emphasis on that interval of time—for each successive ring.

The use of the hand in art-making can convey extraordinary psychic depth and physical density when time is part of the process. Vija Celmins' thickly built-up drawings and paintings of galaxies, oceans and deserts exude, for example, what she calls a "fatness" or a "volume." The pieces are "phenomenological investigations," translations of experience into condensed matter beyond a mere idea. Celmins' search for this "rich and complete form" in her work (such as putting eighteen layers of paint on a canvas, and still not being finished) links time and physical matter: "I like to think that time stops in art," Celmins once told an interviewer. "When you work on a piece for a long period it seems to capture time … when you pack a lot of time into a work, something happens that slows the image down, makes it more physical" (Silverthorn 42). Celmins' hand-made paintings, once again, balance the scale between idea and embodiment, emerging as relentlessly consolidated fields of intellectual and physical matter.

THE HAND AND ETHICAL DEVELOPMENT

Finally, for good or bad, the use of the hand in art has often carried overtly moral and ethical overtones in some art circles. This attitude is often attributed to the Arts and Crafts movement at the turn of the last century, and especially to one of its British leaders, William Morris. But in practice, Morris, who wrote and lectured frequently about the importance of handcrafts and who founded the Morris and Company craft and design firm, "never made a shibboleth of handwork" and didn't argue against the use of all machinery, especially when workers were not exploited and the quality of the output was good (Harrod 7). Instead, his real aim was social change; for Morris, who was a socialist, handcraft meant work without the division of labour between worker and designer, unlike the rigidly hierarchical and exploitive industrial workplace of the nineteenth century. Morris linked social and political renewal with aesthetics, arguing that the promotion of handwork not only improved society by reorganizing relationships in the workplace, but that it was also a path to personal and moral development for the art worker. Because of Morris and other Arts and Crafts leaders, "the mark of the hand" became a prestigious feature in decorative art and manufactured goods at the time, no matter what their quality—leading to David Pye's ironic story about a potter who, in discussing his teapot adds, "Of course it leaks. It's hand-made" (Pye 123).

A rigorously pure theory of handwork, however, did evolve from the Arts and

Crafts movement and continues to affect the contemporary craft world today.
Pioneering studio-craft leaders—among them Bernard Leach, Michael Cardew, and
William Straite Murray—began to articulate values that placed less emphasis on
Morris' social crusading and more on craft objects as the equals of painting and
sculpture. By the 1930s, craft had broken with the political Left; to socialists,
making "luxury" items by hand seemed self-indulgent during an economic
depression. No longer part of the industrial or economic base, craft objects
evolved into art objects.

Influenced by the modernists Clive Bell and Roger Fry (who democratized art
hierarchies), the new craft leaders conveyed attitudes that defined them more as
artists than designers or laborers. They emphasized integrity, timelessness and
authenticity in their work, with an extreme sensitivity to materials and the desire
to work spontaneously and simply with them (Harrod 8-9). Leach, at his Saint Ives
Pottery in England, lived out a stringent paradigm of handwork that still influ-
ences craft artists, and which extends from the beginning to the end of the art-
making process, "from digging the clay himself, to throwing and decorating the
pots, to firing them in a kiln he had built, with wood he had collected himself" (35).

This attitude, rather than promising social improvement in general, still carried a high ethical tone: the arduous hand skills (and, consequently, life skills)
developed over time by the artist became the standard for his or her character
development and moral worth. As craft objects have become more like art objects,
a terrible anxiety has arisen in some corners of the craft world: that the crafts are
being corrupted by the fine-art world and its marketplace. In a talk titled "Craft as
Attitude," delivered at a forum called *Re-Visioning the Crafts* at the Penland
School for Crafts in the mid-1980s, ceramist Wayne Higby complained about the
low quality of craft art, saying that crafts were becoming so "slick" that "the
maker's hand is no longer visible." Higby said that the humanistic, spiritual principles originally at work in crafts because of their thoughtful, handmade qualities
are being degraded by an art establishment that rewards artists who are the best
marketers, not artists with the most integrity (qtd. in Malarcher 40).

This, ironically, is a complaint often heard from fine artists as well. Eric
Fischl, for example, in looking back at what he thought was the shallowness—the
inattentiveness to hand skills and art history—in his own early art training, comments angrily:

> Part of the problem is that artists of my generation were not
> educated. We were not given the equipment, because it was
> generally believed to be irrelevant. Drawing, eye-hand coor-
> dination, art history—really relevant stuff—was considered
> unnecessary ... in fact, it is incredibly disrespectful of the

importance of history that we train people to be amateurs. I
deeply resent the kind of flattery that replaced discipline.
We were made to feel from day one that we were artists,
fully sprung from the womb an artist. What experience has
shown me is that it takes your life to become an artist. (qtd.
in Tuten, 79)

As categories continue to be dismantled and mixed together, many fine artists and craft artists alike find that they frequently stand on common ground, especially as their work revolves around the issues of process, materials and handwork. In the craft world, this is called "crossover," and it is often met with consternation—as well as elation. Clearly, a sculptor such as Jim Hodges, who constructs knotted chains of silk flowers and thread into large-scale, delicate webs and floating walls, has direct connections to fiber art through his hand processes and materials. And among politically oriented artists, the painter Sue Williams, who developed a savvy reputation based on her strident, painful images of sexual abuse, has continued those themes, but now through intensely worked oil and acrylic paintings. In fact, the prominence of a number of contemporary painters who are not necessarily affiliated in any other way—Terry Winters, David Ortins, William Wood, Therese Oulton, Hunt Slonem, Juan Usle, Prudencio Irazabal, and Juliao Sarmento—is due in large part to the striking qualities of the hand work in their art.

To acknowledge the importance of hand work in art is not a revelation; early modernist works such as Cezanne's paintings reveal themselves through heavily hand-applied brushwork and materials. And there is a strikingly handmade quality to much of the avant-garde art of the early twentieth century. But handcrafts have been a frequently ignored undercurrent percolating in fine art since Renaissance artists quit the craft guilds for greener—and more prestigious—pastures in the monarchical courts. Many contemporary artists, however, have deliberately chosen a wide variety of hand processes to develop postmodern themes in their art. This is not a regression to a narrow and purist modernist formalism, but rather continues the postmodern journey toward multiplicity, and reacquaints us all with the historical and aesthetic links between craft and fine art.

This article was first printed in the *New York Art Examiner*, April 1998.

Works Cited

Bhabha, Homi K.
The Location of Culture. New York: Routledge, 1994.

Cabanné, Pierre.
Dialogues with Marcel Duchamp. London: Thames and Hudson, 1971.

Crowther, Paul.
"The Postmodern Sublime." *Art and Design* (January/February 1995).

Crowther, Paul.
Critical Aesthetics and Postmodernism. Oxford: Clarendon Press, 1993.

Harrod, Tanya.
"Paradise Postponed." *William Morris Revisited, Questioning the Legacy*. London: Crafts Council Gallery, 1996.

Hoptman, Laura.
Projects. New York: Museum of Modern Art, 1997.
n. pag.

Kaufman, Jason Edward.
"The 69th Whitney Biennial, New York: Made By Hand, Telling Stories And Talking To The Public." *The Art Newspaper* (March 1997).

Leffingwell, Edward.
"Report from Sao Paulo." *Art in America* (March 1997).

Mainzer, Janet C.
"The Relation Between the Crafts and the Fine Arts in the U.S. from 1876 to 1980." *Diss. New York U*, 1988.

Malarcher, Patricia.
"Re-Visioning the Crafts." *Metalsmith* (Spring 1986).

Meyer, James.
"Mel Bochner: The Gallery is a Theater." *Flash Art* (Summer 1994).

Pye, David.
The Nature and Art of Workmanship. Bethel Court, UK: Cambrium Press, 1995.

Schwabsky, Barry.
"Loose Ends, Conceptual Knots, Liquid City." New Art Examiner (September 1997).

Silverthorn, Jeanne.
"Vija Celmins in Conversation with Jeanne Silverthorne." *Parkett* (1995).

Stafford, Barbara Maria,
interview. *Sculpture* (May-June 1994).

Stuckey, Charles
"Interview with Mel Bochner." *Mel Bochner 1973-1985*. Pittsburgh: Carnegie-Melon University Art Gallery Press, 1985.

Taaffe, Phillip.
"Talking Abstract II." *Art in America* (December 1987).

Tuten, Frederick.
"Fischl's Italian Hours." *Art in America* (November 1996).

Wildenhain, Marguerite.
The Invisible Core: A Potter's Life and Thoughts. Palo Alto, CA: Pacific Books, 1973.

Yanagi, Shoetsu.
The Unknown Craftsman. Palo Alto, Ca.: Kodanska International, 1972.

IMPURE CINEMAS: HOFFMAN IN CONTEXT

by Chris Gehman

At the beginning of cinema's second century, it's instructive to remember how recently proclamations of the "death of the avant-garde" (or "experimental film," or "fringe film") were a staple for filmwatchers concerned with developments outside the realms of commercial and art-house production (e.g., Chicago Reader critic Fred Camper, and Village Voice critic J. Hoberman). This imminent demise was seen as arising from an exhaustion of creative possibilities, and, for Camper in particular, the domestication of a formerly independent and vital movement. In a 1989 statement, Camper wrote that

> What began as an anarchic movement with a singular mis-
> sion—that of changing the viewers' sensibilities
> and thereby changing the world—is now a fragmented col-
> lection of "schools." The phrases "avant-garde film" and
> "experimental film" no longer denote works that break new
> cinematic ground; rather, they name a style, almost a genre,
> which has its own set of defining characteristics. (32)

Towards the end of the 1980s this position seemed to solidify into a consensus, and filmmakers too joined the chorus. Australia's Arthur and Corinne Cantrill, for example, toured with a film performance in which they called themselves "the last filmmakers," and Jean-Luc Godard's television series *Histoire(s) du cinéma* was markedly elegiac in tone. Among many artists who shifted their production mostly or entirely away from film (Jordan Belson, Malcolm Le Grice, Al Razutis), American independent Jon Jost "defected" to digital video—and to Europe. There he became an outspoken critic of what he sees as an irrational fetishization of the medium and a hypocritical institutional/critical environment surrounding experimental film.

During the late 80s and early 90s there were genuine signs that experimental film was in trouble. To begin with, many influential independent filmmakers have died over the past two decades. These include Andy Warhol, Hollis Frampton,

Paul Sharits, Marjorie Keller, Harry Smith, Warren Sonbert, Joyce Wieland, Sidney
Peterson, and Kurt Kren. From the mid-80s through the early 90s, most of the
institutions that supported artists' work in film, among them Anthology Film
Archives and the Film-Makers' Cooperative, the Canadian Film-makers
Distribution Centre, the London Filmmakers Coop and Canyon Cinema, experienced crises caused by fractures and antagonism between different factions. These
crises were exacerbated by dwindling state support and often haphazard adminis-
trative practices. In Toronto, the 1989 International Experimental Film Congress,
which was organized partly to respond to the idea that experimental film was no
longer a vital force, became the site and the subject of heated debates that broke
down roughly along generational lines. A younger, more politically oriented group
of artists, theorists and programmers attacked what they saw as an outmoded and
elitist conception of the "avant-garde," particularly a purist formalism, that had
dominated experimental film production and deformed its discourse. Further,
some major art galleries (such as the National Gallery of Canada and Art Gallery
of Ontario) appear to have dropped film programming and acquisition from their
regular activities, while others have cut them back to almost nothing. Acquisitions
of film prints by libraries and educational institutions, once a small but important
source of income for at least the better-known filmmakers, have all but ceased
and a revival of the practice seems very unlikely. And it is probably true that an
increasingly academic environment made for a less vital film culture, at least for a
particular segment of the field, and for a particular period of time.

But experimental film did not die. Many of the key institutions mentioned
above have recovered their stability over the past several years, and new venues
for the exhibition of artists' film have sprung up. Some of these have been short-
lived, while others have settled in for a long life. Critical writing on film is almost
completely absent from general-interest art journals and magazines, but there are
specialized journals that publish serious writing on film. A heartening range of
books has appeared over the past several years, including Scott MacDonald's
three-volume collection of interviews with filmmakers, *A Critical Cinema*.
Ultimately, however, it can only be the healthy, prickly condition of filmmaking
itself that proves these proclamations of death to have been premature. What
threatens the form now is less a matter of creative exhaustion than the possibility
that the basic tools, materials and services needed to complete a film may disappear as the commercial industry turns entirely towards digital media.

What has perhaps passed away is a certain image of the artist as romantic,
visionary hero, and an allegiance to large-scale, often highly purist, abstract models of making. Some very interesting film artists of the past two decades (e.g.,
Jennifer Reeves, Philip Hoffman) have moved between styles and genres in a way
that might have seemed confusing or incoherent to an earlier generation. The

characteristic elements of these films are likely to be philosophical, thematic, and personal, unlike the formal "signature style" or clear progression of artistic development that made up the work of respectable artists in earlier decades.

There has, then, been a significant shift since the "heroic" period of the avant-garde that found its critical spokesman in P. Adams Sitney, and its bible in *Visionary Film: The American Avant-garde 1943-1978* (second edition 1979). This book became a flash point for much of the debate over the canonization of experimental film. Jason Boughton summarizes the critical point of view:

> [Sitney's] book acts and continues to be used as a lexicon of alternative filmmaking practice, not only for the years it claims, but more generally, forward and backwards in history. Like all written history it is not just a locus of memory but also a kind of sleep capsule, an axis of active, official forgetting ... The problem is the form history comes in [in] *Visionary Film*—the confusion of memory and forgetting, the thinly veiled claims of completeness and simple reportage. When one speaks of the Avant-Garde, is it just one era, a single group of friends, great men, a unified field that is referred to? Is avant-garde an idea or an identity? Is it dead, and if not, can we finally let it die, and take with it a back-breaking debt to every other logocentric, exclusionary Avant-Garde ...? (7)

Boughton quarrels with Sitney's tendency to categorize makers and their works according to major art-historical movements, and takes issue with the staunchly apolitical nature of Sitney's analysis. He accuses Sitney, for example, of ignoring the radical socialism of Ken Jacobs in his discussion of Jacobs's works. Boughton points out that Maya Deren is the only woman filmmaker given serious consideration in *Visionary Film*, while Marie Menken is treated primarily as an influence on male filmmakers, and as the wife of Willard Maas. Boughton concludes that "[t]he exclusion of politics in *Visionary Film* would almost be comforting, an easy resting place, were its politics not so visibly exclusionary" (6).

The "death" that the critics of the 80s predicted, then, was perhaps not the death of the experimental film per se, but rather the death of Sitney's particular "avant-garde." Since that time we have seen a general cultural shift, in which the coherent psychological, spiritual and sexual identity of the individual allegedly asserted by the Romantic tradition and examined by Sitney has been replaced by a conception of the individual as a collection of interrelated aspects under the influence of an array of social, cultural, and political forces. This shift manifests itself in film in several ways: through an explicit examination of personal and family histories; through an interest in the social construction of gender, race, and ethnic identities; through a desire to convey journalistic or documentary content without resorting to discredited concepts of neutrality or objectivity; through a renewed use of "staging," that is, the performance of roles and scenarios, though without an attempt at the kind of realism that characterizes the mainstream dramatic film; through the use of language as an integral communicative element; through the recombination of found/appropriated materials in films made using existing film footage, photographs, consumer objects, etc.; through the live "film performance," which challenges the idea of film as a mechanical medium of mass reproduction; and through a burgeoning interest in manipulating the chemical surface of the image.

In short, it is a certain purism of purpose and of form that has been given up by the new generations, but not necessarily a desire to see changes in the world. The development of self-financing, underground "microcinemas," where a good deal of the material shown has both an activist and an experimental character, testifies to the continuing role of film as an art that aims to contest and to challenge social, political, economic and aesthetic hierarchies, as well as conventions of vision and representation. If anything, it is the members of the avant-garde that Fred Camper so fondly remembers who have found their way into the security of academe, while their contemporary counterparts, practising a myriad of hybrid forms, continue to struggle in a social and artistic environment hostile to film art. Yet the degree to which experimental film has not been accepted into the art world as an equal and crucial form, despite its overwhelming cultural importance over the past century, suggests that there continues to be something "indigestible" about the work, something which resists commodification and academicization. As the very idea of a unifying, central identity disappears, the pathways taken by film-makers become ever more labyrinthine and far-flung, so that the job of the would-be taxonomist becomes difficult, perhaps even impossible. My aim below, then, is to account for some of the disparate elements of contemporary experimental film, creating loose categories that are subject to cross-pollination.

Found Images

Critique is implicit in most contemporary found-footage films, and in films which appropriate images through related forms such as collage animation. Recently, we have seen the emergence of the experimental film "remake." Jill Godmillow's *What Farocki Taught* (1998), a remake of Harun Farocki's *Inextinguishable Fire* (1969), and Elizabeth Subrin's *Shulie* (1997), a remake of a 60s documentary about the young feminist Shulamith Firestone, are the best known examples. Implicit in most contemporary found-footage films is a challenge to conventional codes of representation and the social, political and sexual norms that are seen to be supported by those codes. This political intent distinguishes contemporary uses of found footage from the more poetic, symbolic, or formal uses by film artists who began their work in earlier decades (eg., Joseph Cornell, Bruce Conner).

In tiny units of a few frames each, Austrian filmmaker Martin Arnold reworks scenes from Hollywood movies, which he has defined as "a cinema of repression and denial" (Address). Arnold's work emphasizes the mechanical rhythm of the projected image and hearkens back to the idea of cinema as a machine for the analysis of motion. Arnold's films may be the fulfillment of Hugo Musterberg's 1915 essay describing the possibilities of reordering photographed motion in small groups of frames in order to discover a new rhythm impossible in nature. For Arnold, however, the cinematic machine is primarily an ideological apparatus, and he retools this apparatus in order to draw out every drop of meaning latent in the original material. Arnold's *Passage a l'Acte* (1993) reworks a scene of several seconds' length from *To Kill a Mockingbird* (1962), extending it to 12 minutes by repeating every few frames several times. Leaving the original synchronized sound intact, he slowly allows the scene to progress. The effect is vehement, even violent, and creates a portrait of patriarchal family life and racial division from a scene that would pass almost unnoticed in its original context. The actors are transformed into twitching puppets in the throes of an ideological seizure.

Like Martin Arnold, American filmmaker Jay Rosenblatt has a background in psychology, and mounts his critique as a sort of diagnosis of symptoms. Rosenblatt uses found footage for the creation of compact, personal essays on subjects ranging from the construction of masculine identity in childhood (*The Smell of Burning Ants*, 1994) to the idiosyncracies of the 20th century's great dictators (*Human Remains*, 1998) and the historical conflicts between Christians and Jews (*King of the Jews*, 2000). While Rosenblatt's deployment of found images may seem relatively straightforward, functioning as illustration to an argument given in voice-over or titles, he often inverts the images' values, finding sadness, pain and longing in grandiose, aggressive or blustery gestures. In many instances, Rosenblatt isolates and extends brief moments through optical printing, finding in them a nexus of meaning. In *The Smell of Burning Ants*, for example, two boys bouncing up and down on a car seat suddenly look at one another, and this look is extended to emphasize the underlying homoerotic subtext of their shared activity.

Craig Baldwin also uses found footage as a way to mount a critical essay, though his tone is less sombre and his thinking more lateral than Rosenblatt's. In his instant classic *Tribulation 99: Alien Anomolies Under America* (1991), Baldwin orders the film using a system of substitution: a race of alien invaders called Quetzals stands in for Latin American democratic and communist movements, while historical figures are represented by characters from sundry Hollywood movies (e.g., Blacula as Maurice Bishop). The film's text as a whole, which takes

the form of a demented, paranoid, right-wing rant about an alien conspiracy, stands in for its opposite: a factual critique of American intervention against leftist movements in Latin America. Filmmaker Craig Baldwin is replaced by his right-wing equivalent, "retired Air Force Colonel Craig Baldwin." The diversity of Baldwin's source material and his style of optical printing tend to emphasize the material differences from one shot to the next. Baldwin mixes black-and-white footage with colour and documentary, or educational sources with dramatic sources. Much of the footage is worn, scratched and colour-shifted, so that the seams are emphasized and the result continually reminds the viewer that the film has been "stitched" together, like a patchwork quilt, or Frankenstein's monster.

The use of found footage can extend to the presentation of intact fragments with minimal alteration. For instance, Peggy Ahwesh's *The Color of Love* (1994) is presented almost in the same form it was found. Ahwesh has simply made an optical print of the found material and added music. Remarkably, this piece, a fragment of pornography beautifully decaying into organic clumps of colour, fits perfectly into the body of her work. The scene shows two women engaging in sex play over the dead, castrated body of a man, a violent conception of an anti-patriarchal lesbian order. Many of Ahwesh's other films deal with women's relationships in the absence of men, and particularly with moments in which acting cannot be distinguished from "authentic" or unstaged behaviour. Ken Jacobs' *Perfect Movie* (1986) is another noteworthy example of the use of unaltered found images. The film consists entirely of unused 1965 news footage on the assassination of

Malcolm X, with its original sync sound intact.

In contrast, animators and collage artists such as Janie Geiser, Lewis Klahr and Martha Colburn work frame by frame with manufactured objects and images cut from magazines and books, using these as "puppets" of autobiographical or ideological reconstruction in a sense analogous to Martin Arnold's refashioning of Hollywood actors into puppets of the cinematic apparatus. Where Geiser and Klahr tend to conjure lambent dream worlds that evoke the thoughts of a child confronted with a world it cannot understand, or the reveries of an addled adult in the grip of a fever or hallucination of nostalgia, Colburn's animated collages proceed at a manic pace, wringing out perverse combinations of animal, vegetable and sexual images from her source material. Colburn uses pictures from slick magazines, especially pornographic and animal images, in brief and briskly paced films with a distinctly "pop" rhythm and distinctly "anti-pop" production values and morals.

The Documentary Impulse

One of the fundamental tenets of high modernism was that a work of art be a self-contained object, independent of real-world referents. This idea has arisen in many guises, but for experimental film there are two main forms: the Structuralist/Materialist, and the Formalist. The Structuralist/Materialist argument (distinctly different from Sitney's concept of "Structural" film) turns primarily on the issue of presentation vs. representation. The argument attacks as reactionary any film that relies on illusion for its process of meaning formation. Peter Gidal, probably the most insistent proponent of this position, wrote in 1974:

> Structural/Materialist film attempts to be anti-illusionist. The process of the film's making deals with devices that result in demystification or attempted demystification of the film process ... An avant-garde film defined by its development towards increased materialism and materialist function does not represent, or document, anything ... The dialectic of the film is established in that space of tension between materialist flatness, grain, light, movement, and the supposed reality that is represented. Consequently a continual attempt to destroy the illusion is necessary. (1)

In Gidal's conception, documentation and narrative content presume a passive viewer, and most experimental films, including many abstract works, are understood to include some undesirable form of representation. Of the films that make up Sitney's "Structural film" canon (those by Michael Snow, Hollis Frampton, Ernie Gehr, et al.), Gidal writes of how "the discovery of shape (fetishizing shape or system) may become the theme, in fact, the narrative of the film" (1). For all the

revolutionary intentions of filmmakers and theorists like Gidal, these ideas, and
the extremely circumscribed possibilities available to filmmakers working within
their boundaries, quickly begin to seem like a form of Marxist puritanism: *no
dancing, music, or representation allowed.*

The Formalist stream of filmmaking has tended to be less bound by strict
rules and formulae, but it shares a generally anti-representational bent with
Structuralist/Materialist cinema. In Formalist discourse on film, analogies with
music abound. The idea is that film, like music, can engage the audience most
intensely when it does not refer to anything outside its own formal system, when it
does not rely on representation for its meaning or effect. The conception of film as
a kind of "visual music" arose early in the century, and remains an active model
for filmmakers such as Stan Brakhage, whose non-representational films attempt
to embody a type of "pre-linguistic" vision.

If a disavowal of representation was a defining feature of a great deal of
experimental filmmaking up to about the mid-70s, a major shift in the postmodern period has been the emergence of a generation of artists whose work engages
with a specific "extra-filmic" content. However, these artists are not naive about
questions of representation, nor do they subscribe to any particular school (e.g.,
cinéma vérité/direct cinema) that asserts the possibility of a "neutral" or "objective" representation. Rather, there is a general awareness that every work is a construction, an argument, whose formal elements and representational content
together constitute the substance of the argument. In a sense, these artists have
expanded the interest of many structural filmmakers from strictly visual or aural
perception to include questions of social, sexual, and political perception. This
process demands that the artist foreground the mechanisms by which meaning in
a film is constructed, so that traditional documentary techniques (the sync-sound
interview or "talking head," for example) are generally avoided in favour of a
clearly constructivist approach that may combine voice-over, titles, original and
found footage.

In keeping with this awareness, many artists choose to focus their documentary explorations on those subjects closest to them: for instance, their family histories or their sexual, racial, ethnic or religious identities. Su Friedrich maintains a
rigorous intellectual distance in excavating her childhood memories in *Sink or
Swim* (1990), ordering the material according to an arbitrary system akin to those
often employed by structural filmmakers—the alphabet in reverse (beginning with
z for zygote). Elida Schogt, in *Zyklon Portrait* (1999), uses a similar distancing technique for her elegiac account of the death of her grandparents during the
Holocaust, arranging archival footage, home movies and hand-painted film into
two parallel narrative strands. The first recounts Schogt's Jewish grandparents'
lives in the words of Schogt's mother; the second describes the development of
Zyklon B gas, first as an insecticide, then as the means by which concentration

camp prisoners were murdered in vast numbers by the Nazis, the description presented in a neutral tone reminiscent of the conventional documentary. The history of a chemical and the history of Schogt's ancestors inexorably converge in the gas chambers of Auschwitz.

Other artists use the documentary form to question the "truth value" of the image. Jesse Lerner's *Ruins* (1998) uses the strategy of deliberate and announced falsification to call into question Anglo-European interpretations of pre-Columbian societies such as the Mayan, Aztec and Toltec. Combining found footage with (presumably) scripted interviews, footage shot to look like found footage, etc., Lerner explicitly addresses the difficulty of distinguishing between the "authentic" and the fake, including a brief quote from Orson Welles' *F For Fake* (1973). The film also deals with the problem of authenticating pre-Columbian artifacts when the museums are full of fakes and replicas that stand in for "real" artifacts. William Jones' *Massillon* (1991) combines social landscape photography similar to that of James Benning with personal history (his experiences as a gay youth in a homophobic Midwestern environment) and social history (tracing the development of legal constraints on homosexual behaviour). In the film's final section, these elements are drawn together in a visual and verbal portrait of a new California suburb. Jones' method emphasizes the condition of the unseen, and the need to go beyond pure vision, by slowly "filling" his images with verbal information, so that the film's blank and undistinguished locations become inextricably linked to the history and attitudes of the (unseen) people who inhabit them.

THE MATERIAL IMAGE

At no other time in cinematic history have so many artists been working directly with the chemical surface of the image, using a multiplicity of techniques: hand processing, colour toning and arcane chemical treatments; homemade emulsions; application of paints, inks and dyes; scratching, abrading, and applying various materials to the film surface; collaging of cut-up pieces of film; and organic decay processes. A direct approach to the film surface is not new, having many precedents in avant-garde practice (e.g., Man Ray's inclusion of strips of "rayograph" film in his 1923 *Retour a la Raison*, or Stan Brakhage's 1955 *Reflections on Black*, in which the protagonist's eye-images have been scratched away). Beginning as early as the 1930s-40s there are also examples from experimental animation in the cameraless films of Len Lye, Norman McLaren and Harry Smith. However, partly for economic reasons, but largely because of the enthusiastic interest of a new generation of makers, the sheer amount of this kind of work has vastly increased over the past decade.

Unlike Brakhage, whose cameraless hand-painted and etched films are

intended to express an inner reality, a spiritual energy (he could be considered the most prolific abstract expressionist ever), many of these artists emphasize the material of the image in order not only to defeat its illusory qualities, but to draw attention to the physical presence of the film strip in the actual immediate space of the screening room, a concern that derives in part from the earlier Materialist discourse discussed above. This critical intention is confirmed by the frequent use of found footage as a source material for assorted physical alterations. The attack on the chemical surface of the film is implicitly an attack on the intended meaning of the original source images and on the "transparency" of conventional photographic reproduction.

In Germany, in films such as Jurgen Reble's *Zillertal* (1999), and the Schmelzdahin collective's *Stadt Im Flamen* (1984), artists subject films to organic decay processes and chemical treatments that create swarming masses of colour, often rendering the original images printed on the film barely legible. The sensory appeal of these films is considerable, given their highly textured and often brilliantly coloured surfaces, but the idea is as much to criticize the meaning of their source material as to provide visual pleasure. *Stadt Im Flamen* (*City in Flames*), for example, humorously exaggerates the source "text" to the breaking point. Here, the filmmakers work from a super-8 print of a disaster film about an uncontrolled urban fire along the lines of *The Towering Inferno*. By burying the film underground for an extended period, colonies of mould and bacteria developed, drawing the pigments in the emulsion into new forms, often intensifying the colours. Under the influence of these processes, the system of representation breaks down, falls into disaster like the crashing buildings and fleeing citizens in the original film's story.

The Armenian-Canadian filmmaker Gariné Torossian also works directly with the film surface, but in a manner more closely related to Carolee Schneemann's *Fuses* (1964-68) than to the chemical approaches described above. Torossian chops her films up, dyes them, scratches and tattoos them, and tapes them back together in new configurations, mixing super-8 and 16mm footage at will. Often this footage is already refilmed from a video image of an artwork or photograph, so that the number of generations of remove from any real-world referent is multiplied irretrievably. This becomes especially poignant in *Girl From Moush* (1993), a brief, haunting poem in which Torossian's longed-for homeland of Armenia is seen only in borrowed images that have inhabited and fermented in the artist's mind.

Film Performance

Some artists working in film reject its status as an impersonal, mass-reproducible object, mounting live film performances. These works partake of the film projection not as "text," but as event. In these performances it is not enough to run industrially reproduced materials through a projector. The presence of the living artist is required, as in the performance of a piece of music, with the film and the projector as instruments to be played. Prolific Toronto super-8 filmmaker John Porter, in his ongoing *Scanning* series, uses the entire theatre as a screen, moving the projector by hand to create magical illusionist effects which simultaneously make the spectator acutely aware of the theatre space. San Francisco artist Luis Recoder creates cinematic paradoxes and time loops using found footage by the simple expedient of looping a piece of film so that it runs through the projector twice, allowing images from one section of the film strip to overlap with those from a later section. His *Moebius Strip* (1999) uses documentation of sports events: we see a racing car tearing down a track from left to right, the camera panning with it, and simultaneously, the same car racing from right to left. The result is one of frenzied motion that cancels itself out. Recoder's *Magenta* (1997) uses a badly colour-shifted medical film demonstrating the proper methods for bandaging. Again, by running the same film through the projector twice, a visual echo is developed in which each action overlaps upon and repeats itself. The sensation is created of a continuous caress in the context of medical damage, a feeling both soothing and disturbing.

Philip Hoffman In Context

Philip Hoffman's highly diverse body of work in film, beginning with *On The Pond* (1978), shares many interests and approaches with the work discussed here, but is distinct in its relation to the documentary tradition (which is of particular importance in the Canadian context)[1], and in its concern with personal and family history. From *On The Pond* to *Destroying Angel* (1998), Hoffman has balanced an awareness of film as a constructed object with a desire to explore specific extra-filmic themes. This has led him to a complex, first-person cinema very different from the formal approach of an earlier generation. When Stan Brakhage films his family in his famous *Window Water Baby Moving* (1959), or in *Scenes From Under Childhood* (1967-70), the viewer does not learn the names of the people shown, does not hear their voices and discovers nothing of their past. The effect is two-fold: on the one hand, unencumbered by language, the film is able to hold in its form the very specific moments and energy of a particular time with particular people. On the other hand, everything is universalized: the children become all children and represent a state of "childness"; a birth becomes every birth, a symbol for all generative efforts.

In Hoffman's work the drive is very different and this leads to the inclusion of names and places, and the tracing of specific relationships. However, Hoffman's acute awareness that the medium is never a neutral carrier of information leads to a variety of representational approaches, which often contain contradictory cues about the "truth value" of the material (see for example *?O,Zoo! (The Making of a Fiction Film)* (1986)). Alternatively, in a manner analogous to Craig Baldwin's indirect treatment of his subject in *Tribulation 99*, Hoffman's "absent presences" refuse explicit visual representation of their subjects. For example, both *?O,Zoo!* and *Somewhere Between Jalostotitlan and Encarnacion* (1984) have at their centres the story of a death, and in neither case is the dead person or animal represented visually. In varying proportions, Hoffman's films play documentary content against fiction within a complex and shifting formal treatment.

Hoffman engages in an intense process of self-examination that is also an exploration of the capacities of his medium. In finding an appropriate form for his themes and ideas, Hoffman has developed a multiplicity of styles. But these are not arbitrary exercises; in each case, Hoffman demands of a film that it communicate certain crucial ideas to the viewer while promoting an intense awareness of the film's means of construction. It is ultimately this foregrounding of the means of construction and Hoffman's casual hybridity of genre, balancing the concerns of documentary, fiction and formal experimentation, that mark Hoffman as a filmmaker allied with the impurities of contemporary practice and engaged in a critical dialogue with the "straight" documentary tradition that has been so important in the Canadian context.

Hoffman's influence as a teacher at Sheridan College and York University has been as important as his artistic influence. For example, although Hoffman's films evidence a relatively gentle engagement with the chemically altered image, the summer film retreat he founded with his late partner Marian at their rural Mount

1. Michael Dorland even asserts: "I entertain the thesis that 'avant-garde' in Canada is an instance of misprision and that the notion of experimental documentary may prove more productive in a Canadian context" (*International Experimental Film Congress* 33). R. Bruce Elder treats the influence of the documentary tradition on Canadian experimental film in great detail in his book *Image and Identity: Reflections on Canadian Film and Culture* (Waterloo: Wilfrid Laurier University Press, 1989).

Forest home has been inspirational to scores of young makers by teaching the basics of first-person hand processing and other chemical treatments of the film surface. This workshop has been a key catalyst in the explosion of first-person, hand-processed, cameraless and chemically-worked films in North America over the past several years.

The balance of interests in Hoffman's work has shifted markedly from film to film. Much of his work enters into the relationship between documentary, fiction, and formal experimentation described here, while some of his films favour more generally formal visual and aural approaches (e.g., *Chimera*, 1992-3), and still others venture into aleatoric construction (*Technilogic Ordering* and *Opening Series*, 1992 ongoing project). In *Opening Series*, Hoffman gathers together several separate rolls of film, packaging each in its own box with an unrelated image or text on the outside. Audience members are asked to change the order of the boxes as they enter the theatre prior to the screening. Hoffman splices the film together in the order arrived at by the collective choices of the audience members; the film will therefore be projected in a different edit at every screening, moving his work into the realm of "film performance."

The richness and complexity of Hoffman's greatest works, which include *passing through/torn formations*, *Kitchener-Berlin* and *?O,Zoo! (The Making of a Fiction Film)*, have made him one of the important experimental filmmakers of the past twenty years. The insistent hybridity of Hoffman's practice also marks him as distinctly postmodern, and his particular relation to the documentary tradition as distinctly Canadian. To assert that experimental film is no longer a living force is to ignore the challenge offered by Hoffman's films and those of many other active filmmakers. If an earlier generation found its identity through a purity of form and identity, the strength of today's experimental filmmakers may lie in a canny "impurism" that allows them to traverse the boundaries that separate documentary from fiction, abstraction from representation, and political from personal.

Works Cited

Arnold, Martin.
address, Pleasure Dome screening. Toronto, 18 Feb. 2000.

Boughton, Jason.
"Laid to Rest: Where the Forward Guard, and Their Regrettable Victory, Are Finally Dismissed." *Pinhole Cinema Project*. n.p. 911 Media Arts Centre, 1993.
5-7.

Camper, Fred.
International Experimental Film Congress. Toronto: Art Gallery of Ontario, 1989.

Gidal, Peter.
"Theory and Definition of Structural/Materialist Film." *Structural Film Anthology*. Ed. Peter Gidal. London: British Film Institute, 1978.
1-21.

FILMS AND FAIRY DUST

by Cara Morton

It started with this dream: I am surrounded by lowing cattle. The moon is pregnant, promising, full. The air is sweet and warm and I am on my back, floating in the grass, while Maya Deren pulls a tiny key from her mouth again and again, while Maya Deren pulls a tiny key from her mouth again and again, while Maya Deren … Kazaam! Hang on a second … this isn't a dream at all. This is real. I am on a filmmaking retreat taught by Phil Hoffman on his enchanted property just outside Mount Forest, two blessed hours from Toronto.

still: *We Are Going Home* by Jennifer Reeves.

I'm fully awake and it's the end of the first day. Nine of us, eight women and one guy ("the guy on the girl's trip") have just spent an amazing day playing with the camera. For some it was a time for rediscovery; for others, it was that first glorious encounter between magician and medium, otherwise known as the Bolex. Now it's around midnight, and we are lolling in the grass like the cattle in the field next to us, chewing our cuds and watching *Meshes of the Afternoon* flicker off the outdoor cinema (the side of the barn). For me, this is film at its best: fields, forest, cattle, countryside and total immersion in the process of creation.

I went on the workshop in the first place because I hate film. I mean sometimes I have to wonder, what has gotten into me? Why am I putting myself through this agony? I've spent most of my grant money. I'm in the midst of editing and I find myself asking, what is this damn film about anyway? Why am I making it? What am I trying to say? At this point those of you who run screaming from process-oriented work can laugh at me. I don't plan much (what do you mean, storyboard?). I like letting things happen, letting that creative, unconscious self reign. But sooner or later that insightful (not to mention delightful) self turns on me and I'm left stranded in a dark editing suite with the corpse of my film and that evil monster self who thinks analytically, worries about money and who just doesn't get it! So, 'round about May, that's where I found myself. But then, the cosmic wheel turned and I went on the workshop, hoping to exorcise this critical, anti-process, monster side of myself. And it actually worked. I opened up to my instincts, started trusting myself again. (So what if this sounds like a new-age self-help tirade. Just go with it …)

One of the first censors to go was the money-obsessed self—the self that abruptly grabs the camera away when you're trying to have fun. Now, in the mainstream film world, this may sound subversive, or certainly weird, but if you can shoot without analyzing every detail, without worrying about money, money, money … Imagine! You can experiment! You can try things, be free with the stock! How? Cheap film! At Phil's we were shooting the incredible Kodak 7378, at 12 bucks/100 feet. It's cheap because it isn't actually picture stock, but optical print stock. It's black and white and has a varying ASA somewhere between twelve and thirty depending on how you process it. And it's gorgeous: very high contrast with a fabulous dense grain.[1]

OK, so we can shoot cheap! But there's more! Remember Polaroids? At the workshop it became clear to me that I had been missing that sense of wonder about film—that sense of playing an important role in a magical process. Thanks to Phil's workshop I got that feeling back. How? Hand processing. It's better than Polaroids because you can control the process of development. You can develop your film as negative or reversal, you can solarize (a personal fave), you can underdevelop, overdevelop—anything you want—in minutes. Imagine, you wander around the countryside shooting to your heart's (and wallet's) content and then run back to the barn, where the darkroom's set up, and process your film. It's hard to describe the feeling you get when you hang your film out to dry. It's a mixture of wonder, accomplishment and connection to the medium. And all this for less than one quarter of what you usually pay.

At this point, you can tint or tone your film with other colours to get some far-out, moody effects. Most of us favoured the potassium permanganate, which

photo: film farm 1999.

eats away at the film emulsion. This brings us to scratching. Imagine not only not worrying about scratches, but trying to make them! Nothing, I mean nothing, beats stomping on your film, rubbing it against trees, rolling around with it in the grass or even chewing on it like bubblegum (OK, no one actually tried that, but it would be fun, no?).

These experiences totally changed my relationship to film as a medium. I became equal to it; no, I became the master of it. No more God-like can of film handled with white kid gloves: I shot it and I can fuck with it, and if I don't like it, well, I can re-shoot for the price of a new pack of crayons. Film can be a truly plastic medium.

Believe it or not, the mythical last day arrives. We have our final screening (most of us have actually finished a short piece) and then a discussion. Later that evening, as we are striking camp, the sun is miraculous, huge and orange, setting over the marsh. It's so beautiful that we stare, but after five days of total immersion in beauty, we are saturated by it. It's too much, all we can do is ridicule how goddamn perfect it all is.

On the way home I realize I've achieved more than I imagined possible. I've found the magic in film again. My next dream goes like this. I'm in Toronto, in a basement, surrounded by streaming ribbons of film I've shot and processed myself. I start chewing on it. I chew and chew until my film turns into a tiny perfect key, until my film turns into a tiny perfect key, and I pull it from my mouth …

This article was first printed in the *Liaison of Independent Filmmakers (LIFT) Newletter*, Summer 1996.

EAR STONES

by Sarah Abbott

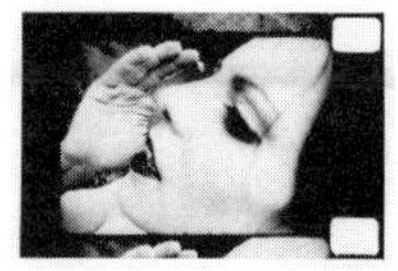

still: *The Light in Our Lizard Bellies* by Sarah Abbott.

For that to which one lacks access from experience, one has no ears.
People have the illusion that where nothing is heard, there is nothing.
Nietzsche, *Existentialism from Dostoevsky to Sartre*

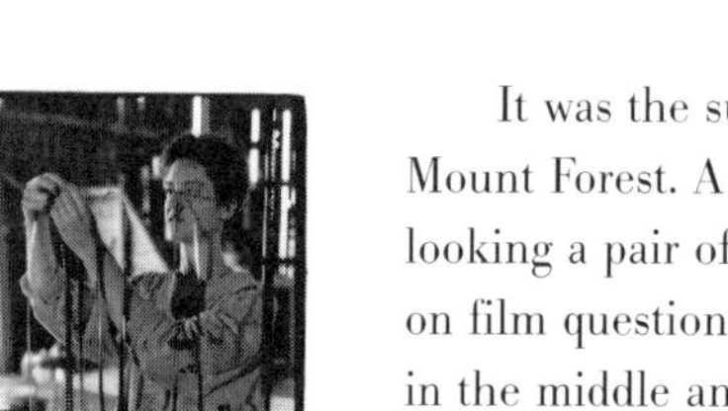

photo: Sarah Abbott hand processes film.

It was the summer Marian and I walked down the dirt road: June 1996, Mount Forest. A few days before that walk, I had stood next to bookshelves overlooking a pair of flatbeds in the sunroom as Phil and the "film farm" gang buzzed on film questions. I pulled a random book from the shelves, opened it somewhere in the middle and found my finger on Nietzsche.

Marian and I had set off in the heat to try and ease my frustration at not being able to release my feelings into the film that would be *Froglight*. It was a dream-like hour, punctuated by roadside, emerald-green plants, a river sparkling through gaps in a bridge, and an intense, windless sunlight. I was following our conversation, helping to build it, yet our words and the surrounding air were swirling and ungraspable. Something I hadn't encountered before kept oozing into my breath, but I couldn't break its surface. All I could do was keep treading under water.

Back at the farm, I scribbled fragments from our conversation into my blue journal.

> We have to resist others' truths about ourselves. Yet we,
> ourselves, can't tell or know the truth about ourselves.
>
> The self.
>
> What I was experiencing versus what I was told I should be
> experiencing.
>
> When what you believe is never validated, your vision
> becomes limited and you can't see as far.

As I kept treading under water, Marian spoke of how you walk through life with a stone in your shoe that shapes your gait, informing your every action, thought and interaction. We don't often think of removing the stone—if we realize it's there at all—and so become paralyzed, blinded by the habits it forms. To remove it would mean we'd have to negotiate unfamiliar territory, and this blindness in ourselves is terrifying.

Film is a neutral zone until we approach it as makers and viewers with our sundry of stones.

I was re-neutralizing film when I first came into contact with it at the age of six. In an obscure craft class, I scratched blackened emulsion off 16mm stock with a pin. Since then, nothing has been that neutral. Countless times I have come pin-width close to jumping on a plane at the close of shooting a film to find a person to fill my soul and a "better life."

If, as movie viewers, we are enlivened by the illusion of escape, we move only further from ourselves. If, as makers, we lack self-knowledge, we will produce work that reflects the storm of manufactured thought surrounding us, instead of the light and reality of our own worlds. In denying our own worlds, we deny the worlds of the viewers. The magic of film is released when we can move inside it with independence, imagination, and self-reflection to places beyond our habits of hearing and seeing. The magic of film helps us pick the stones out of our shoes.

The innards of what would be *The Light in Our Lizard Bellies* flicker back at us, as Phil and I sit, stuffed as far back in the den as possible, flanking the hum of the projector. It is August 1999. Again, Mount Forest. Susanna Hood had danced alone when I circled her with the camera in Toronto, but now she dances with a light that softly punctuates her movements, licking the space around her and adding rhythms of its own. But I can't see this. In my eyes, I still have pristine pictures of Susanna's body in the jet black of a controlled studio, captured in the crisp perfection of 35mm film frames. Now my film is a leaking, dirty mess that I wish I had not processed by hand.

You've got some beautiful things happening here.

It was only months later that I would actually hear Phil's words and learn how to make film. I had to surrender to the thing itself, listen to its description of my stones and ditch them.

SITE SPECIFIC SYMPTOMS

by Deirdre Logue

stills: *Enlightened Nonsense,* by Deirdre Logue.

#1 NIGHT DIARY

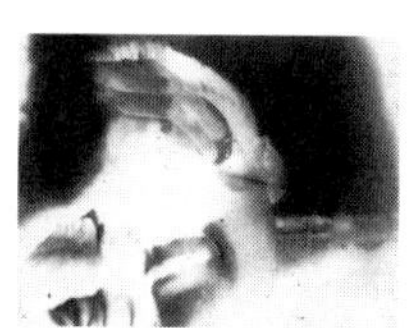

The overnight sleep study showed difficulty initiating and maintaining sleep, associated with a significant alpha-EEG disturbance. There was no polysomnographic evidence of significant bruxism on this particular night. Psychologic self ratings indicated considerable emotional distress including symptoms of depression and anxiety, which may require further psychiatric assessment. She indicated an average consumption of twenty alcoholic beverages per week, which may be compounding her sleep-related symptoms. Sleep questionnaires indicated a tendency to restrict sleep, especially during her work week. Please advise as to whether you require further assessment for this patient in this clinic.

#2 THE SKY IS FALLING ... THE SKY IS FALLING ...

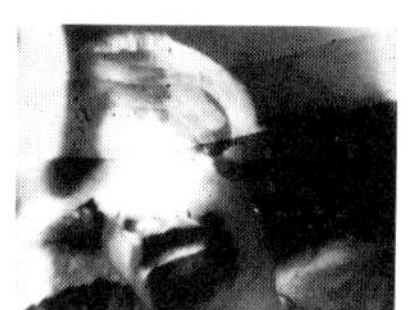

I can't remember if it was Chicken Little or Henny Penny or both, but someone spoiled optimism for me with that insane story of the sky falling onto the fragile heads of all the adorable farm animals. I can't recall if the sky falls or if it's bread crumbs, acid rain, a plague of frogs or a swarm of locusts. Or if it's simply the threat of something so final that makes this story so terrifying to me still. Its stupid ideas have set in motion a group of associated symptoms that in turn have set in motion a set of associated films. A syndrome.

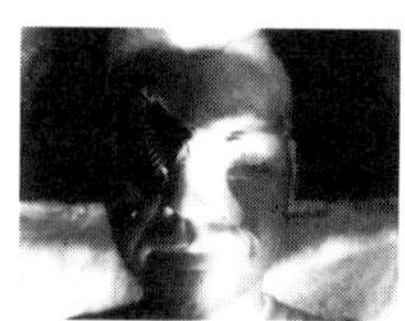

It is on uneven ground that I have felt my unconscious body for the first time. My body is alive, and in the moment I discovered this, I also discovered that the harder the ground under my feet, the worse the anticipated fall. A sinister side of me that I have never really known has worked its way out—it grows more beautiful as each day passes, and more threatening still as I move through these ten films.

#3 DIRECTIONS TO PHIL'S FARM

After the Mount Forest exit, things get a little dark no matter how bright the day.

The last half-mile to the farm is the best part. A bridge built for one swings slightly, and it is there that the coolness catches you. Once you have passed the first bend in the dirt road and can't yet see around the second, you leave one place for another. When I travel to the farm I always get a headache, which makes me salivate and think about basketball, and my best conversations of late have all been in the darkroom. These conversations remind me of dreaming, and they leave me unsettled. Standing in Phil's driveway, I realized that a willow tree is glorious when ripped from its root hold and thrown across a pathway, and that it's not just about a place but what happens to you in that place.

D: Hey.
B: Hey.
D: You got time to give me a quickie?
B: Pardon.
D: A haircut.
B: Don't do women's hair here.
D: Well, I went to the salon across the street but they are all busy, prom weekend you know, so they told me to come and see you, and seein' as you're not busy …

B: Don't do women's cuts.
D: I don't have women's hair.
B: (pause) Sit down.
D: Are you sure? I don't want you to do it if you're going to give me a half assed haircut. I got a big weekend myself …
B: I'm sure.
D: Last chance …
B: Yep.
(Trimming back and sides)

B: Where you from?
D: … just in town for a couple of weeks, up at Phil Hoffman's farm, you know Phil Hoffman? He's got a nice place out the berry farm way, does these film workshops in the summer. People from all over the world go there to make films.
B: That so.
(Clipping top and thinning sideburns)
B: What kind of farms did you say you make films about?
D: Oh, we make films about all sorts of stuff.

B: You go to different farms?
D: No, we pretty much stick around Phil's farm, but folks go all around Mount Forest to shoot stuff …
(Shaving neck)
B: Yeah, they came in here last summer. One of them got a haircut …
D: Yeah, yeah, made a great film too. Shop looks great in it.
B: That right?
D: Yeah.

#4 Plan A: Excerpt From Grant to the Ontario Arts Council

My work relies on myself as the primary source. This approach to my production, a way of making work "internally," has contributed not only to the performative style but to the formal aesthetic of each piece. They are process based, further emphasized by hand-processing and tinting techniques, surface manipulation and in-camera editing. The subject matter ranges from gender ambiguity and sexual difference to masochism, psychoanalysis and somatic illness.

Each work begins with a specific physical action, (e.g., a ball hitting a head) which is compulsively developed through repetition and intercutting related images, sound and text. Sexual deception, humiliation, injury, fear and failure are common themes, however humour plays a critical role. Though dark, the works have a curious, nonsensical quality, which provides the viewer with some distance as well as comic relief.

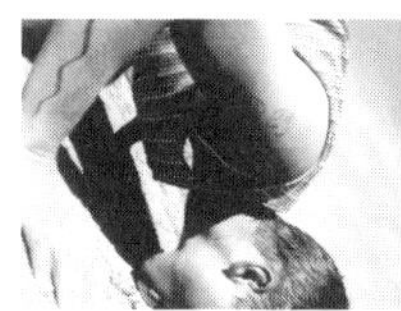

#5 Backup Plan and Other Psychic Noises

Since my first visit to the farm four years ago I have shot ten films. Having completed six of them to date, over the next three weeks I will finish the remaining four. Now, as I write and edit, I can feel the essay and the films about to collide, like siblings running in opposite directions around the kitchen table, each one thinking they know what the other's strategy is, trying to watch themselves, each other, the floor and the table at the same time, picking up speed and hysteria along the way. When I write all I can think about are the films, and when I work on the films all I can think about is what to say about what I am doing. I start to wonder what I've begun, what I am trying to finish and what will be left when it's over. Or if it ever will be over. What if I'd just spent more time scripting instead of wandering around myself like a tourist? Everything was fine until I started taking pictures: putting myself in between you and me, waiting for the flying object to land and watching the clock, stitching up my wounds, controlling my control, processing my process and trying to fix my mistakes. Now the monsters move and they move faster than my camera can.

#6 Trouble

Step 1: Try to Calm Down

This can be accomplished in a number of ways, though two are recommended. First, let your body go limp and allow your dead weight to drop directly to the ground. While on the ground try telling yourself over and over that you will sur-

vive this, and that if you really think about it, this is the best time of your life. You are making some really interesting work. It's difficult, yes, but imperative that you keep things in perspective. If this doesn't work, carefully insert one small handful of common garden thistles into your underpants and wait.

Step 2: Call a Friend or Your Local Therapist

Under trying circumstances it can be very useful to pick up the phone and have an intimate conversation with your therapist or an old friend. They will tell you that the ideas you are working with are difficult and hard to manage but that you are doing fine while trying your best, which is what really counts. After all, being a filmmaker is an honourable and fascinating profession and people admire what you do. This conversation may compel you to drink twelve to fourteen litres of ice cold, vitamin-enriched, homogenized milk while lying on your back. (Note: Milk may cause drowsiness).

Step 3: Try to Identify the Problem

If you don't know what's bothering you sit down for a moment and think. While sitting and thinking, take a three-inch-wide roll of clear, plastic, sticky tape and wrap up your head so that your thoughts can be contained. Hold your breath. Wait several seconds before removing the tape. Upon removal, notice that the problem is stuck to the recently discarded tape. Look at the problem and ask yourself, what is its shape and size? Continue breathing in and out.

Step 4: Fantasize

Creativity is uniquely linked to your imagined self, to fantasies of who you are and who you may wish to be. Let this concept take hold of you for a moment. Inhale deeply and plunge your head into a bucket of cold water. With your head submerged you can imagine that the things you wish for are real and that these things make you feel fulfilled, satisfied, even if it's just for a second or two.

Step 5: Call Your Friend or Local Therapist Back and Tell Them You are Fine

Having survived all of this, you realize that it's not so bad, that this is the best time of your life, that your films are the most important thing right now, that you have things in perspective, that you have great friends and a terrific therapist, that ideas can be difficult, that internal chaos is part of the process and that you can be anything you want to be. Go directly to the phone and call those in whom you have confided. Tell them that you have figured out a few very meaningful things and that you are back on track and doing fine now, thanks. Thanks a lot.

#7 Cure (A Syndrome)

I am the primary performer, director and technician. I arrive at the actions and events through fantasy, impulse and intuition. I perform the actions with a repetition that I have come to know so well in myself. I am most often there alone so that I can see myself without your reflection. The films demonstrate that I am permeable. When I am there, I feel relaxed with this idea, even though it frightens me. I have found a place where I can drown out my sorrows, doze off, fall down, lick the ground, bite off more than I can chew, chop off my head, watch it split open, patch it up and tape it back on. Miles and miles of empty fields make it possible for me to hide in the tall grass and sneak up on myself when I least expect it. I can pretend I am the surveillance camera's well-hidden lens, the physician looking for a diagnosis, the patient looking for the cure. I am the moving target, the illness, the antigen and the antidote.

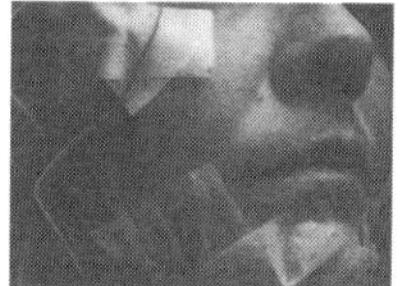

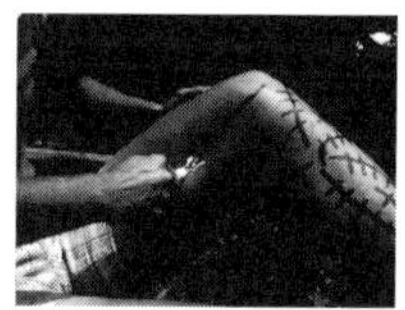

BY MYSELF

by shary boyle

Shary Boyle 1998

the practice of secretive play

is not undertaken by day

a habit picked up as a child

alone in the closet, reviled

halloween

unseen

teen queen

FILMS OF LIFE AND DEATH:
REMARKS ON THE DIARY FILM

by Matthias Müller

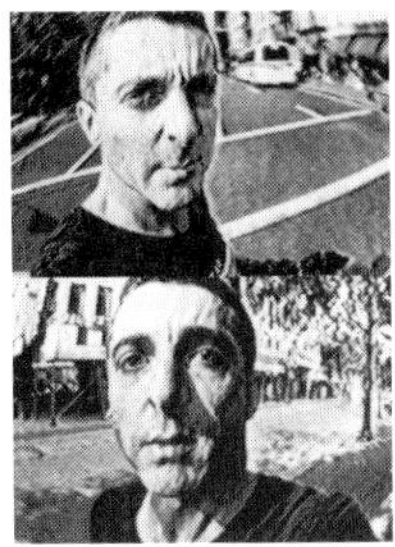

still: *Sullivan.*

Diary films pinpoint an "I" so omnipresent that the world fades to a mere etcetera. In the diary videos of Nelson Sullivan, for instance, the wide angle of his hand-held camera seldom allows the maker to slip out of view. Sullivan usually fills the entire image, pushing the reality of the outer world to the edges of the frame. When he tells us, "You can walk in my shoes. I want to share it all with you," (1989) Sullivan reminds us that diary films invite the viewer to visit a private world. "Welcome to my world, won't you come on in …" bubbles an old pop song. Formulated in the first person, diary work dialogues with its viewer using the persona of the maker. As film critic Karsten Witte writes, reducing the film's focus to its maker "limits the radius, but deepens the perception" (1983).

The written diary is usually hidden, sometimes under lock and key, and it seldom leaves the private sphere. By contrast, the diary film is made for dissemination. Both genres involve the author's interest in recording personal incidents in order to recall patterns of becoming. Me, myself and I: it's about the manifestation of the self. But in the cinema, factors that are irrelevant to the clandestine and private journal may come into play, like vanity, shame, or the consideration of others.

Like any written diary, the diary film is created after the fact, distanced in time from the events described. But in the moment of recording, the film demands spontaneity and flexibility. Analysis and reflection lend the raw material structure, but editing follows associative connections rather than classical principles of narrative continuity. It is through editing that these "objective" documents transform into fiction, though they may be all the more "authentic" for it.

Diary film makers such as Sadie Benning or George Kuchar self-consciously employ role-playing, parody and travesty as well as thoroughly conventional rules of narration. Kuchar edits much of his material directly in the camera. In his videos, one senses a boisterous pleasure and virtuosity (resulting from years of experience in working with fictional films) in the dramaturgical editing of his own daily life. As Kuchar suggests, "Most of us see life in the form of a Hollywood movie anyway. So in diary videos you can add music at just the right time, and orchestrate the shots of mom making potato blintzes so that it looks like she's in a Brian de Palma movie" (20).

There is no unifying code that accompanies the autobiography. For instance, Birgit Hein's challenging *Baby, I Will Make You Sweat* (1994) and Michelle Fleming's sophisticated *Life/Expectancy* (1998) are reflections on the mid-life situations of the filmmakers, and yet worlds lie between these works. Hein defiantly reclaims her right to her own sexuality at the age of fifty-six, simultaneously pushing the limits of "direct cinema." Fleming's eclectic montage combines psychoanalytic intertitles, moments of her own life recast as noir fantasy and the bickering of Taylor and Burton from *Who's Afraid of Virginia Woolf?* Each maker invents a shape for her own experience, as unique and individual as a thumbprint.

Styles from the diary film (first-person narrative, hand-held camera, jump cuts, etc.) have been adopted by other film genres. Faked diary sequences have long been a staple of Hollywood fare, where grainy, home-movie memories become codes of truth and authenticity. As Godard writes, "In order to make fiction, you have to begin with documentary, and in order to make documentary, you start with fiction." Yet many diary films are craftless and crude, deliberately unsophisticated. Mainstream audiences often recoil, in part because these films ignore the usual social distance that regulates our dealings with each other.

In accordance with the formula "low tech, high fidelity," many makers prefer amateur equipment. Super-8, 8mm camcorders, and even the Fisher Price video camera (originally marketed as a children's toy) have been used to make diary work. Easily obtainable, simple to use, and very mobile, this kind of equipment is ideal for unpredictable, extended projects with minimal budgets. The camera becomes the travel escort, the longtime companion, even bedfellow.

The diary film continues to face accusations that it is little more than a vehicle for narcissistic, egomaniacal self-promotion. In our vicarious-living society, all human interests appear to be represented by others (lobbies, clubs, political institutions). It is considered inappropriate, impolitic even, to speak in the first person. In Anne Charlotte Robertson's seventeen-minute litany *Apologies* (1983-90), only the author is shown, endless apologizing for taking herself so seriously and for robbing the viewers of their precious time. For many diary makers, the need for representation arises out of their absence on the public screen. As Yann Beauvais, curator of the diary film series *Le je filmé* ascertained, directing the camera at oneself is often "the liberating act of an individual, who is normally forced into the social background" (198). Due to the close relationship they bear to the amateur film, one could think of many film diaries as emancipatory home movies.

Marginalized groups, such as gays and lesbians (Sadie Benning, Su Friedrich, George Kuchar, Nelson Sullivan, Remi Lange), displaced persons and immigrants

(Jonas Mekas, Robert Frank, Rudy Burckhardt), or the mentally ill (Anne Charlotte Robertson) formulate commentaries about their lives in diary films. For Robertson, who has been diagnosed as "temporarily mentally disabled," producing a diary film is a daily therapeutic exercise. She writes, "Making my diary has literally saved my life." Diary filmmakers use film to oppose their social oblivion, and to show themselves as individuals, as opposed to the case studies rendered by more orthodox documentary practice. They want to oppose a neo-scientific objectivity and all-knowing voice-over with an eccentric subjectivity. Even when they appropriate scientific texts, these films add the personal pronoun. One striking example of this kind of subversion is Birgit Hein's *The Uncanny Women*, where the maker borrows from ethnological and psychological texts, but connects them with a decidedly obscene language.

Diary films are often studies of memory and family. In the films by Robertson or Frank, which appear improvised, one has the feeling of real, unmediated time unfolding. But relics of the author's past—such as mementos of Frank's dead children—find their way into the lens. In a scene from Frank's *The Present* (1996), the filmmaker's co-worker attempts to wash the word "memory" (which Frank had written a long time ago) from the studio wall. Frank's camera stops when only "me" can still be read.

Lawrence Green's *Reconstruction* (1995) is also a melancholy meditation on memory. With the aid of old home-movie clips, the filmmaker conjures up moments from a distant childhood, though this is not an escapist longing for a deceptive idyll. Green allows these images to collide with the report of his sister's adoption into the family. Kept for many years, this secret was uncovered in the making of the film. So these family documents are never quite what they appear to be, and this overturning of heritage and repression is typical of much autobiographical practice.

We are accustomed to images that show the diary filmmaker shouldering the camera in order to begin a journey of discovery. The delegation of camera work, so we imagine, might harm the material's authenticity. Since the beginning of the 1980s, however, there has been a growing interest in exploring the possibilities offered by found footage. This most anonymous of film processes appears to stand in sharp contrast to projects centered in a unique and steadfast individuality. But those diary films that admit scraps from the media world cast doubt upon the naive belief in the unity of identity. Dissolving the borders between inner and outer worlds, these films place their protagonists in a tense situation between self-insistence and the dissolution of self in a surplus of media stimuli.

In my own films, appropriated material often serves to expand the autobiographical, to tie introspection to a world of collective images. Drama, dynamics, pathos and sentimentality—found footage is used without irony to tease the latent

still: *The Memo Book*
(1989) by Matthias Müller.

content out of my own pictures. In *The Memo Book*, it would have been natural to counter the lavish production values of the appropriated Hollywood films with the impoverished circumstances of my own production. Instead, I balanced their inequities by subjecting each citation to my aesthetic agenda. This was done by color matching, editing according to the direction of movement, and the use of my own body as a sliding screen in front of the TV monitor.

The Memo Book is my most personal film. It began after a friend died suddenly of AIDS. Working on the film clarified how strongly my own feelings are determined by traditional media images, no matter how toxic these might appear. The fear and self-loathing, the insistent quest for a story (Why did it happen? Why now?) were all borrowed emotions, but no less real. The long period of gathering and revising made it possible to distance myself, to consider my own creations as if they were found in a flea market. This raises the fundamental question of where one's own images begin.

Working on *The Memo Book*, I recreated myself in crisis, with the camera acting as interlocutor and intermediary. Cameras can change the visible, and restage even the spontaneous and unprepared. Take a diary project such as Sophie Calle's and Greg Shephard's *Double-Bind* (1992), which was conceived as a human experiment with unknown results. Calle drives with a stranger across America, trying to persuade him to marry her. Shephard has no idea what is going on, and the audience is welcomed as Calle's accomplice. The camera is used as a magnifying glass to heat up their relationship: its presence fuels the intensity of the clash between the protagonists.

The use of the camera as an intrusion into the personal realm shifts our attention from the content of the work to the terrible complicity at stake in the act of looking. Yet the shamelessness with which George Kuchar's camera cruises the men around him produces an openness unattainable through subtler strategies. Using tactics of intrusion, Robert Frank's insistent questioning of his son Pablo in *Conversations in Vermont* (1969), or Abraham Ravett's merciless and unceasing demand that his old mother remember the Holocaust in *The March* (1999), are painful attempts to drive the exploration of the self to the edges of confrontation with the Other.

Filmmakers have rarely gone as far as Tom Joslin and Mark Massi in traversing the divide between self and the world. In *Silverlake Life: The View From Here* (1997), the makers document their slow death of AIDS and the strength of their love. Cocteau's definition of film as the only art that can show death at work finds its painful confirmation here. When Tom dies, Mark wants to close his eyes, just like in the movies. But this is not possible, because real death is different. In diary films, perhaps we have only the practice of life and death, and as Montaigne ironically instructs us, "To begin to strip death of its greatest advantage over us, let us take an entirely different way from the usual one. Let us rid death of its strangeness, come to know it, get used to it. Let us have nothing in our minds as often as death ... It is uncertain where death awaits us; let us await it everywhere" (60). To practise death, Montaigne propounds, is to practise freedom. In *Silverlake Life: The View From Here*, the gap between industrial cinema and the diary film, and between life and death, has seldom been more intensely presented.

Translated by Allison Plath-Moseley

Works Cited

Beauvais, Yann.
"Le Je a la Camera." *Le Je Filme* Eds. Yann Beauvais and Jean-Michel Bouhours. Paris: Centre Georges Pompidou, 1988.

Kuchar, George.
The George Kuchar Experience. Ed. Steve Reinke. Toronto: YYZ Artist's Outlet and Pleasuredome, 1996.

Sullivan, Nelson.
"*Monologue for TV Show*" (video tape). New York City, July 2, 1989.

Montaigne, Michel de.
"That to Philosophize is to Learn to Die." *Complete Works of Montaigne.* Trans. Donald M. Frame. Stanford: Stanford University Press, 1943.
56-68.

Witte, Karsten.
"Es Werde Licht!" *Frankfurter Rundschau* (newspaper), Frankfurt, Germany, 1983.
3.

EXCUSE OF THE REAL

by Steve Reinke

Steve Reinke's 100 videos began in 1989. This monumental project has altered the face of Canadian video, spreading like a stain, changing everything. Reinke's intention was "to complete one hundred videos before the year 2000 and my thirty-sixth birthday. These will constitute my work as a young artist." *Excuse of the Real* is the first of the 100 videos. In it, the following text is read by Reinke in voice-over while a series of home-movie excerpts, originally shot in super-8 and transferred to video, play in looped succession. They show a family on Christmas morning, children mugging for the camera in delight, all smiles.
Mike Hoolboom

I've made a few documentaries before and I like making them. Documentary material is usually more interesting than anything I could imagine and I don't have to be bothered with all the tiresome specifics of a fictional creation. Also I can't be held responsible for material which purports to an actual reality. I'm not personally implicated and therefore can't be blamed. I call this the excuse of the real.

Like everyone else I wanted to do something on AIDS, a close, personal look at a guy dying. Wanting the work to be as effective a documentary as possible, that is, as visceral as possible, I would want to include my subject's death. In fact, the video would not be complete without his death. So I set out in search of a subject. These were my initial parameters. In order not to confuse or blur issues: a white, anglophone, homosexual male, and for added empathy, he should be under thirty. Due to budget restrictions, I would prefer one who would die six to eight weeks after taping was to begin, yet would be strong enough in the initial days of taping that I could get his basic life story in a few days of interviews before settling down to watch whatever complications the guy has play themselves out. What I had in mind seemed fairly simple. Him talking of his childhood and adolescence, his emerging identity through a series of stories, personal remembrances, anecdotes, dreams. The audience would be constructing an image of him even as he himself crumbles away. I would need some home movies, flickering super-8. I would use these as visuals. If my subject didn't have any, another's could be used. Everyone's

home movies are basically the same. It would simply be a matter of matching hair colour and body types.

This is something else I'd want to show. The steady degradation of his body and mind. Medical charts would be included, reports on blood cells. I would want to provide a record of each lesion over time, a shifting map of epidermal sores.

This became my problem. As my search continued, I began imagining with increasing specificity the things I would like my subject to say and do. That is, the longer my search took, the more specific my criteria became. And the more specific my criteria, the more difficult, and therefore longer, my search. It seemed an unending spiral. Two sets that might never overlap or share any common points. And even if there were specific points of juncture, how could I find the individual that would be at each point? My project risked degenerating into fiction.

DAMNED IF YOU DON'T: 4 NOTES ON HERSELF

by Su Friedrich

1. *Sink or Swim* was completed in June 1990. It runs forty-eight minutes and was shot in black and white. The film consists of twenty-six stories and an epilogue, which are read in voice-over by a thirteen-year-old girl, Jessica Lynn. These stories proceed alphabetically, in reverse order, with title cards that begin with Zygote and end with Athena, Atalanta and Aphrodite. The only story that is re-enacted is the chess game, Pedagogy, while the rest are accompanied by images shot from daily life, street life. These usually function on a symbolic or metaphoric level, providing an additional commentary to the ideas conveyed in the text. All of the stories are based on my experience but were written in the third person, so that the distance provided by a less subjective voice might allow the viewer greater access to the material. Here are four excerpts:

JOURNALISM

On her tenth birthday, the girl's sister gave her a diary with a green cloth cover. It came with a lock and a small key, which she carefully hid under her bed. On the first page she scrawled a large note that declared: If anybody reads this diary, they are very mean! It is personal.

For the most part, the girl filled it with stories about doing punishment assignments, fighting with boys and playing with her friends. Because she didn't write every day, there were still empty pages left when her parents told her they were getting a divorce. The girl was too ashamed to tell anyone, and even kept it a secret from her best friend for more than a year, but she did confess it to her diary. It felt as if the act of writing it down would make it really come true, so she used a pencil instead of her favorite cartridge pen. The next time she looked inside, the entry had been erased. Her mother was the only possible suspect.

INSANITY

The girls were out of control, the house was falling apart, nothing made sense anymore. In the middle of dinner, their mother would burst into tears and say

"Maybe I should kill myself. Then he'd realize what he's doing to us."

Early one evening, her father came over to pick up a few things. The girl
hoped he would stay for awhile, but her parents got into a fight and he left a short
time later. Her mother was furious, and called the girl and her sister onto the
front porch. She opened one of the casement windows and had the two girls climb
onto the sill. As she held her arms around their waists, they stared in fear at the
sidewalk far below. Their father was halfway down the block by now, and their
mother had to scream to get his attention. He stopped, turned around slowly and
looked up at them. The girl had an urge to wave, but she felt her mothers' grip
tighten around her waist. Then her mother leaned forward and began to shout
down at him, "You think you can just leave us like this—just walk away from your
home and your kids. But what if we all jumped out the window now and landed in
a pile at your feet? How would you feel then?"

The girl waited for her father to do or say something, but he just stared at
them for another long moment and then shook his head and walked away.

HOMEWORK

One of the first things to enter the house after her father left was a black-and-
white TV. And because her mother had gone back to work, the girl could come
home every afternoon and spend hours watching her favorite shows. She also
started getting a small allowance, which she spent entirely on candy.

GHOSTS

(This one is shown being typed rather than being read as a voice-over.)

Dear Dad,

After you left us, Mom used to come home from work, make us dinner, send us to our
rooms and then sit in the living room in that dark orange armchair and play an album of
Schubert Lieder over and over again.

There was one song I particularly loved. I never knew what the lyrics meant, but it was the
one that made Mom cry the most. We would come in and tell her we loved her, and we promised
to be good so that you would come back again. I recently got a translation of that song, "Gretchen
at the Spinning Wheel." Do you know it already? It's the one about a woman who yearns for her
absent lover and feels she cannot live without him. It's so strange to have such an ecstatic melody
accompany those tragic lyrics. But maybe that's what makes it so powerful: it captures perfectly
the conflict between memory and the present.

P.S. I wish that I could mail you this letter.

2. Letter to a filmmaker about *Gently Down the Stream*

March 4, 1983
Dear Leslie,

I thought I would write in my journal but then I decided to write this to you. Tonight, *Gently Down the Stream* was shown at the Lucky Strike, a club on Stuyvesant Street (across the street from where A. lived after we broke up, down the street from where A. and I lived when we first moved to NY and were happy together, and where we lived also when we split up). It was a group show—I think I earned seventy-five cents for it. Manuel DeLanda, Benning/Gordon, Kobland, von Zeigesar, et al. Two women from the Heresies Film issue whom I really like were there—and the monitor (E.) from the Millennium which, in some way, rounded out the picture. I was extremely nervous before the film, and got stoned, and hence got more nervous. I was worried about what C. and G. would think. But secretly I felt as if I was going to surprise them with the film—as if the film's strength wouldn't be determined by their response to me, but by their ability to fall prey to the film. It was as if I'd laid a trap for them and was waiting to see if they'd fall into it. I watched the film, clutching at my sides, with a secret smile on my face (embarrassed to show my cowboyish Yippee! Attago! Waowiee! Looker that frame, looker that cut!) because for once I was enjoying the film. I felt as if I'd made it for myself. That it was a gift to myself. That every choice was made completely for my pleasure. And yes, it was. But I also started feeling strange, as if the film had its own determined, predetermined trajectory. One that I couldn't see before, because I was making it. And so it took me, forced me, dragged me headlong through the paces until the moment that I knew it was complete (when the words MY TONGUE first appear in the last dream), and whatever that means, I was forced to stare it straight in the face, though I felt like a kid pulling HARD in the other direction from where "grown up" is trying to drag me. So then of course I got the shakes with a vengeance, and when the film ended I was so embarrassed. G. was the first to give me a good word. C. eventually admitted that she thought it was good. And yes, I was pleased and flattered to hear that; I started stuttering and reached for my beer, and we spoke a bit more. But I suddenly felt very apart from them, settling away and down into some private, noisy little corner of myself. Because I knew beforehand that they'd probably like it (though of course I left the possibility wide open that they wouldn't like it or would have strong objections to something in it, and I could even relish that event), and I felt discouraged. I knew that I was beyond the experience of that film: not in quality, but in some more horizontal manner. It had done its work on me, I had given it all I had, and so necessarily it would speak some truth to those who would want to hear or enjoy hearing what I needed to hear and what I enjoyed hearing when I made it. But somehow, tonight, seeing through the film to the essence of what it offered me in certain pleasures, I felt as if I'd suddenly turned my hunchback away and started plodding on to the next thing, which at first will/would (must?) seem like a torment until I can find what specific pleasure it will offer me. Because I can't go back to that old film for any (unfamiliar, surprising, unnerving) pleasures anymore—I know them, and I'm still afraid and ignorant of the next ones. I'm in a no-man's land right now.

When I know what delight or spark of thought I can give or share with someone, I get bored. When I know pretty much how a film can or can't affect someone (what its strengths and weaknesses, limitations, failings are), I get bored. There always must be something that's unfamiliar, if only so that one can overcome fear enough in order to make it familiar. Yes?
much love, susi

P.S. Has anyone ever talked literally about what happens when they "break up" with a film they've made?! And what we stand to learn and suffer from that?

stills: *Gently Down the Stream* by Su Friedrich.

3. *Gently Down the Stream* (1981)

The text of *Gently Down the Stream* is a succession of fourteen dreams taken from eight years of my journals. The dreams were shuffled out of their original chronological order for the purpose of coherence, and because often we know/dream something long after, or before, we can use it in our lives. The text is scratched onto the film (with approximately eighteen frames per word) so that you hear any voice but that of a recorded narrator. The images were chosen for their indirect but potent correspondence to the dream content. I am not interested in recreating a "dream sequence" on film: dreams do it infinitely better themselves.

I chose to work with dreams that were the most troubling to me, that expressed my deepest fears, anxieties and longings, or ones that had forced a sudden awareness about a nagging problem. Anything repeated often enough loses its mysterious ritual power, and so I hoped that I might exorcise certain personal obsessions while using a language that was direct enough to allow others to recognize their own demons (assuming that our desire for attachment, and our fear of it, can be equally demonic).

What intrigues me about the dream state is that our self-generated "special effects" initially disguise the basic meaning of the dream, but then, paradoxically, we are enticed by the dream's fragmented and flashy form into admitting hard truths we might not have been willing to confront more directly. The fireworks we create are a necessary seduction, but we must recognize our own heartbeats in those explosions.

4. "Radical Content Requires Radical Form"—panel[1]

Making films has been a way for me to periodically grab hold of the elusive world, untangle the questions surrounding my past and articulate the fears, disappointments, and aspirations I have about life. With a camera, I'm able to sort through the incessant stream of images that life offers, and by framing and movement I'm able to show life as I see it. In addition, I have language—the text I generate and the words others give me—as well as music. While I'm writing and shooting, I don't know how these disparate elements will work in relation to each other, but through the trial and errors of editing, I work to make the images and text so dependent on each other that they form a meaning utterly their own and quite different from what each means by itself.

My urge has always been to make my interior sense of life (that bundle of ruminations, memories, and desires) become part of the exterior world expressed through images that I find in the present: in this city I inhabit and those I visit, among many different people and buildings and trees and animals and bodies of water. I like to take what I find in the world and then make of it what I will. But I'm not a purist, and there are times when the world has its limits, so sometimes I

1. The Second New York Lesbian and Gay Experimental Film Festival, September 13-18, 1988, Millennium Film Theatre.

depend on images made by others or ones fabricated by myself.

A lot of experimental films have portrayed alternative ways of living and asserted that there's more to perception or experience than linear narrative can ever convey. There's a great freedom in seeing these films. But just as often, experimental films portray, if through a radical use of the medium, things that are fairly mundane or familiar. Stan Brakhage is a good case in point. His use of the medium has been truly radical; he has forced us to see through a lens as few others have, but I couldn't say the same for his content. He's made a few too many films about his family, his wife as Muse, and himself as the artist-as-genius. I've felt as aggravated and oppressed watching some of his films as I feel watching a sitcom, even though these feeling are often mitigated by my interest in Stan's formal devices. In the long run, I appreciate the risks he's taken with form enough to allow, somewhat grudgingly, for his conservative sexual politics and his self-mythologizing. Stan Brakhage and many others stand as good examples of the split between radical form and content, defending—by the very nature of their genre—the superiority of a radical approach to form. On the other half of that divide exist many fine documentary and narrative filmmakers. It's hard for me to choose an example, but suffice to say that during the past fifteen years, I've seen innumerable films that have exposed me to the lives of people with whom I might never be in direct contact. I've been taught about how others live, think and feel, and this experience has made me re-evaluate my own prejudices, taught me the narrowness of my own thinking and experiences, and compelled me to put my life in the context of all those other lives out there. I'm grateful to those films for giving me so much.

Yet, just as I feel after many experimental film screenings, I come away from these other films distressed by their inconsistency. How can they push me so hard, work such a transformation in my thinking without even beginning to address, let alone challenge, my sense of narrative structure or the alleged veracity of film as a "realistic" medium? It's such a weird feeling to sit at one of those films and watch myself be worked on, watch as the film gradually feeds me all the familiar narrative hooks, pulls me in and keeps me going until we arrive together, breathlessly, at the long-awaited conclusion. If this sounds a bit like having sex, it's no coincidence …

I go away from these films with a sense of loss, a sense of potential only half realized, and continue to imagine that the combination of transformative experience through the content and a radical approach to form would take me halfway to heaven. But unfortunately we live on earth, and I still believe in the separation between church and state. Hence I've come to accept, albeit reluctantly, that there are, and will be, many good films made that do provide a fairly radical content without giving the least hint of a radical form. And so it goes.

Every subject has a mind of its own and needs to be treated with a respectful and sympathetic understanding of its intrinsic properties. The form it takes—the choices, the images, and how they're combined—grows out of a collaboration between my propensities and the subject's nature. I cannot force it to be shot or written in only one way: just as we expect to be treated as complex beings, the subject usually has to be approached from many angles. It may require that I employ all my means: that I call on the fantastic, the factual, the quotidian, the passionate and lyrical, though sometimes only a few of these are required. It may be sufficient just to call upon my own history, or I may need to include many other voices. The subject may sometimes need an actor, because it can't express itself through what I find on the street or in the voices of the living, the real. Each subject has its own degree of vanity: one may want to be made more beautiful while another is best when it's hand made and a little grubby. And, like all living things, it always needs more love and attention or courage and anger than I thought I had to give.

INCARNATIONS

by Janieta Eyre

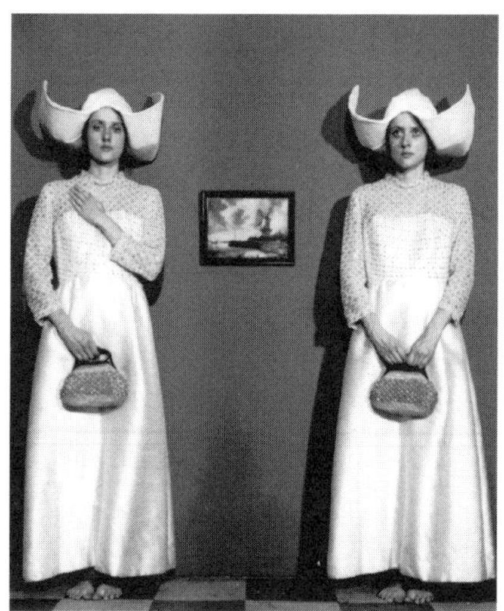

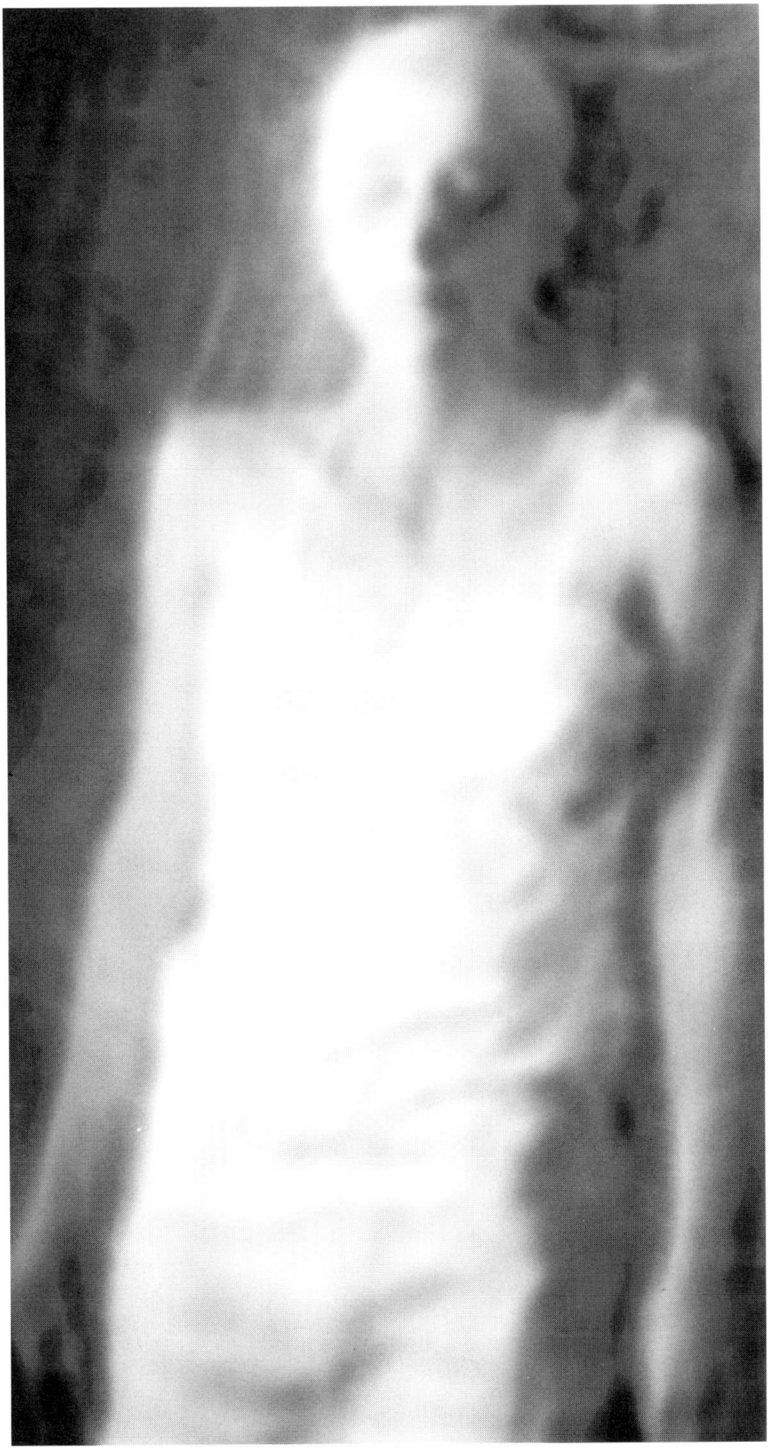

DIARY DEAREST

by Tom Chomont

Diary is an integral aspect of most filmmaking because, unlike other forms of art, the filmic image is rendered from a recorded likeness, however altered or unrecognizable it may become. The diary aspect may or may not be apparent to viewers, but there is an indelible relation between the film and the maker. With the camera prosthesis, each act of seeing requires a frame, which necessarily excludes more than it embraces. These rectangles of intention, these dividing lines between the visible and invisible world, are also a part of each maker's personality, a signature of seeing.

June 27, 1992

There is a place from which everything emanates, that is all light and all sound in harmony, and this light is shaped to our own individual experience, projected onto worldly matters. Pure light and sound is the beginning and the end, but short of that are the infinite heavens and hells that we make of it. (Is all action reaction?)

This preceding paragraph is based on the memory of a reverie experienced while riding the Enterprise at Coney Island. The open cart is connected to a carousel and spins along the ground; then the carousel tips and the cart hurls up to the sky, then back down to the earth in a continuing circle. In my mind, this action describes the space between that very inner private chamber and the earthly domain, the vertiginous path between heaven and earth taking place at every moment. For heaven can just as well be hell. I sense the internal space of my mother, Peter, all those I have known and who have known me, separated forever as individuals by the borders of our limited identity. I know the cart will return to earth, but I will disembark into a world plainly shaded by my own private approach.

Quite suddenly, after not seeing much of each other, and my being quite unconsolably sad, Clark and I decided to live together. Much uncertainty, unspecific directions, undefined situation. Currently unspeakably happy.

My initial impulse to film was intimately bound to creating souvenirs of moments, people, places, objects, feelings, enactments and the like. This was motivated by the desperate realization, already at the age of five, that all things were subtly but surely changing and that no moment could be re-experienced. This was followed by the more disturbing realization, around age ten, that even the most vivid memory grew dimmer and less detailed, and that subtle but unstoppable changes in who "I" was made it impossible to go on recapturing the past, even with the literal evidence of a photographic likeness to preserve it. But I was simultaneously becoming aware of the power to render something trans-mutable. Each moment, as it is lived, dies instantly, or with the trailing blaze of a shooting star, but art held out the possibility that something from the past could be propelled forward by an alteration of form.

November 28, 1995

The day before Thanksgiving, Clark and I went to an anniversary party at an S/M bar. I had a design drawn on my chest after Clark put a dog collar on me. Then my head was shaved (and my pubic hair) by a barber dressed in leather chaps with a black rubber jock. At the party we ran into a friend who was in the "adult video" I did in 1991 (just sold a re-edited, harder version to a distributor). A friend of his said, "Hello," and without another word began to pinch him by the nipples, bringing him to his knees, at which point Clark and I grabbed his arms and legs, stretched him over another man's knees, pulled down his pants and slapped and strapped his ass. All four of us took turns, and then Clark got some ice cubes from the bar and cooled down his butt before shoving the ice in. The day after Thanksgiving, this man came over for a take-out dinner to talk about shooting another video at his house in West Virginia …

Image gathering always has a sentimental aspect for me, though the final form of a work requires a merciless rending of the material. Even my most apparently confessional and/or anecdotal works, such as *Phases of the Moon* (1968), *Oblivion* (1969), *Razor Head* (1984) or *The Dog Diary* (1996), are far from literal records.

"While I was making *Morpheus in Hell* (1967), I was working as a typist in an office. I began to feel like a machine, and developed mechanical rhythm periods in my sleep that were like dreams; then eventually, even when I was awake, I would sometimes see landscapes and faces in front of me when I closed my eyes. We would be talked into working until two or three in the morning one night a week when a deadline came due. Once, I came home and stood in front of the mirror, talking to myself, saying things I didn't even know. The odd thing was that

I experienced both talking and listening to the face in the mirror. Sometimes I would look at the face and see the lips moving and hear the words coming like they were someone else's. That was the beginning of *Phases of the Moon*, which was shot in the same mirror, and explores the divide in our personalities. But I soon realized that two wasn't enough—it's really millions, because all the faces are us, and we have to split into more than two. We have to keep splitting until we know all of them.

"Back then, I'd lived almost a year near Central Park West and never realized it was a gay cruising area, and then one night I was walking and suddenly noticed men looking at me. My mouth just dropped open. I was aroused! One man approached me and I must have looked petrified. I immediately felt he was a hustler. I was afraid to bring him to my room, but I finally relented. I knew him for over a year on and off; he would disappear and come back, and that's how *Oblivion* began. It was shot on two separate evenings, but had elements of many of our visits. We would sit and talk, he would smoke, and at some point one or both of us would feel aroused. Usually he would take off his shoes when he wanted to have sex; that's in the film, where his hand untying his shoe is blended with a pan of his body on the bed. While this material was highly personal, I was conscious from the beginning that there had to be a formal side. The experiences themselves had broader meanings of identity and role-playing and the face as a mask. I wanted to give the film the feeling of being between dreaming and waking. Much of the imagery had symbolic meanings for me, like the apple and the canopy of lights, which I thought of as the nervous system or the circulatory system.

"There's always a tension for me between seeing someone from the outside—as a body, an object—and seeing the dissolution of identity that usually takes place during sleep. If the dissolution happens when we're awake, it's disturbing; we want to avoid it. But objectifying this man was a tendency in our relationship. At that time, I think he had trouble accepting his sexuality. He said it was easier to accept performing sexual acts for money, but the fact of the matter was, he would sometimes take the money he earned and go buy another prostitute to have sex with him as he wanted it. Twice he asked me to pay him for sex, and I thought, 'This is a very bad precedent, and besides, I can't afford it.' While I resisted, it still appealed to me to ask, 'What will you do for this much?' After many years of trying to follow what I was taught—not to do certain things sexually—I had a lot of very intense fantasies. During this time I began to act out my fantasies and, in doing so, the experiences became more important than the fantasies. This all became part of the film."[1]

Approximately thirty images comprise *Oblivion*. Most obsessively repeat themselves. Although the images appear to be

1. From an interview with Tom Chomont in *A Critical Cinema*, by Scott MacDonald.

solarized, the film was actually contact printed, combining high-contrast black-and-white negative with a colour positive of the same image. The high contrast accounts for the tendency of shots to flood. Images in the film swell and contrast, often disappearing into pure colour … *Oblivion* employs extremely rapid cutting. Some of the images last as briefly as two frames. The fact that we see so few frames, that a shot is representationally ambiguous, or shown upside down and sideways, often causes the viewer to project his/her own fantasies … When Jean Genet was asked to what end he was directing his life, he responded, "To oblivion." (Murphy 122)

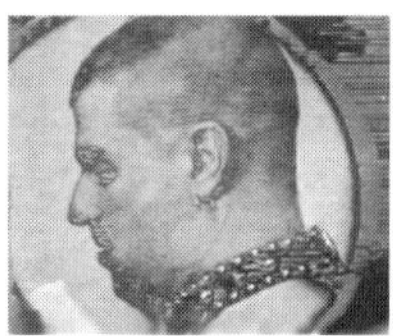

stills: *dog diary* by Tom Chomont

July 23, 1996

July 4th weekend turned out to be a crisis point in my relationship with Dog. I had pushed Dog into a three-way relation with Clark and me, and he began to feel that he was in the middle of our relationship. Just at that point he was obliged to go to Washington to help an ex-lover pack and move to New Jersey. I became insecure, although he assured me it was just an old personal debt with very bad timing. Finally, I realized he wanted to feel I was taking a decisive role and wanted him as my Dog. And I did! He had to go to California again this week for more training. Clark thinks he may be a stray Dog; I'm inclined to feel he is a faithful Dog. I've done unsafe things with both Clark and Dog. Keep both informed what is going on. But, does Dog keep me informed? The insatiable appetite for Dog is on hold, I probably needed the rest. Miss him, trust him. We had a great time before he left.

The film diary questions the relation between reality and illusion in art. For instance, some viewers understand *The Dog Diary* (1996) as literal documentation. But while it is based on video material gathered during several days over a six-week period, the original recordings run over five hours, and the finished tape is just twenty-two minutes. Alongside montage and several video "effects," the film also features superimposed sounds and pictures. In its finished version, it has a closer approximation to memory than the original footage. The largely erotic relationship with Dog was based on sexual fantasy, and the tape works to convert some of these moments into reflections on identity, power and representation.

In the case of *Razor Head* (1983), my brother had provided two rolls of film, asking me to record a private, erotic, shaving ritual which would last two days. My brother had shaved many men and taken polaroids of them, and he later produced his own S/M tapes for an underground market, but this was the first time we had worked together. For my film, I used an effect produced by lighting the colour images with strong shadowing and sometimes fading or moving the light. This comprised the A roll and was combined with a high-contrast print of the same images on the B roll. Printed together, these two rolls show the colour image etched into or evaporating into the white light of the screen. Although I had originally used the effect to approximate the use of blank paper as part of the composition in drawing, by this time I had come to think of it as expressing the transient and spirit-manifesting aspect of material form.

OCTOBER 5, 1999

Dear Mike,

Hoped I would hear from you but then, I said I would call if you didn't, so I probably will. You sounded a little tired and said you had been "up and down," so I worry that you've had fluctuating health. You had written about starting pentamadine treatments and I remember Ken (who had them from early on after his diagnosis) told me that the infusion was unpleasant and often followed by nausea. He did say there was less of a reaction after the first month. My own nausea-producing medicine (sinemet) has been altered to a time-release prescription, which is less irritating because not as much enters my system at one time. However, it is not always 100 per cent effective until the next dose.

I'm less in touch with it at present, but I remember how in connection with the light I had that near-death experience. You know, the one of going into the light and presences being there on the way. All sound and light were there as I drifted into it. Fragments of voices and sounds and people were present, and if I let go and passed into it, the light and sound would gather into a single sound like a heavenly choir. I felt some apprehension, because entering fully into it seemed like dying or leaving the world forever. Then just at the last, concern for someone I knew pulled me back and I wondered if it were possible to go into the light and still be in the world.

It began like a dim star in the very centre of the darkness. I had seen it many times while meditating. Sometimes it was blue or red or outlined by haloes of changing colour, and sometimes it took forms that I came to feel were projections of my mind. When I began drifting fully into it, the forms would pass away. It seemed like the sounds and voices created there were the result of the mind's attachment to worldly things. This primal light and sound felt like home; it was the place my personality drew from to create experience. Some would say that this feeling is the last stimulation of the phosphenes (that are credited with stimulating dreams) as the brain shuts down in death and that the ringing sound is similarly a last vestige of hearing when outside stimuli are shutting off. I don't know.

I also talked to my brother about this when I arrived at the hospital the day he died. He was unconscious and in intensive care on a respirator. The hospital staff said he had reached the point where they suspended the rules about only one person at a time visiting, and they encouraged us to talk to him because they said patients seemed to hear although they might not respond, and that voices of loved ones sometimes brought them back when nothing could be done medically. I told him many things, but then began to remind him of our talks about the light. I asked him if he could see the light and told him he could go into it. I told him he could swim back to the shore where I was with Howard and Andy and Andy's friend Peter (who came to show Ken his new, green-dyed mohawk haircut). I told him I wanted to show him some old photographs from when we were children, but I told him that if he felt too tired to swim back he could let himself drift into the light. I stroked his arm while I spoke. His pulse raised once while I was stroking his arm. But later I was told that he had been administered a stimulant to start his pulse up again, and that when it only perked momentarily, the doctors knew he was probably going to slip away.

Everything in this world is constantly changing. Eventually everything is gone or not what it was. Our attachment to it causes pain and joy, satisfaction and frustration. The light and the sound have a feeling of eternity but they may just be the dot on the TV screen when it's turned off, fading away. Practising at non-attachment is a preparation to deal with the gradual loss of everything. I write this as one who cried and wailed with grief at the death of my cat Spider. I am writing these thoughts because they relate to that moment in my kitchen when we speak, and what happens to us. Hope to talk with you soon and that you're feeling a bit better.

All my love,

Tom

Works Cited

Chomont, Tom.
A Critical Cinema: Interview with Independent Filmmakers. Ed. Scott MacDonald. Berkeley: U of California Press, 1988.

Murphy, J.J.
"Reaching for Oblivion." *Millennium Film Journal 3* (Winter/Spring 1979): 122-123.

BLIND SPOTS

by Chris Kennedy

I've been putting off making films for a while. No one wants to do mediocre work, less so an emerging artist. The missteps of inexperience may bring wisdom, but they still sting with pain and embarrassment. The effort it takes to move beyond the mediocre to the sublime requires patience—a demand which, added to the fear of failure, often makes it hard to create at all.

As a young image-maker, my sense of the art continues to develop. I still have images formed by textbooks rather than the flickering light against a white screen. One of these pictures is from the ending of a Jonas Mekas film. He and a few friends had just been turned away from a prestigious film seminar and wound up on a hill overlooking a beach. Instead of being disenchanted, they spent the afternoon cavorting with their Bolexes, passionately engaged with their new form. The film ends at this point, captioned with Mekas's final title card, declaring his cohorts "the monks of the cinema." This title denotes a spiritual and sensual aspect of this personal form of filmmaking, a form that P. Adams Sitney, who danced that afternoon, would later call "visionary cinema."

This term captures the freedom and beauty of Phil Hoffman's best work. His investigations of personal history, tragedy and the mythos of filmmaking have shown that he knows something about being a monk. His cinema gave us the image of the cobblestones floating by in *Kitchener-Berlin*—in one transcendent sweep of the steadicam, past and present were joined with the mysterious. The power of this image endures, despite the many films I've been absorbing recently. Instead of trying to create—instead of facing the keyboard and then the camera— I've found it easier to watch. I've spent countless hours at festivals, where easy access has permitted me to gorge on the medium. Gluttony has its drawbacks.

I find myself in the second stage of discovery, where the initial excitement for the art fades into impatience. Outside the cocoon of college, where only the canon is kept, there are discoveries and the inevitable disappointments. Too many disappointments. Initiates like myself are still learning sight, but even the chosen have fallow periods. Maya Deren couldn't finish *Divine Horseman*. Bruce Baillie gave us

the awful ending to *Quick Billy*. Stan Brakhage shows us everything he does. How do visionaries lose their way? It is painful to witness, especially when it reminds you of your own failures.

Philip Hoffman, too, has suffered through bad periods. None of his recent films have matched the power of *?O,Zoo!*, *Kitchener-Berlin* or *passing through/torn formations*. *Sweep* belabours Hoffman's favourite themes: the relationship between family and history is rehashed, intruded upon by graceless self-reflexivity. *Technilogic Ordering*, uncharacteristically impatient, loses an important political moment to an enervating structural conceit.

When the filmmaker comes out of the cloister, bearing their latest, there is great expectation, though just a moment lies between a masterpiece and an opaque, uninteresting work. Moments of truth require an inspired commitment to process—the willingness of artists to explore themselves is as important as the images they make.

I once read a Marxist who called films "allegories" of their production. The view was materialist, reading economics back into every image. I think there is also a spiritual side to this allegory, where the process of making becomes evident. The best experimental films show their scars. The bandages are splicing tape.

A life of vision includes the missteps—when faced honestly. It includes the good films with the bad, the prolific periods with hibernation. The worst reveals how stunning the majestic is. Asking "Why do great filmmakers make bad work?" is like asking "Why do bad things happen to good people?" No answer.

My grandfather, the first artist I knew, would have little patience for all this. "You paint because you like to paint. It's what you do. If the painting fails, then learn from it and start again." I had a camera trained on him when he said this, trying to memorize his words, wishing wisdom would transfer to youth.

He knew that you have to wrestle with the angel—muddy your hands, do bad work to cleanse your soul. You have to work at intuition, gift giving, and chance.

The true gift to the audience comes when an artist steps back. The image of the cobblestones considerately condensed the weight of Philip Hoffman's experience. The myth of personal filmmaking insists that there is no need for rigour when the image comes from the soul. But the introspective quality that can make an image so resonant can also render it untouchable, too dear to cut. How to be cowed neither by the blank page nor by an overload of experience? Whether it faces drought or deluge, real vision encounters its subject straight on.

As I watch for inspiration, I am beginning to recognize the author's second pass, when the experience of shooting is reshaped. I still see Mekas frolicking on the hill, but I also see the time he took to reflect upon and craft his film. His gift was not just the moment when the camera rolled, but when he realized, "On that day we were monks."

Soul searching is not separate from filmmaking; a part of you is always on the line. But in the end you create and, with luck, you're back on the hill, with a Bolex in the afternoon light.

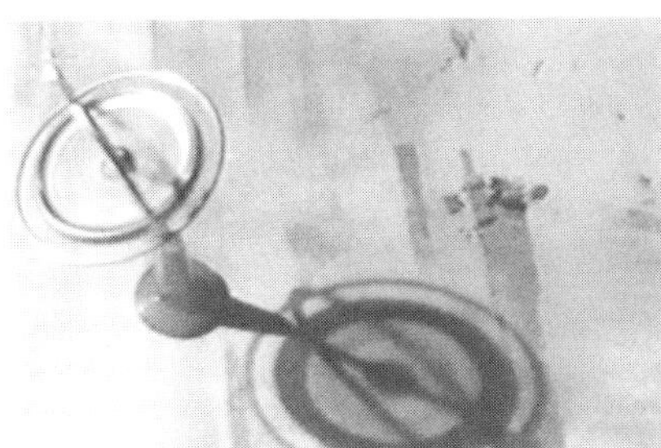

still: *Faultlines* by Chris Kennedy.

THEORY IS SEXY

by Roy Mitchell

still: *Christian Porn* by Roy Mitchell.

Ionce had a professor who taught a course on postmodern film. He kept going on about some pre-cultural relationship that existed between a mother and child. I would go have a coffee and wait until that evening's film was screened. On the nights where the film was unbearable, I'd say I forgot my glasses and leave early. He wanted us to be experimental and postmodern in the final essay, so I was. I played with the text fonts and line spacing on my computer, incorporated big gaps and shuffled the page order. I got a B+, quit university and never went back.

Experimental film is just like that class. It takes a keen eye to discover if someone is serious about being serious, or just playing with whatever is the equivalent to text fonts in film.

Experimental film can be so damn earnest. It is deep. It is made by people who like to think a lot. They usually have degrees and like to wear black.

Oh, I know you want to disagree. You can name oodles of laugh-riot experimental films, right? But I am not writing about the exceptions. I am here to talk about the last time you sat in a semi-renovated, drafty, exposed, brick-and-wire space on cold, metal chairs and watched "work." Chances are you left the place wondering if you understood what you had just seen.

Experimental film does not require a beginning, middle or end, but the longer the work, the more important the ending. The best experimental work is short. The end is what we are all waiting for. Then, as the lights go up, you can turn to your companion and say, "NOT BAD." Do not expect to share much beyond that, because any more discussion could ruin the impact/engagement/connection with the work. You can quote theorists, because believe it or not, that scratchy piece of celluloid is based in theory. Whoever said the brain was the sexiest organ must have been an experimental filmmaker, curator and/or writer. Or trying to sleep with one.

But everyone knows what is sexy. Money is sexy, and film is full of it. In my limited research into funny experimental film, I have found that the more serious the film, the more money the maker comes from. It takes money to wear a good black. After years at university studying theory, the kids do not want people saying they are spending mommy and daddy's money on FUN. No, they want to be taken seriously. As they get older, they sell out to Hollywood, use more narrative, get funnier or become web-page designers.

Whenever someone mentions experimental film, I get nervous. I drift off into a vision of the experimental film experience, as I want it to be. My experimental cinema would have no rows of uncomfortable seats, just bean-bag chairs scattered around the room. These would provide an audible indicator of just how boring the work is. Fidgeting equals bad, doesn't it? While viewing, people could walk around, stretch, get a drink and talk. And there would be a cappuccino machine in the back. It would keep the audience awake with its hissing and caffeine. In my experimental cinema no film would be processed in negative, and no voice-overs would be delivered in whispered tones. There would be more footage of figure skating and very small people surrounded by very large landscapes. After the short films had screened, people would be honest and astonishingly provocative in their analysis of the work. I would charm the pants off of some filmmaker, curator, and/or writer. We would sleep together. Because theory really does turn me on.

DESTROYING ANGEL

by Robert Lee

Where our language suggests a body and there is none: there we should like to say is a spirit.

Wittgenstein, *Philosophical Investigations*

Learning to read was like climbing for some. Each word, a step in the direction away from an unwanted ending. It felt like a progress upwards, but reading was an inevitable descent. Every word led to the edge of the page and then down.

He pretended to be an ESL student to help the instructor meet the enrollment quota for a class that would otherwise be canceled.

Drawing cartoon daggers on a yellow-lined notepad.

The sounds of well-meaning language teachers, the tired students, the many unison drills out loud, heard through the walls.

They seemed happier when speaking the language they would never master, events from the past forgotten without the words to describe them.

Sometimes all inessential verbs left out, as if any extra efforts were too much.

He listened to someone pronounce the silent letters, who used the same word eleven times. He waited for it again.

They sat and thought before they replied, sometimes half a minute or more would pass before they opened their mouths to deliver the economical answers.

When asked to use a particular word, a student said he had "melancholic" features, then paused to indicate a search for a euphemism. His features not found in the word.

He did not want to be the subject of the sentence.

Unable to mourn the lost object, the melancholic internalized the loss. He turned the lost object into a loss within himself, felt he was missing something of himself.

The man seated beside him said, I write too, in my journal, you would like to read it sometime and see all the bad things that have happened to me.

The "I thinks" and "maybes" stricken out of his speech, so that now the man spoke with the blunt authority of someone among equals.

It was the first time he had heard him speak, but it always seemed that way, whenever anyone said anything.

Speaking quickly as if to finish the sentences before they became afraid.

They did not like him in the second grade because he knew how to spell every word in the spelling bee.

They beat him up without explanation, possibly because he asked for none.

His business to be accomplished behind a closed door, with all evidence removed at the end and no reference to them afterwards.

After class, the instructor was talking in an assured, non-stop voice to one student while others waited outside his office or sat on the stairs nearby.

He wasn't interested in meeting people, but knew it would be impossible to skip steps or find a shorter way.

They stared at him and noted his details and then their own.

The way you looked for something hidden in a kitchen drawer, behind the worn-out can opener, the toothpick dispenser, the instruction manual for a food processor.

The instructor took him to a place built by people who had nothing to lose by being overheard. They were about to close.

A party of drunken office workers lingering at the largest table.

Co-workers who often discussed each other, but seldom thought about each other when they were alone.

Loud-talking boyfriends were explaining and explaining. They did not need to convince him of anything, but they tried.

They offered detailed accounts of their workout routines.

A bad suit and haircut can travel faster and with more precision than all the best intentions.

Their self-involvement spared him from having to comment.

They kept talking like there would always be room for whatever they had to say.

An old waiter refilled his water glass, exhibiting the utmost concentration, holding it critically to eye level.

Everything the waiter did somehow had the quality of an accusation.

Delivering a whole speech with his face: You are going to be sorry and I look forward to the apology.

The kind who asked a lot of questions, then peered into your eyes as if he expected you were lying. What it might be like to be interrogated, each word chosen could be false.

He watched advertisements on the overhead television for wonderful cars with almost no money down.

Then menacing men entered a beauty salon, drew the shades and flipped the window's sign over so its OPEN side faced inside.

The painful bugles of bus brakes from the stop just outside.

A forehead glowing with sunburn and three beers blocked his view and made it easy to focus in one direction.

The rest were not simply closed books, but closed books that he had no interest in reading.

The owner had skinny legs and one of those wide, flat bodies with a little belly. If he lied down flat, he'd be a pancake.

He thought about how the heavy books in his room had been leaning far over to one side and sprawling open for so long that their covers were warped out of shape.

How he had begun to leave out the letters of certain words and had to read the words over again carefully, adding the missing letters and afterward printing some words a second time above the illegible script.

The words were plainly not his, anyone could see that someone had typed them and then he squeezed things in here and there.

The sort of words that he used himself all the time but didn't care to see written down.

The floor had been mopped and would never dry.

still: *Destroying Angel.*

PHILIP HOFFMAN'S CAMERA LUCIDA

by Brenda Longfellow

For years, Hoffman has been introducing his work with an apocryphal story about how, at the tender age of fourteen, as the designated documentarist of family life, he was asked to photograph his dead grandfather in his coffin. It was an indelible experience for the young man—his first dead body, his first photo assignment. So traumatic was the experience, in fact, that he put the film in a freezer and could only develop it years later. This story is recreated in Hoffman's latest work, *What these ashes wanted* (2001), and whether or not this event represented a primal scene in the gestation of Hoffman the filmmaker, what is apparent in the body of films he has produced over the last twenty years is a profound meditation on the relation between death and the image, on the distinction between the sensual, phenomenal world and the moment of time frozen in the flatness of a mortuary image.

still: *What these ashes wanted.*

In *Camera Lucida/Reflections on Photography*, a book that serves so resonantly in reading Hoffman's work, Roland Barthes argues that photography has a historical relation with the "crisis of death" which he sees evolving in the second half of the nineteenth century. Instead of trying to locate photography "in its social and economic context," he argues:

> … we should also inquire as to the anthropological place of Death and of the new image. For Death must be somewhere in a society; if it is no longer (or less intensely) in religion, it must be elsewhere; perhaps in this image which produces Death while trying to preserve life. Contemporary with the withdrawal of rites, Photography may correspond to the intrusion, in our modern society, of an asymbolic Death, outside of religion, outside of ritual, a kind of abrupt dive into literal Death. Life / Death: the paradigm is reduced to a simple click, the one separating the initial pose from the final point. (92)

Even with the incredible proliferation of image culture, the representation of death, actual death, as opposed to the plethora of fictional deaths that fill popular culture, remains, as Amos Vogel puts it, "the one last taboo in cinema" (qtd. in Sobchack, 283). If natural death in previous centuries was integrated into the life of the community and culturally naturalized through ritual and religion, the increasing medicalization and technologization of death in the West removes the experience from everyday life and places it within impersonal legal and medical institutions. In these new contexts, death remains antiseptically invisible and shrouded in a veil of prudery.[1] Outside of the consistently diminishing power of official religion, the personal, emotional and philosophical content of death has barely begun to be addressed.

Vivian Sobchack has argued that the taboo of representing death in our culture is powerfully connected to "the mysterious and often frightening semiosis of the body" (286). Death, in this instance, represents one of those primal threshold states, marking the distinction between being and non-being, the transformation of human matter from one state into another. The act of photographing a corpse is experienced as trauma precisely because the corpse confounds these distinctions. "The dreadfulness of the corpse," as William F. May notes in *The Sacral Power of Death in Contemporary Experience*, "lies in its claim to be the body of the person, while it is wholly unrevealing of the person. What was once so expressive of the human soul has suddenly become a mask" (qtd. in Sobchack, 288).

A corpse conveys the shocking transformation of the subject into a brute objecthood, devoid of consciousness, devoid of intentionality, devoid of what May refers to as "the revelatory power of the body." For the young Phil, what I believe was traumatic about photographing his grandfather's corpse was not only the cruelty of the silent and still body of a loved one but the insight the experience yielded—that photography, as a technology of reproduction, is inherently complicit in the transformation of subject into object. Every photograph, Barthes writes, is a reminder of Death because every photograph opens up that irreparable gap between the intentionality and sensuality of the lived body and the "flatness," as he puts it, of the photographed body. Every photograph confronts us with the real absence of the loved one and with the irreversibility of time's relentless progression. Every photograph is tinged with melancholy, the loss that is ontologically inscribed in its very technology.

On the Pond (1978), Hoffman's first film, is paradigmatic of the importance of this insight in his work. This is certainly the film where the role of the photograph as an organizer of memory and index of an irretrievable past is the most prominent. The central structuring element in the film is a series of black-and-white family photographs of Phil, his parents and three sisters. The photos are all related to winter recreation, mainly ice skating and playing hockey at a pond in front of the family cottage. The sound is entirely non-synchronous. Mapped onto

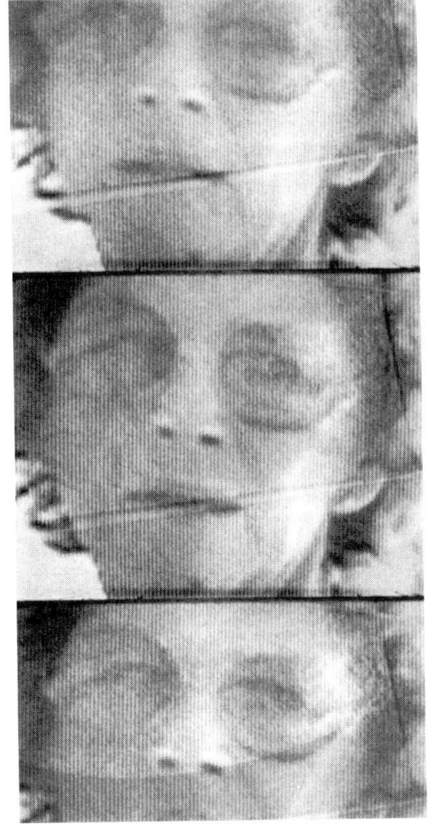

this division between sound and image, moreover, is the irreparable gap between the past of the images and the present of the auditory track which is filled with the family's shrieks of recognition, delight and unabashed nostalgia. At one point, Phil's sister laments "I want to go back," and it is precisely this desire and its ontological impossibility that structures the emotional content of the film. The voice of the filmmaker, however, is rarely heard in the family chorus although he implicates himself in the general family nostalgia through a visual recreation featuring a young boy playing hockey on a pond. In this repeated image of the boy, Hoffman seems to take up that desire articulated by his sister, dissolving the veil between past and present through an act of imagination and filmmaking that revivifies a moment from the past. But it is a false and impossible note, a fantasy of a return to boyhood only made possible through the intercession of a fictional signifer that is as removed from present reality as the archive of family photos.

As other writers in this collection are providing detailed readings of Philip's middle works, I want to linger on only the opening images of *passing through/torn formations* (1988) as an additional indication of the thematic that I see running through all his work. *passing through/torn formations* opens in silence as a hand-held camera continually pans over the face of Babji, Phil's maternal grandmother, who lies dying in an institutional setting, a hospice or hospital with a cool institutional veneer that has been somewhat humanized by the family photos, mementoes and cards pinned to the wall by her bed. Phil's mother is feeding Babji, whose face, without her false teeth, is ravaged and skeletal. The camera lingers over the protruding veins in Babji's thin arms, her stiffened hands, her gaunt cheeks, her eyes black with pain. Her "creatureliness," as Sobchack puts it, is foregrounded by the palpable fragility and vulnerability of her all too human body. Here again, Hoffman finds himself in a room recording a death. The trauma, however, is acted out by the persistence of movement, by the repetitions of the camera's pan refusing to rest in a final composition, continually moving toward the curtain on the window as if to escape the claustrophobia of a room of the dying and of death. The eerie silence confounds the sequence's location in a real time and sends it, reeling, into the future—an image "catastrophe" in which the knowledge of certain death is already vested in the present/past of the image (Barthes, 96).

In *Camera Lucida*, while Barthes claims that the cinematic image (as opposed to the still photographic image) avoids this sense of catastrophe through the continual unfolding of one off-screen space into another, it is clear that he is referring to the shot/reverse shot grammar of classical cinema and not to any particular ontology of the moving image. Indeed, in an essay that might in some respects be seen as the inspiration for Barthes' insights in *Camera Lucida*, André Bazin argued for the inextricable connection between photography and cinema precisely through their mutual capacity to "embalm time" against the certainty of death (1967). Bazin erases the traditional difference between cinematic and photographic relations to time through a more profound consideration of how both media are produced (through the photo-chemical action of light on film) as traces of the real.

A crucial distinction needs to be made, however, between fictional and documentary signifiers in film and photography. Vivian Sobchack argues that this difference inheres not so much in the property of an image as in the phenomenal experience of a spectator. As spectators, we have an entirely different relationship to the representation of bodies that we believe share the same world as we do. Unlike the fictional signifier of death or of bodily destruction which can be figured solely for entertainment value, the indexical nature of the body image represented in documentary (and in experimental documentary) calls forth an ethical space, according to Sobchack, "the visible representation or sign of the viewer's subjective, lived and moral relationship with the viewed" (292).

This is why, for me, the image of Phil's mother feeding Babji is so moving. It calls forth a flood of memories of feeding my own parents on their deathbeds. And while using all of the experimental cinematic codes that defy realism—repetition, overprocessed stock, silence, etc., the sequence, nonetheless, conveys the past/presence of an actual lived body, one that solicits our profound empathy.

If the body in the opening sequence anchors the film in a relationship to the real and to the acknowledgement of impending death, the remainder of the film proposes memory, storytelling and retracing the past as defences against that inevitability. As rich and layered as a dream, the film voyages between Poland, the land of Babji and Phil's mother's birth, and Kitchener, home of Uncle Wally, the crazy one, the black sheep, the family skeleton. If family history was registered as overly bucolic in *On the Pond*, *passing through/torn formations* delves into the other side, the dark histories of madness and murder, abandonment and depression, the stories that the public archive of family photos does not tell. Supported by the richly textured pans of stones, crumbling fences and pavements, *passing through* is metaphorically associated with an archaeological dig through history; the result, however, is not a seamless whole artifact but a jagged and disjointed assemblage of multiple shards of stories. Like the dream, these stories are as layered, as the images themselves, one on top of the other to form a palimpsest of memory—memory as palimpsest. No coherent gestalt or linear family history can be forged from these fragments. What is left to the filmmaker is to bear ethical witness to that impossibility, to continually record and photograph life, hunting and collecting images of everyday life against loss and against forgetting.

Early in Hoffman's new film we see a long, silent sequence featuring his late partner, Marian McMahon, frolicking in the snow near what would eventually become their farmhouse in southwestern Ontario. Marian, as she was in life, is full of spirit and mischief—playing to the camera with that goofy quality that Canadians take on in the dead of winter. There is something so fundamentally idiosyncratic about her image: the funny, red earmuffs, the vintage striped scarf, the thickness of the woolly socks pulled over her jeans—those stubborn details that affirm the irreducible uniqueness of the individual, that persist despite the inevitability of human mortality. They are what Barthes defines as the punctum—the accidental, the coincidental, the telling detail which "pricks the spectator." For Barthes, this is the order of love:

> … the Photograph mechanically repeats what could never be repeated existentially. In the Photograph, the event is never transcended for the sake of something else: the Photograph always leads the corpus I need back to the body I see; it is the absolute Particular, the sovereign Contingency, matte and somehow stupid, This … in short, what Lacan calls the Tuché, the Occasion, the Encounter, the Real, in its indefatigable expression. The off centred detail … the materiality of the particular that won't and cannot be named. (40)

If so much of Phil's work involves a meditation on death and the image, that meditation has its most personal articulation of this theme here in *What these ashes wanted*. It is a film explicitly about death, about the particular death of Marian, lover and life partner, and about the emotional fallout experienced by the filmmaker as a result of that loss. It is a film about mourning, about how to mourn, about styles of mourning. In the latter part of the film a question is posed by Marian in voice-over: "What ritual would you invent for death? Would it be public or private?" Hoffman responds "Public." This film is his public elegy and while intimately and achingly sad, it is also a film about redemption and the redemptive possibilities of that mourning.

In *Mourning and Melancholia* Freud describes mourning as a process "so intense" that it resembles a temporary psychosis. Overcome with grief, unable to reconcile oneself with the painful actuality of loss, the subject clings to the lost love object "through the medium of a hallucinatory wishful psychosis … Each single one of the memories and expectations in which the libido is bound to the object is brought up and hypercathected," but each is met by "the verdict of reality" that the object no longer exists (253). In normal "successful" mourning the narcissistic satisfactions of the ego win out and, though a painful and slow process, libido is eventually withdrawn from the lost object and transferred onto a new one. Proper mourning, according to Freud, is like a narrative—it has a beginning, middle and end (in that order) and its goal is to restore order, to reintegrate the subject with the world and the reality principle.

But what if the proper route is resisted and the subject refuses to disassociate affective connection with the lost loved one? In one of the most lyrical sequences in his new film, a text by Hoffman dissolves over a photo of a seaside landscape taken by Marian in Spain:

> … if I could brighten up this part of the picture, I might
> illuminate the conditions of her death, the mystery of her
> life and the reason why, during the instant of Marian's
> passage, I felt at peace with her leaving, a feeling I no
> longer hold.

His body still longs for her, he confesses, his mind still imagines her, his soul still aches. The loss remains fully present.

In *Mémoires: For Paul de Man*, Derrida puzzles as well with this issue of "proper" mourning.[1] In Freud's view, successful mourning is equivalent to the assimilation of the object into the self and to an eventual forgetting of the loved one. But does this assimilation, this "eating of the other," Derrida asks, not erradicate the irreducible alterity of the other? This is a profoundly ethical question for Derrida: how to honour the otherness of the other while at the same time acknowledging that within the act of mourning, the other is always an object—"image, idol, or ideal" that one constructs oneself.

For me this is the resonance of the film's second long sequence, which uses video footage of Marian working in her day job as a VON (Victoria Order of Nurses). In the footage, she is the most punky and weird of VON's—butch haircut, smoking cigarettes, speculating philosophically on the issue of touching a stranger's body. At one point, however, she confronts Phil (hiding behind his heavy 3/4-inch camera in the back seat), accusing him of not understanding how difficult it is to be filmed and how much the camera mediates and makes strange their relation. It is an important moment precisely because it honours the otherness of the other. The only sync sequence in the film, it anchors Marian in her lifeworld not simply as an image, idol or memory, but as a sensate and intentional subject in her own right, and one, furthermore, who explicitly defies the naturalness of a camera recording her image.

What one misses in mourning, speculates Derrida, is the response of the other, the voice of the other, the return serve in the dialogue that has structured the couple. Making the film in her absence, with the bits of images and audio fragments left behind, allows Hoffman to reconstitute that dialogue. In one sequence, for example, images of a trip to Egypt fade in as the voice of Marian,

1. Much of my argument re Derrida is drawn from Penelope Deutscher, "Mourning the Other, Cultural Cannibalism, and the Politics of Friendship (Jacques Derrida and Luce Irigaray), *differences: 4 Journal of Feminist Cultural Studies*, vol.10.3 (1998), 159-184.

photo: Guadalest, 1997.

waking up from a siesta, recounts a dream: "We went back to Canada. Everything had changed but it was somehow familiar. Mostly I remember walking in the snow with you." What the film does is implicate itself in this dream, remembering and imagining for Marian. The recounting of this dream, of course, lends a retroactive meaning to the opening sequence of Marian in the snow and is linked, associatively, with later sequences of shadows of two people falling on a snowy lane.

The recovery of the loved one's voice is also undertaken in the sequence featuring the photograph Marian had taken in Spain, although the voice can only be present in its absence, as a printed text superimposed over the image. In many ways, this sequence in which texts by Marian and Phil both endeavour to tease out a meaning ostensibly hidden in the photograph, acts as a fulcrum for the entire film. For Marian the image "reawakens a bodily memory" and reminds her of a time when she was becoming acutely aware of extraordinary bodily changes that, retroactively, seemed to signal the return of an illness she felt she had been cured of. Going through her effects after her death, Phil discovers this text written by Marian and clipped to the back of the photo. His text introduces and closes the sequence, reflecting on Marian reflecting on this image, seeing in the photograph a mysterious and cryptic relic that might reveal "the conditions of her death" and "the purpose of her life." The photograph itself is banal, a seaside landscape, a tourist image, conventional and undistinguished. Yet the photo functions as a blank slate, a void whose meaning is produced associatively entirely through personal memory and projection. In this way, the sequence condenses the series of questions that I've argued are central to Philip's work. How does meaning adhere to an image? How do images organize memory? How does death and the absence of the loved one imbue the image with its beauty and mystery?

In *Mourning and Melancholia* Freud experiences some difficulty in definitely distinguishing between the two psychic states. In one instance he posits melancholy as an unresolved form of mourning, where instead of assimilating the other into the ego, the ego identifies with the lost object: "the shadow of the object fell upon the ego [and] the ego is altered by identification" (258). For Derrida this is one formulation of love where the other is taken into oneself, not to obliterate difference but to preserve otherness, an otherness whose effect is to alter one's being. While I do believe this is the style of mourning and love that Hoffman proposes in his film, let me suggest that Freud's alternative conceptualization of melancholy may be of some use here. In the second formulation, melancholy is without a specified object. The subject experiences overwhelming sadness but cannot attribute it to any particular cause: it is a generalized sense of loss. This generalized sense of loss has an uncanny resonance with a thematic that I have argued is central both to Barthes' formulations in *Camera Lucida* and to the cinematic oeuvre of Philip Hoffman. In these instances, melancholia is inspired, not only by the particularity of this death, but by an acknowledgement of Death itself—its inevitability beyond the fleetingness and ephemerality of life. It is this emotional quality which makes photography and experimental film among the more melancholic of arts.

Works Cited

Barthes, Roland.
Camera Lucida: Reflections on Photography. Trans. Richard Howard. New York: Hill and Wang, 1983.

Bazin, André.
"The Ontology of the Photographic Image." *What Is Cinema?*. Trans. Hugh Gray. Berkeley: U of California Press, 1967.

Sobchack, Vivian.
"Inscribing Ethical Space: Ten Propositions on Death, Representation, and Documentary." *Quarterly Review of Film Studies*, vol.9, no.4, 1984.
283-300.

Freud, Sigmund.
"Mourning and Melancholia." *On Metapsychology*. Trans. James Strachey. Middlesex: Penguin Books, 1984.

DUETS: HOFFMAN IN THE 90s, AN INTERVIEW

by Mike Hoolboom

Philip HOFFMAN: After finishing the autobiographical film cycle, I wanted to play again. I brought a super-8 camera along with me to Banff in order to do some sketching. I began exposing a frame at a time while zooming, or moving the camera. The result was a Cubist kind of taking apart of the world. It splays the frame, making the image move. Because of its extreme speed, it was necessary to slow the image down afterwards, controlling the speed via re-photography on the optical printer. The lightness of the camera allowed me to play along with my subject in a musical way. This kind of shooting, or being in the world, marked the end of one kind of working, which was much more personal and traditionally "documentary."

still: *Chimera*

HOOLBOOM: Why was it important to break the space up?

HOFFMAN: It was in the air. The Berlin Wall had fallen, film had become media, computers were everywhere and fragmentation ruled. The cycle of personal film work I'd finished allowed me to travel and show the work, and *Chimera* (15 min., 1996) was the result. It was photographed in Banff, Finland, Russia, Egypt, England and Australia.

HOOLBOOM: Despite lensing for years all over the globe, your shooting style is very consistent.

HOFFMAN: I felt electric. Like I was touching eternity. These camera gestures create rhythms at the speed of light following an inner-outer sympathy. I was doing a fair bit of inner work at that time—trancing, meditation, yoga—so what was coming to me in image was symbolically meaningful. I had my own narrative, no matter how abstract it might appear to others, but instead of people and places, which are a part of a social world, it became another kind of journey. *Chimera* began in 1989 during the Banff residency and took seven years to shoot and edit.

HOOLBOOM: The shooting blends one place into another.

HOFFMAN: It shows a world breaking down, and the images express the energy of change. The film doesn't insist that market people in Cairo's Khan Khalili and London's Portabello are the same, but that they share an energy related to colour, shape and form. That's why some of the film is abstract, to evoke these pleasures of sharing.

photo: shooting *Chimera*.
Photo by Marian McMahon.

In *Technilogic Ordering* (1994), by contrast, the fragmentation is political, reworking of media images of the Gulf War. The collisions mean more because lives are being lost, along with their representation. This sketch of *Chimera* is simply one way to experience the world. As a viewer you're only moving forward, like the stream of images that come to us through TV, or the Web. *Chimera* is a representation of that way of being in the world. Gathering speed. But in the third and concluding part of *Chimera*, I finally go back, and this return offers a critique of the first two sections, where each image replaces and erases what's gone before. In the final section a man plays electric piano in a Russian square, and this is intercut with scenes from a Finnish rave, and the great rock Uluru. Uluru is a sacred Aboriginal site, which I photographed from a distance. It stands boldly through it all. This speed finally brings us back to making pancakes in the kitchen because, despite virtual velocities and cyberspace, at the end of the day you have to go home and make supper.

I had a lot of trouble finishing the film, in finding the shape for these sketches. I finally returned to its original idea, which is contained in the title. *Chimera* is an animal in Greek mythology that combines the head of a lion, the body of a goat and the tail of a serpent. For the first time in my making, I didn't have a narrative to hang the structure on, so I was guided by myth, and the beast's embodiment of diversity and fragmentation. The first section begins with a roar on the soundtrack and proceeds with an accelerated drumbeat and a scream, which I associate with the roar of a lion. The second section has a very ethereal soundtrack, which is the goat on the mountain, "up in the clouds," where he finds his place. The final sec-

tion is the serpent. It is filled with sibilant chanting, which brings on transformation.

There were many things in my life that I pinned to these scenes. They are returning now in my making because I couldn't deal with them at the time. I encountered three deaths while shooting this way. The deaths are not shown or even
alluded to in these films, but they lie underneath each of them. Waiting.

Chimera's original super-8 footage was being blown up to 16mm by Carrick
Saunders in Montreal. I gave him a call to see how it was going and his wife
answered. There was some commotion—she left the phone and didn't return. I
phoned later that night and discovered he'd had a heart attack and passed away.

> HOOLBOOM: He died while you were on the phone?
>
> HOFFMAN: Yes. And you don't know why you're part of it. Of course this is an
awful tragedy for Carrick's family, but I didn't know him. As a witness to his
death, I felt I was being given a gift, and that I had to do something with it. I just
wrote it all down in my journal, but couldn't figure on how it would become part
of *Chimera*.

In the second instance, I was crossing a bridge over the Thames, just coming out
of the Moving Image Museum, where I'd shot their history of cinema exhibit. I
was blurry eyed. I stepped out on the bridge, where a stranger looked me in the
face, got up on the bridge and jumped. I spied him through the cracks, already
going underwater without a struggle. Dazed, I wondered if I should film him. And
didn't. A man came by and asked if he'd jumped. A woman arrived from the other
side of the bridge and said she'd call the police. That's when I came 'round. I'd
been stuck in that existential moment where you see someone who wants to die.
Do you let him? Should you do something? Can you? I ran to the other side of the
bridge and met up with a policewoman who didn't have a walkie talkie. I kept
running until I found another cop who said they'd got him. A pleasure boat had
come by and picked him up. What a coincidence, this man wants to die but a boat
chances along. I asked the cop if he could let me know what happened, and that
night I got a note: "The bloke who jumped in the creek is alright." Both these
events made me think about death, and how little control we finally have.

> HOOLBOOM: Tell me about *Technilogic Ordering* (30 min., 1994).
>
> HOFFMAN: The Persian Gulf War was a made-for-TV affair that filled me with
anxiety. I watched the war with some of my students at Sheridan College, where I
was teaching. A couple of them—Heather Cook and Stephen Butson—began to collect images as a way of thinking about the broadcasts. It's like when you have a
lot of nervous energy you go for a skate. You have so much anxiety watching this
stuff and you have no control over it.

During our gathering I found a VCR with a computer chip that fragmented the
image into Muybridge-like box frames. This machine allowed you to play the
image, change the size and number of the boxes onscreen—do you want nine, 400
or 1600?—and scroll them from left to right, like reading or media literacy.

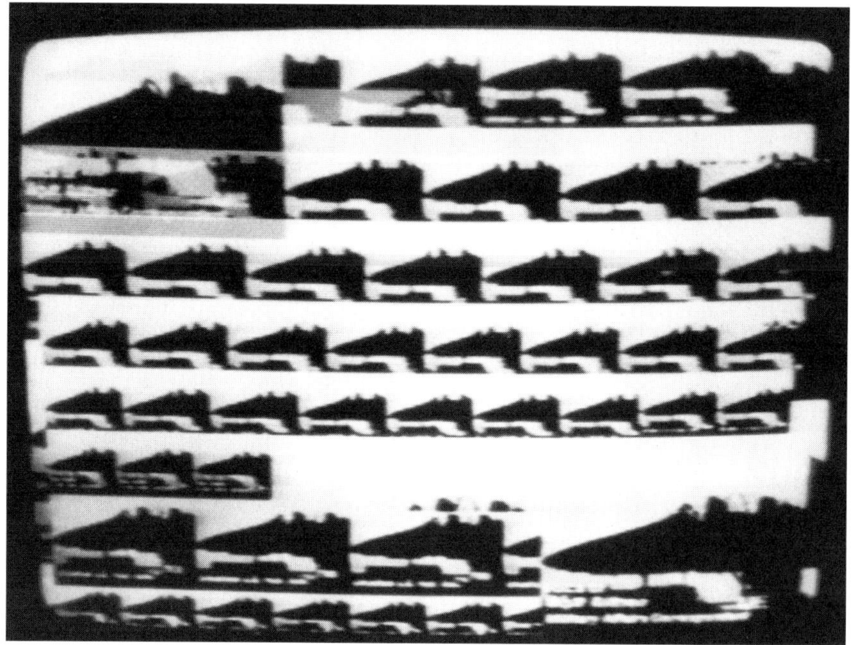

We collaged some of the different footage we'd collected, inserting commercials, movie fragments and sports into news broadcasts of the war. Among other things, we wanted to show the difference between Canadian and American coverage. While many Canadian commentators questioned the necessity of the war, the Americans were blindly patriotic. As we discovered later, all the war footage had been cleared by the Pentagon, so it appeared bloodless and techno-centric. It was mayhem at a distance. The boxes were a visual way of commenting on the reports, making patterns out of this destruction and allowing the pictures to critique themselves.

The montage featured many heavy-handed collisions. Kitchen cleaners were juxtaposed with images of the Iraqi army being "cleaned up." Airplanes from *The Wizard of Oz* smoked messages across the sky: "Surrender Dorothy." There was a nationally televised football championship going on at the same time, which blurred the line between sports and war. Both featured the same mass hysteria. Once the editing was done, the video footage was transferred to film because in order to really see television, you have to look at it somewhere else, in a movie theatre for instance.

HOOLBOOM: Like much of your work in the 90s, this film began as a collaboration.

HOFFMAN: After my personal work in the 80s it was time for the author to die. I wanted to relinquish control, explore ways of making that would expand the palette. In the early 90s I started three projects that had in common sketching, collaboration, and smaller-format technologies [other than 16mm]. With the help of Vesa Lehko and other friends in Finland, *Chimera* was turned into an installation. *Technilogic Ordering* was made with Stephen Butson, Heather Cook and

Marian McMahon, who naturally helped with all of them.

In *Opening Series* I collaborate with the audience by offering a film in parts, each in its own painted box. I ask the audience to arrange the boxes in the order they would like to see them on screen. The film not only runs differently each time, but provides a picture of its audience. *Opening Series* arose out of questions of inter-activity, which too often means people watching computer screens instead of relating to one another. In moving the boxes around the audience has to collaborate and eventually come up with an order.

Following *Opening Series* are three collaborations: *Kokoro is for Heart* with Gerry Shikatani, *Sweep* with Sammi van Ingen and *Destroying Angel* with Wayne Salazar. By the mid-90s, I'd committed to hard-core collaboration.

HOOLBOOM: *Kokoro is for Heart* (7 min., 1999) has a feel of daily ritual and naming.

HOFFMAN: I met Gerry Shikatani at Sheridan College, where he worked in the writing department. Gerry's a poet, a Nichols protegé. He writes sound poetry, novels, and food reviews for the dailies. One morning Gerry came up to the farm and we went for a drive, not thinking about making a film at all. We wound up at a gravel pit, and I pulled my camera out of the truck while Gerry interacted with the space of the pit, moving rocks and branches around. I shot two rolls of 16mm reversal. When I got the footage back I noticed the registration pin was slipping, so there were periodic stutters in the image. Trained as a cinematographer, I saw these as flaws, though Marian said they were like Gerry's voiced poetry. He works with the structure and gestures of language, and the flipping frame reveals the structures of vision strained through the machine.

I optically printed the whole film one-to-one and two-to-one. So each picture had a double, one for each of its makers. Then I cut the film into twelve parts, and put them into twelve separate boxes for *Opening Series 3* (7 min., 1995). The audience would choose the order they'd be screened in. I made the paintings for the box covers by using natural materials like seeds and sunflowers, along with family photographs and paint. Then I put a blank canvas on top of the painted ones, laid them on the ground and drove over them with my truck, so every picture is doubled as well.

As an interactive work, the film began its life as part of the *Opening Series* experiment, where the audience affected the order of the film by arranging the boxes. We also ran it as a performance at Cinecycle, where Gerry sat in front of the projected image rapping out his sound poetry. Later, we fixed the order of the film, made a final print and renamed it *Kokoro is for Heart*. So the performances served to find a satisfying fixed order. But it can still run as an open-ended work in the performance setting.

Kokoro is the Japanese word for heart, or life force. Here, it's the heart of the land, speech or breath. Gerry is shown as part of the landscape but separate from it, and his words on the soundtrack [a blend of Japanese, French and English], are a way of knowing or naming the land. They're the language of the land or a landscape of language.

HOOLBOOM: Tell me about *Sweep* (30 min., 1995).

HOFFMAN: One of my interests in making the film was to go to Kapuskasing, because that's where my mother settled when she first came to Canada. My grandfather, Driououx, came to Canada to work as a lumberjack. He eventually ran a poolhall and pushed moonshine on the side. The area they lived in was actually called Moonshine Creek. My grandmother, Babji, ran a rooming house. I asked my mother to recollect Babji's stories for the film, which she does while looking at family photos. One of these shows the family gathered for Christmas dinner. Mom says this picture makes her feel happy, because at Christmas everything would go well. But I knew from my own growing up that visits to Babji and Driououx's would always start in fun, but often end with a plate of food hitting the kitchen wall. I pose these questions to my mother through narration, and her answer is evident in the grain of her voice. The violence and abuse in the household remains in her trembling speech. This is where our forgetting and the things we care not to tell come to reside.

This makes me think of Marian's work, how the past lives in the present. The fears we don't get over become part of our everyday life.

My mother's image returns at the end of the film when I zoom in on her, followed by a zoom on me, as a reminder of that repressive pain, which flashes forward from the beginning of the film to its end, as suddenly and ferociously as the past takes over the present.

HOOLBOOM: Your collaborator is Sami van Ingen and his journey is also a personal one.

HOFFMAN: Sami's great-grandfather was the American documentary filmmaker Robert Flaherty. He made ethnographic "classics" like *Nanook of the North*, which was shot in Canada. While it is considered one of the first verité documentaries, most of the scenes were staged and rehearsed. It offered a particularly white view on native practices, and was made in a time when white meant "objective." Sami wanted to return to some of the places that his grandfather had been in order to deal with this part of his family's history.

While we were making the film, a feature-length, France-Canada-produced drama was released about Robert Flaherty, which reveals a love affair he had with a native woman. Everything was suddenly out in the open. Sami and his family already knew this, but no one dared to speak about it. They were keepers of the legend, the great genius, the family name. Our film begins with a suggestion that we will hear details of family history, but Sami didn't want to go further in that direction, so the film arrives at more general conclusions. We used archival home movies showing white men's journeys to appropriate the north. Sami's great-grandfather was just the most famous person who went up there. So while we couldn't speak of the family legacy, we could show white men hanging around the native camps, and the effects they had. These scenes are intercut with shots of Sami and I dozing around a pool on our way home amidst spring blooms, implicating us as part of another wave of white explorers. The film has a strong visual thesis, but parts are missing. It's like the deaths I encountered while making *Chimera*: real life overwhelmed its representation.

HOOLBOOM: The film shows the two of you traveling north by car, meeting people along the way and entering a Cree reservation. This journey ends when one of the native guides takes you across the water to Fort George.

HOFFMAN: Fort George was one of a series of British forts built in the north, and Flaherty would have traveled through there. The Fort is gone, but we found an old Hudson Bay Company trading post still standing, which we filmed. I say in voice-over: "You're not going to find your grandfather here. It's gone now. It's over." Around the building we discovered a lot of beautiful driftwood. Earlier in the film we showed the dam, and talked about how the need for hydro-electric power overwhelmed native protests, and how their burial grounds were flooded because the dam raised the water level. This driftwood is also a result of the dam. These are the bones of the forest, the ruined culture. The driftwood was shot in high-contrast stock, with the haunting call of Canada geese in the distance. Then we have a lunch of canned fish and tomatoes, which we film because all we can do now is film ourselves. We've come all this way to shoot the making of a sandwich.

Throughout the trip many of the native people we met asked us to film them. During the dam protests, so many white journalists had been up to visit they were used to it. They'd even built a motel just for visiting politicians. A motel in this small village, which had a huge teepee as the local supermarket! We always refused, saying we don't want to tell your story, this is up to you, and it always has been. So the film's critique of ethnographic filmmaking shows the failure of white culture to integrate, proposing a movement alongside instead of the usual pictures of control.

At the end of the film, during dinner, I showed our native host Christopher Herodier how to use the camera, and he shoots us eating. I left him with the camera, saying, "Give me a surprise." When we got back to the city and processed the roll we discovered that Christopher had filmed a teepee against a backdrop of new housing, and the two of us against a sunset, slightly out of focus.

When the film was finished, Petra Chevrier invited *Sweep* (1995) to screen at the YYZ Gallery. I called Christopher and asked if we could show our work together. He had made a videotape called *Chiwaanaatihtaau Chitischiinuu* [Let's go back to our land]. It shows a Cree protest against the building of another dam, the canoe voyage from Fort George to Great Whale, the singing and the outrage. The two pieces played together for a month and it was very satisfying. It reflects our approach of living cinema.

HOOLBOOM: Can you tell me about the title *Sweep*?

HOFFMAN: To shoot the drive northwards we rented a motor that ran the camera very fast, giving us super-slow motion. At the head of the shot the motor's still gaining speed, so you get a fast motion that is overexposed, which then turns into slow motion at a regular exposure. This gives a sweeping motion to the image, a sweeping of landscape and driving. *Sweep* is also sweeping the road clean, trying to start over again, sweeping away Flaherty.

HOOLBOOM: *Destroying Angel* (32 min., 1998) features another collaboration. How did that begin?

HOFFMAN: I met Wayne Salazar in Australia in 1991 at the Sydney Festival. The curator Paul Byrnes had invited me to show all my work. In Sydney, Paul would take you to supper every night with a small group of filmmakers and curators, and Wayne was party to that. It was a marvelous time. Soon after the festival I visited Wayne in New York, and awhile later he called to tell me he'd contracted AIDS and was very sick. He was going to tell his mother, who lived in New York State, so I invited him to come up to the farm and relax and meet Marian. That's when we started shooting. I don't know how these things start. Maybe it's just that you're always shooting film, and when people come you keep shooting and then films start.

The farm reminded Wayne of his rural youth, the day trips he used to take with his father, who worked as an insurance salesman. Wayne's bad health made him wonder how long he was going to be around, and he felt compelled to deal with his father, who had abused him as a child. They hadn't seen each other for years, but Wayne decided to go see his father and tell him he had AIDS. This all became part of the film. The first weekend he came he got along well with Marian, and they spoke about personal histories, and her themes of remembering and forgetting. He was very sick then, and taking a lot of pills. The drug cocktail hadn't been introduced yet, so he was tired and depressed. It was Wayne's idea to make the film and I felt my role was to assist. He'd made a short video about Cuban artists, had seen a lot of films as a curator and had been painting since art school, but really had no experience making personal film work. Which is fucking hard. During the making, I felt I was back working on *Road Ended at the Beach* (1983), because the struggles were the same. *Road Ended* took seven years to make, trying to give shape to these concrete bits of memory, working without a script, and letting the camera respond to experience as it's happening. I stayed patient, trying to help give Wayne an outlet. I learned more about his struggles of growing up gay, dealing with his macho father's disappointments, and how he and his lover Mickey were finding a way to live.

It began as a film about our fathers, but it quickly became clear that mine was no match for his. The stories of Wayne's abuse created too much of a contrast to my father's sympathetic parenting. I shot sequences and told stories that were part of an early cut, that might one day join another film. But there was so much anger and need on Wayne's part that I had to withdraw. The decision was made when my partner of twelve years, Marian, was diagnosed with cancer, and a week later, during a biopsy, she died. We stopped making the film, and when I climbed up out of the hole, that's when I moved my voice out of the film. I needed to make my own film about Marian, her life and the grieving. Marian was already part of *Destroying Angel*, asking Wayne questions on video about his meds, and AIDS and everyday life. Wayne felt close to her and asked if her story could be developed more in the film, if we could show this passing, and I felt that would be right.

HOOLBOOM: You show Wayne and Mickey getting married.

HOFFMAN: Back in San Francisco, Wayne got healthier, which was partly the drugs, diet and exercise. But the film had a lot to do with it as well. Wayne and his partner Mickey decided to get married. Mickey is Austrian, so an Austrian TV crew arrived to shoot them for a news program on San Francisco gay life and marriage. And I thought, yes, we have to have this in the film. Their reportage was typically television. It opens with a shot of the Golden Gate Bridge, then moves into the gay bars, and sexual activity and dancing and high-pitched screaming, but in our film, we inserted a shot of Wayne and Mickey walking down the street buying flowers. Very everyday. It's a nice moment because it shows how television creates stereotypes.

HOOLBOOM: Why did they want to get married?

HOFFMAN: They were in love, of course. But I think it was a political decision as well. In a culture that doesn't accept their sexuality, it was a step towards gaining the same rights as heterosexual couples.

HOOLBOOM: Wayne speaks of his father surrounded in darkness, directly to the camera, outlining a history of ignorance and abuse. But when we meet his father at the wedding he looks so benign.

HOFFMAN: The film reveals how the monsters of our past live in us. He's become an old man, no longer shouting abuse at Wayne. But it doesn't change what he did. He hurt Wayne, and neither of them could deal with it. They held onto this pain for years. At the ceremony, Wayne says it hasn't always been easy with his father, who then breaks in and proposes a toast to Wayne and Mickey. He says that he's from Guatemala, a culture where gay people exist only in the closet. And then he wishes Wayne and Mickey happiness in their life together. But it took the making of our film to release this fear. It's Wayne who's done the work to recover his past, and the evidence of this work is *Destroying Angel*. While the early passages of the film are drawn from Wayne's point of view, the ceremony at the end is shot in a verité style by the Austrian video crew. Finally, we're seeing something outside of Wayne's frame. He's no longer telling his story using voice-over. We enter another side of him, and this adds in a profound way to the information we get about his relationships.

Wayne called me last week, a year after his father died. He said, "I don't recognize that guy in the film." He was referring to himself. People use different tools to create change in their lives. Some use work, or alcohol, or art. Wayne doesn't need to talk about his father that way anymore. This is a familiar feeling for me. *passing through* (1988), for instance, was a grieving for my grandmother Babji. You hope these rituals of filmmaking resonate for others.

Marian's death is revealed in *Destroying Angel* and people say, "You must find that hard to watch," but I don't. I love her images, her voice and her writing. After Marian's death, while looking up references to bring her Ph.D. thesis to completion, I dwelt for hours on the small, hand-scribbled writings she left on the texts she was reading. No matter how esoteric or academic the text, her response would always tune in the personal, the everyday. She came back to life for me through her writing. The film I'm working on now attempts to deal with the traces she's left behind, so that I might better understand our time together and learn something about death and life. The dead carry on longer than the living, and it seems that the force of a life lived is stronger once it ceases to exert itself … its silence and mystery … majestic.

    HOOLBOOM: The title *Destroying Angel* suggests an angel that returns to wreak vengeance, a once purity that's now armed.
    HOFFMAN: It's also a mushroom, one of the most deadly and poisonous. The poison is the virus, which brings pain and suffering, but also transformation and change and growth.

There's an eating sequence in the film shot at the farm, where Wayne is making us dinner. In the early 90s there was still such a fear of casual infection, you know, he could cut himself and infect us, but instead there's only celebration. We're living right now, the camera's floating around the food and we're having a ball in the face of it all.

    HOOLBOOM: Much of your work in the 90s is more hermetic and difficult than your autobiographical cycle. What would you say to those who feel your work, along with others in this small field, is willfully self-enclosed, unnecessarily obscure, interested in formal issues in a medium that itself is coming to an end, and on the other hand suffers from solipsism and narcissism?
    HOFFMAN: Yes—and? It lives with me and that's what is important. Often circumstances collect around you and you have to make the film as well as you can without knowing why until later. Sometimes you get a song out of it, sometimes a mumble.

    HOOLBOOM: Is it important to finish work or is it just the process that's important?

Hoffman: I need to bring everything to some kind of completion. I learned from my dad how to start and finish things in the factory when I used to make boxes every day. Screening your work and receiving feedback is an important part of the process. We experimentalists may not get the TV audience, but that's alright. Our work has a different purpose. We're the people behind the stage sweeping up the old act and getting it ready for the new show.

People who try and push boundaries are part of a lineage that's a much thinner thread than CNN or Cineplex, but it's continuous, it's a living history. We're carrying this on, and maybe I'll make just one film that's important, that will have an effect on people. I hope I haven't made it already. If I've always held on to the personal it's because I believe that what I've lived has a shape, an organic world that can be shared, through film, with others.

photo: Philip Hoffman.

LANDSCAPE WITH SHIPWRECK

by Mike Cartmell

You've left out a lot.

> No doubt. But is it ever possible to avoid gaps, ruptures, deficiencies, omissions, even ignorances and stupidities, in a commentary of this sort? Isn't every reading (viewing) always and only partial, the "taking" of a reading, as if checking temperature or humidity or rainfall, which must be re-enacted a vast multiplicity of times before any reasonably valid conceptualization of the climate can be gauged? And isn't that conceptualization at best only "reasonably valid," since at bottom the climatic system is chaotic, borne by uncertain and ungauged disturbances, critically unpredictable, in the last instance outside representation or symbolization? You can never be sure when you'll wind up in peril.

You seem obsessed with the weather. What does this have to do with anything?

> Well, you see where I'm living. But I don't think the metaphor's inapt. I've tried to say (as is true for all that we can, with integrity, call "art") that at the heart of this "body" of work lies coiled a disturbing, chaotic, unpredictable, unmasterable "something"; compelling while repulsive, terrifying yet enchanting, offering a serene forecast of shelter, warmth, comfort at the same time that it bodes implacably the perilous risk of absolute loss, fracture, desheltering.

Or, to shift ground a little and bring you back to your theme, we could call this precarious "something" (following your beloved Blanchot) "that marine infinitude which both buoys and engulfs."

> I hear that, cher! I'm beginning to think I might have a twin brother.

Well, we've been spending an awful lot of time together; perhaps we've come to resemble one another. But let me ask you this: I understand your lack of enthusiasm for the seamless text, but this is a pretty herky-jerky collection of observations, quotations (the relevance of which is often questionable), theses (on occasion possibly half-baked, or once in a while even over-baked), reminiscences, rhetorical questions, and so on. It seems at times that you barely have a plan. How is the reader to make sense out of this?

> I have no desire to instruct readers on how to read, any more than I'd be

inclined to instruct film goers on how to view (if it can be put that way). All I
can say is that the bits that I've put in place to make up this piece arrived via
some form of compulsion; in a way, I don't trust them any more than you do.
I could go out on a limb and say that these fragments somehow coalesce
around the influence of some "strange attractor," which could be the film
that you and I have only heard about, but which the reader will have seen
presumably. I guess I can hope that at least some combination of my various
bits will operate as a productive node to which the reader can link his or her
(in principle unique) experience of Phil's cinema, and carry on that experience in an otherwise unlikely direction. I will say that although I haven't tried
to be cryptic, the subject at stake here has something to do with the crypt.

OK, another thing: I have to say that this piece sometimes seems as much about you
as about Phil's films. I mean, you've been monkeying with the metaphorics of shipwreck for years now, and then there's the Blanchot, the psychoanalysis, this idea of
singularity, the various references to Mobile and to the blues …

I'm going to take those out, I think.

… all right then … uh, but also Sam, Jazzbo and his (or your) toothpick, and even
your current status as (may I say it?) a bit of drifting debris. And of course (what a surprise!) you work Melville into it. Isn't this a bit hobby-horsical?

In attending to the singularity of the work I recognize the singularity not of
its maker, but of myself. This would be true, I would say, for any attentive
respondent to any work. But this encounter with my own singularity is neither simple nor simply satisfying. It is precisely that which overwhelms the
subject's capacity to grasp it. It defies intelligibility, symbolization; one can't
put it into words. And even to talk here about "recognition" or "encounter"
is imprecise: maybe I can say that the experience of the work offers, or
maybe only figures, an approach. And it is this experience (let's say again,
"risky crossing") that draws me into the dangerous unknown of that aspect of
my subjectivity that everywhere cuts against the grain of everything I take
myself to be: that lacerates my "identity," let's say. And so, while enthralled,
I'm also engulfed; while exhilarated, I'm also dispossessed. And therefore it's
normal that I or anyone would be inclined to cling to whatever familiar flot-
sam drifts to hand, and to use it! After all, what else is there? (By the way, I'd
say that something like this—or even precisely this—goes on for the maker in
the process, the experience of making the work, as well.)

I'm not sure I buy that, but I'll think about it. The last thing I have to say you're probably not going to like. But really, this idea of putting our discussion at the beginning
of the piece bothers me! Isn't it going to look like some sort of disclaimer, or worse,
some obsessional dodge that seeks to qualify or clarify or otherwise perfect or render
more palatable (and thus somehow subvert) what you've already written? Can't you
just let it stand?

Maybe I just can't stand it. Anyway, aren't prefaces always produced after the
fact, after the work is done, and don't they often bear little or no relation

either to the style or the substance of what they purport to introduce? They
frequently appear to have different projects or agendas from the work proper,
don't they? Well, maybe I'm just joshing. But the serious answer would be
that one has to start with something, somewhere. I know it could look like
an inane stratagem; it's even possible that this part was in fact invented, and
written first!

That's true. It does seem odd that we could be eating this succulent black mess (it
really is good, by the way!) if you've already washed ashore in Buffalo! After all, where
would you have gotten the shrimp heads?

Well, I don't care that readers may think it's completely fictional; surely they
realize that even within the realm of documentary film such things can be
employed to productive purpose, so why not here? Reality is by no means a
sure access to truth. It may be utterly no access. Besides, you know good and
well my spintrian history with the act of writing. I need every tool and trick
that might ease the release of the thing. Maybe this will only shed more
obscurity on what I've written, but that doesn't matter. I'm not trying to clarify or even interpret; certainly not to analyze. I'm here to respond, as atten-
tively as I can, and if it has to be from the saddle of my hobby-horse (or
from somewhere between the stirrup and the ground) then so be it. If I've
done a good job, then perhaps my experience of Phil's cinema (at least inso-
far as it appears in desultory translation here) will resonate, in consonance or
dissonance, with some readers, to what I hope would be some useful effect.
Finally, I take my maxim from a wonderful former student who, of her
poignant, moving and absolutely singular films, once said, "I do what I do." I
hope I can live up to it.

Well, thanks for the gumbo. Maybe we should go out. I bet it's cooled off some.

I'm not sure I'm ready. You know I like to be stationary. I think I'll just stay
inside for now.

photo: Philip Hoffman and
Marian McMahon.

Here at one view are our blighted prospects and the reward of our toil scatterd to the winds.[1]

It is a film as yet unseen, as yet, at this writing, unfinished, perhaps unnamed, which is the occasion for this and the other writing in this book, or at least for its collection here. An absent film; a lost object. A work of mourning that I somehow mourn in its absence, its yet-to-be.

I can testify.

I was present when Phil and Marian met. This is what I remember: it was about eighteen years ago, in the late spring or early summer of 1983, after a screening of Alan Zweig's *Where's Howie?* at the Funnel. There was a gathering at AZ's place on Palmerston. I remember Marian telling stories of private-duty nursing in Los Angeles involving Alfred Hitchcock, Michael Jackson and Larry Flynt. I remember the rich intimacy of her voice; the fierce grope and exhilaration of her intellect. I can still see (am I imagining it?) the mad glint of wild hilarity in her enormous eyes. At the end of the evening Marian stood at the door to leave and, as if addressing the company in general, asked "So who's gonna take me home?" It was a question the undertones of which were in no way concealed. Phil was on his feet in no time. They went home and remained together for twelve years. The message always arrives at its destination.

Marian after Marian Day, the feast of Mary, the birthday of god as a mother. Marian the stoneskipper, burrower, grubworm, worker in memory, digger into the past. That past, too, as maternal: we can go there for safety, comfort, knowledge; to find, as Wayne Salazar suggests in *Destroying Angel*, "peace before we die, contentment not confusion." A refuge, a safe harbor. And Time itself as supramaternal; in Paul Celan's formulation, *zitzenprächtig*: splendid with teats. Nourishment without remit, the source, the fountainhead—the stuff of cinema.

On a seashore in Newfoundland, at the close of *The Road Ended At The Beach* (1983) (the apotheosis of the "road film"), we hear a little girl singing a vaguely menacing improvised song about who her mother loves and doesn't love and why.

But none of the temporal as maternal without an attendant threat: Marian wondered if bad memories could cause illness. Wayne asks, "When we reclaim the past, what do we unleash?" Is the devouring, superegoic aspect of the maternal apt to assail us as we pursue our personal archeologies? Does it threaten to invade us and operate within us—like a cancer: silent, invisible, ferocious—until we are consumed? Must we go there anyway? Marian thought we must.

1. The passages in italics are from the "Desultory Sketches of Thomas Nickerson" (1876), who, at fourteen, was the youngest crew member of the whale-ship Essex, stove and sunk by a sperm whale in the south Pacific, 20 November 1820.

MAURICE BLANCHOT: "Reading is anguish, and this is because any text, however important, or amusing, or interesting it may be (and the more engaging it seems to be), is empty—at bottom it doesn't exist; you have to cross an abyss, and if you do not jump, you do not comprehend" (*The Writing of the Disaster*).

I want to extend what Blanchot calls "reading" (would it be "the experience of literature?") to include the experience of cinema, and point out what may be obvious: that to take the risky leap does not guarantee the abyss will be crossed without incident, or at all.

photo (above): Marian McMahon.

still (right): *Cartouche* by Mike Cartmell.

A Cano-centric bowdlerization of the first line of Charles Olson's *Call Me Ishmael*: "I take the LAND to be the central fact to man born in Canada, from the last Ice Age till now. I spell it large because it comes large here. Large and without mercy." Unlike the American SPACE, which is Olson's concern and which is precisely space in that it exists to be occupied, the hostility of our LAND was and is unmasterable, impossible to fill up. It remains there, pitiless, pernicious, pristine (the Bowron clearcut and similar inanities notwithstanding).

It is well established that the landscape figures crucially in Canadian art; critical discussion of Phil Hoffman's cinema has often embraced that thematic, and not without reason. Consider just about any of the films: the camera frequently dwells on fields, forests, rocky shores, horizons, even visually interrogates in close-up detail the elements that give the land its scape: bark of trees, surfaces of rocks, beach sand, tide pools, grasses and leaves, and so on. And *Sweep* (1995), a film in part about cinematic forebears, opens with an Arctic landscape followed by some clips from a film called *On To Ungava*, which was the site of the limit-text of Canadian (we might as well say all) landscape film: Michael Snow's *La Région Centrale*.

[I recall that around fifteen years ago, in a spurious gesture toward taxonomy (if not taxidermy), some wag came up with the idea that a particular set of stylistic features or themes (I forget which) could be discerned in a group of films, which he designated by the major geographic formation near which the makers worked and/or grew up. It was called the Escarpment School, and in its uncontrollable sprawl eventually came to include, along with Hoffman's films, the work of Richard Kerr, Rick Hancox, Gary Popovich, Steve Sanguedolce, perhaps even Mike Hoolboom. Maybe there were others. I think that my own work was implicated. I'm fairly sure that this started out as a joke, but I can attest that I've since seen it referred to in critical articles of the most redoubtable nature.]

I am interested here not in the landscape, but in what appears in the landscape of Hoffman's cinema: something unsettlingly homely and disturbingly familiar precisely in its brokenness, fracture and disjunction. An unapproachable, uncanny, impossible yet enabling fragmentation of the true, without which this, Hoffman's, or any truthful testimony would not be possible.

Here lay our beautiful ship, a floating and dismal wreck—which but a few minutes before appeard in all her glory, the pride and boast of her capt and officers, and almost idolized by her crew, with all sails neatly set and trimd to the breeze presenting to the eye the fac similie of a ship about to leave the harbour on a summers day under the admiring gaze of hundreds to witness such a scene.

I can call it shipwreck.

When I taught filmmaking, I described it as a process of fragmentation, of dealing with the fragmentary. One used a camera and possibly a sound recorder to fracture the profilmic world into bits: *decoupage*. Through selecting, realigning, combining, adding to, superimposing and mixing those bits one altered their contexts, gave them new power and meaning: *collage*. And by giving the bits a definitive arrangement, a final and intractable temporal order, one had a film: *montage*. I think this is a fair, though perhaps idiotically simplified, account of what filmmakers do, and I think it's more or less what Phil Hoffman does. But what Hoffman doesn't do is respond to the pressure toward an ultimate seamlessness in the final product. It's obvious from where this pressure comes; there's no need to rehearse its origins here. Hoffman responds, is responsible to, a different calling, a distinctly inexorable, though perhaps more discreet, demand.

A speculative etymology, in the manner of Blanchot: *the fragmentary asks a question* (Ger. *fragen*, to ask or to question).

If we give the name "reality" to that which corresponds to the field of the symbolic, to that which can be, precisely, symbolized, represented, given fully to experience, then it is the impulse of its other to which Hoffman responds. We can call this other "the real:" that which escapes or exceeds symbolization; the unrepresentable, the impossible, the fragmentary, the disastrous, the unconscious, the sublime; the singular. Perhaps it is not exact to speak of a response to this call, since it is unclear in what way it might actually be "heard." Say instead that one maintains an openness, an availability; a passivity before and beyond any possible activity. One is responsive by being responsible to and for one's own passivity which, although it resides with the subject, is encountered (passively, passionately) as if it were an exterior force; one suffers it, endures it and remains (by means of this passion, passively) available, open to the possibility of the impossible, the presence of non-presence, the inexhaustibly, intransigently other, the negative. Or, I will say again, the singular.

George Oppen: "The shipwreck of the singular" ("Of Being Numerous").

Emmanuel Levinas: " … two world wars, totalitarianisms of the right and left, massacres, genocides and the Holocaust—have already signified (if one can still speak meaningfully) an experience torn to shreds, one impossible to put back together. It also points out the failure of the 'I think' … doing its utmost to reassemble the fantastic of the real into a world. A defeat experienced not so much as a contradiction or failure of philosophical audacity, but already, as a cosmic catastrophe, like that mentioned in Psalm 82, 5: 'All the foundations of the earth are shaken'" (*Simulacra: The End of the World*).

When experience is already torn to shreds, what does the film become when it, when its maker (as subject), responds to the radical demand of what I am calling the singular? There is no need to repeat (unless we are, as I am, unable to avoid the compulsion to do so) that it cannot be seamless, cannot achieve a total closure; can't, in some sense, ever be wholly finished. It can't in any way pretend to be an imitation of life or a representation of reality. It can't look to the modernist consolation of formal purity, and it must stand on the other side of modernism's melancholy, nostalgia and regret. Instead, this is the cinema of the accidental stab, the innovative risk; it follows no rules other than the rules invented in the immediacy and responsibility of its every instance of making.

Father: "What is a catastrophe?"
Daughter: "The first stanza of a love poem."
Jean-Luc Godard, *Passion*

Not documentary cinema, but the film as essay. And I take "essay" here in its full-dump etymological sense: to try, to try out, to test, to test the value, to take a chance, to experiment (OFr. *essai, assai*, a trial; Vulgar L. *exagiare*, to weigh out; Late L. *exagium*, a weighing, a balance; and more speculatively, L. *exaggerare*, to pile up, exaggerate, from *agger*, pile or heap). In the film essay, it is not the fragment as an end in itself that is at issue (that would be modernist nostalgia), but rather the fragmentary as the infinite heap of fragments, whether found or made. A cinema of the collection, the miniature, the gigantic, the souvenir: elements of longing, but not a melancholic longing that abides incomplete, caught in the defensive web of desire; rather longing that motivates, that moves and impels, that tasks and heaps the maker in the making, invoking the unpresentable in presentation itself.

JAMES JOYCE: "Pity is the feeling which arrests the mind in the presence of whatsoever is grave and constant in human sufferings and unites it with the human sufferer. Terror is the feeling that arrests the mind in the presence of whatsoever is grave and constant in human sufferings and unites it with the secret cause" (*Portrait of the Artist as a Young Man*).

The encounter of desire with the beautiful arouses pity, gives rise to intelligibility, and leads the subject into the domain of knowledge (the symbolic). The non-encounter of the drive with the sublime arouses terror, gives rise to nonsense, and leads the subject into the domain of truth (the real).

If modernist cinema is a cinema of desire, whose affect is pity attended by pleasure, and whose nostalgia for some lost plenitude of the past leads to a melancholic (and so, in principle, incomplete) mourning for the trace of that loss in the ruined fragment as such, then I will say that the film essay exemplifies a cinema of the drive, whose affect is terror attended by enjoyment, whose mourning is accomplished in the future anterior, whose movement circulates, and circulates around, its fragmentary objects, and whose passive passion/passionate passivity gives itself as an approach and a witness to what will have been made. The film essay is in this sense postmodern.

still: *Somewhere Between Jalostotitlan and Encarnacion.*

In Mexico, during the collection of footage for what eventually became *Somewhere Between Jalostotitlan and Encarnacion* (1984), a bus on which Philip Hoffman was riding stopped, and a woman came screaming across a field. Her little boy had been run over and killed (by the bus?). Phil watched from inside with camera in hand, trying to decide whether or not to film. He didn't. He can attest to the event, he says it happened, but he doesn't have evidence to back up his claim because he didn't turn the camera on. Later, at the Grierson Seminar, *Somewhere Between* is screened, an entire film structured around the death of a child and the absent image of it, and a news correspondent who'd made a number of films about Vietnam approaches Hoffman: "Phil, I really enjoyed the discussion, but you know when you were in the editing room, didn't you just wish you had the footage?"

I put the camera down. The film is a cinemato-poetic account of an event, of the experience of an event, the evidentiary image of which is missing; the maker attests that it never existed, was never made, and does not reside undeveloped in some freezer. So what we have is his testimony. He testifies to what was apparent to him, to the visible, to what was available to experience: "on the road dead, lies a mexican youth … /the white sheet/is pulled over the dead boy's body/the children wept … /the little girl/with big eyes/waits by her dead brother." He testifies to the unseen, the non-experience, as well: "the boy's spirit left through its blue." But he doesn't have the hard evidence, the documentary proof, for either sort of testimony: we know the camera never lies, but it's possible that Phil could.

For testimony to be what it is, to remain precisely testimony and thus retain its character as something other than a direct access to "truth," it must necessarily be haunted by what it excludes: the documentary evidence that we suppose never lies, but also, and more to the point, the possibility of the lie itself, of perjury, mistake or lack of fidelity. In short, testimony is inevitably haunted, even possessed, by the possibility of fiction. The witness is himself riven by this possession. His passion is a desire to avow, to confess without reserve, to bring forward an utter truthfulness in the face of the other's "Tell me everything!" But this passion is also to be understood as a martyrdom (Gr. *martis*, witness) in the sense of putting oneself on the line, making truth and bearing bodily witness to it through the attenuation of one's being, as martyrs bear witness with their bodies in dying; as passivity in its autonomic or heteronomic relation to the Law of Truth; as endurance of some indeterminate limit that invites the inclusion (potentially) of everything and is at the same time overwhelmed by this everything, raising the question of how to include by not including.

*They might for aught we could know have founderd during that awful night, and
ourselves be the only survivors to tell the tale of woe. And we too might at any
moment sink beneath this vast extent of ocean leaving scarcely a momentary buble
to mark the spot or tell that we once was.*

On our way to the death. So I'm saying that experience cleaves the witness,
foregrounding both the split in the subject itself (inside/outside, consciousness/the
unconscious, desire/enjoyment) as well as a rift between what can be made available for public attestation and something else, some secret testimony, evocative yet
incomprehensible: "the boy's spirit left through its blue." The elements resulting
from this cleavage are radically asymmetrical and incommensurable; they threaten
to engulf each other and the subject, are ruinous to any simple transparency in
truth-telling, and bring the word "experience" closer to the disaster secreted in its
etymological root (L. *experiri*, to try or test, to lead over or cross something per-
ilous). The witness, as he testifies, feels the hot flush of colour in his cheeks; the
possible pride he might feel in doing his duty gives way to embarrassment, or further, to something else.

Primo Levi (on the arrival of Russian soldiers at Auschwitz on 27 January 1945,
the definitive moment of the prisoners' liberation): "They did not greet us, nor did
they smile; they seemed oppressed not only by compassion but by a confused
restraint, which sealed their lips and bound their eyes to the funereal scene. It was
that shame we knew so well, the shame that drowned us after the selections, and
every time we had to watch, or submit to, some outrage: the shame the Germans
did not know, that the just man experiences at another man's crime, at the fact
that such a crime should exist, that it should have been introduced irrevocably
into the world of things that exist, and that his will for good should have proved
too weak or null, and should not have availed in defense" (*The Drowned and the Saved*).

Levinas: "What is shameful is our intimacy, that is, our presence to ourselves. It
reveals not our nothingness but the totality of our existence ... What shame discovers is the Being that discovers itself" (*De l'évasion*).

Shame is the lack of distance; too much intimacy, too much proximity, on our
way to the death. It is precisely the lack of lack itself (our lack of lack of presence
to ourselves). The subject has no other content than its own desubjectification; it
becomes witness to its own disorder, its own fracture, its own rivenness, its own
oblivion as subject. A double movement, both subjectification and desubjectification: shame.

Having now consumed their last morsel of food the captain with his three surviving companions after a due consultation agreed to cast lots.

LEVI: "It is no more than a supposition, indeed the shadow of a suspicion: that each man is his brother's Cain, that each one of us (but this time I say "us" in a much vaster, indeed, universal sense) has usurped his neighbor's place and lived in his stead" (*The Reawakening*).

The flesh of those unfortunate men constituted the only food of the survivors whilst it lasted.

"If I make films instead of children, does that mean I'm less human?"
from *Soft and Hard* by Godard and Anne-Marie Miéville

Father (not my father, but me, a father): "What is a catastrophe?"
Son (toothpick jauntily engobbed, eyes demonbright, gleeful): "Goddammit!"

SUSAN HOWE: "Love changes besides he's / damned ... " (Pierce Arrow).

Date: Sun, 23 July 2000 23:14:09 -0500 (CDT)
From: <bmlaugh@southalabama.edu>
To: <mick@yjhammer.com>
Subject: Re: your email

Dear M,

So what were MY reasons for wanting out of the situation? One reason was the atmosphere of gloom that permeated the household. Nothing ever seemed to create joy for you, and I was/am under the impression that to be happy is not one of your goals, and not one you would advocate for others.

Another reason is that I didn't see you taking much responsibility for your life—it always seemed to be up to me to make your life worth living. And as I've said before, I don't think that's an appropriate burden to put on another person, even if that person is your spouse. I felt very oppressed by the weight of that responsibility, and I don't think I'm one who takes the easy route. That is to say, I don't think I am a carefree, callous type who shirks accountability or responsibility, but I think what was being asked of me was unreasonable, and although I tried to take it on for a number of years, I just couldn't continue to do so. It was making me miserable.

I also felt that I was always on duty as caretaker, and that I never had an opportunity to be the sick one. It seemed to me that you were constantly complaining of not feeling well—feeling old, etc., as if your life were over—and so I never got any relief. I always had to be well. Perhaps that's why I lost so much weight in the early months of this year: I was sick myself but didn't have much of an opportunity to be so and then recover. And although I'm turning 41 tomorrow, I certainly don't think my life is over. It's still in high gear, and I want to continue thinking in those terms until I'm on my deathbed.

Another thing that was very troubling to me was our inability to communicate. There were moments, far too many of them, when I felt as if we were from completely different planets. Your reasoning/logic seemed to me to be upside down, or skewed so that there was no way for me to respond to it. Except with silence ... which you hated, and which I hated, too, but I could think of no words that were up to the task.

I feel ridiculous saying all of this, because I've said it all so many times before that it seems completely shop-worn.

Well, I'll continue nevertheless.

Yet another thing I felt quite acutely was the lack of action that we took. I can't blame this on you because I felt a kind of inertia myself, but I HATED it. This may be ego discourse speaking, but I think I am generally a person who likes to take action. If I say I want to do something, I'm not just blowing hot air. I do it. Damn it, you must remember that there were times when I'd say, "Let's do this, or let's do that," and you'd say, "Not now. We'll do it tomorrow." But "tomorrow" never came. I couldn't stand the paralysis ... the procrastination ... the dwindling hope that anything was EVER going to get done.

Anyway, I hope you're beginning to recover from the horror of these events. There really IS a way to put it into perspective, if you want to do that, and there really IS a way to think beyond the (stupid) confines of a (stupid) institution such as marriage. As someone once said, "Don't live in the penitentiary. Try bemusement." Or, as I might amend it, "Try laughing heartily at yourself and your predicament on occasion." In fact, that's what I'm trying to do.

love, B

Here she now lays, snatched untimely from her stateliness, into a mere shadow of what she was, and our selves deprived of the home which her goodly sides had so long afforded us.

Roland Barthes: "Whenever you give anybody anything to read, you are giving it to your mother."

Blanchot: "To be lost. To capsize" (*The Writing of Disaster*).

Date: Wed, 23 Aug 2000 19:09:46 -0400
To: bmlaugh@southalabama.edu
From: mick@yjhammer.com
Subject:

Last night I had a particularly horrible dream in which I came to Mobile to see Jazzbo. You had several people staying in the house, including a young girl whose hands did not function properly and which were supported/contained within a web-like contraption that moved the fingers for her. When I finally spotted Jazzbo he was standing with his back to me and wouldn't answer me when I called his name. I went up to him and turned him around to hug him, and he was limp and thin and pale and silent and wore glasses and had moist swollen lips on an impossibly large mouth; he looked like an infantile Stephen Hawking. I was so shocked at this I immediately woke up, relieved that it was a dream, but stayed awake the rest of the night feeling awful, both because I had invented this, and also because it somehow meant that he was lost to me forever.

I don't know if I can stand this much longer. I have been thrown out because I no longer have any value as a husband or as a father. It's still not clear what I have done to deserve having this judgement passed on me, and while I rationally know that neither of its propositions are accurate, I nevertheless cannot avoid buying into its "truth," at least on some level. This is having very damaging effects. I do not know if I will ever see Jazzbo again, but I do know that I will not be permitted to participate, in any important way, in raising him; I will miss seeing and helping him grow and develop and learn and I will be deprived of the pleasure and heartache of all that those things entail (and I know what that pleasure and heartache is). I can't understand what I did that made this deprivation necessary, and I do not see how it can possibly be construed as "best" for me, or for Jazzbo, although I guess I can imagine how you might see it being in your interest, though the only reasons I can come up with for that pertain to some version of your symptomology.

For me, this is a disaster in the fullest sense. I have lost my bearings completely, am totally separated from the star that ought to guide me somewhere. I tried very hard to act and to be OK, and was able to do that for a while, but I've lost it now and I don't know how or if I'll find it again. If there is some inherent gratification in shipwreck, I must be wallowing in it. There is little doubt that the drive seeks its fullest satisfaction in annihilation.

To shake things up, to "jolt" out of paralysis, would seem to me to be a preservative act, an effort to keep something alive, to prevent its loss. It would not be the way one would describe the termination of a marriage, of a family, especially when a child is involved, and when one's feelings can still be described as "love." I think your rhetoric betrays your confusion as to what you've done or are doing. Not that this inspires me with any hope.

When will I see Jazzbo again? It's been two months, already too long in some people's minds. Upon whom does the onus reside to facilitate my seeing him? Given the distance, and my present circumstances, it seems like a pipe dream, a fantasy. Do I want to see him? Yes, I want to see him, hold him, talk with him, kiss him, and love him and keep him near me until he's grown up. Is that going to happen? No. Why? Because you've decided it is better if it doesn't. Why? I don't know why.

Well, I don't know what to say beyond this. It's not easy to write anything. I'm not getting anywhere with the Phil thing, let alone writing to you. I can't sleep, I can't read because I can't see worth a damn. I can't stop crying so I'll just stop.

m

If I make children instead of films, does that mean I'm less inhuman?

The moment of inscription: I am in Buffalo in my tiny, boozesweat-besotted apartment, $325 a month including heat, of which there is either none or too much. It is Wednesday, 20 September, 2000, 7:34pm EDT. I'm listening to Blind Willie Johnson's "Dark Was The Night, Cold Was The Ground" (1928), perhaps one of the greatest blues recordings ever made, in part because it's postmodern avant la lettre. If you don't believe me, listen to it. Like Babji, Johnson lived through the influenza epidemic of 1918, and he wrote at least two songs about it.

Marguerite Duras: "C'est un lieu de détresse, naufragé" (*L'Amant*).

I am way late with this, but I'm distracted again (I almost want to say, distracted in the etymological sense, i.e., torn limb from limb). Yesterday after work I made a tape for Jazzbo on which I read some stories, and sang a few songs. His favorites, since he was a baby, are "Death Letter Blues" by Son House ("I got a letter this mornin', how do you reckon it read? It say 'Hurry, hurry, you know the gal you love is dead.'"), "The Greenland Whale Fisheries" and "Lord Franklin" about the shipwreck in the Northwest Passage.

It is stunningly pointless to say that I miss him. Somehow writing this makes the anguish more acute, as if he is in some way implicated in the domain of film-making; as if making or even writing about films somehow demands writing or making films about him. I guess that's how it was with Sam too. Once James Benning stayed at our house in Hamilton, and Sam made him a picture, a city seen from a distance, with the caption, "Keep your eye on the brown structure." When I went to visit Jim in New York a couple of years later, Sam's picture was still on his fridge. Did you know that the boy flailing the stick through the dewy field in *passing through* is Sam? I'm his da now, but then I was his daddy.

Memory is always construction; a remembering, a re-articulation (in every sense of the term) of pieces, fragments, members. In some sense it raises the problem of the psychoanalytic "primal scene:" the moment of trauma invented as pure construction. One's memory, what one remembers, becomes reified precisely as fact (*this* is what happened; I can testify), as the truth of the past, but it is everywhere and always founded upon, foundered by, the personal, the equivocal, the aleatory, the fictitious.

A certain fetishistic modality is apt to be entailed here in the visual domain of cinema, namely the instance of the (memory) image as such: plenitude, seamlessness, completion, talismanic charm, the maternal as ideal. The film essay, Hoffman's films, operate to oppose this entailment; they seek to remain open to the rents, fractures, the "torn formations" that the fetishistic is concerned to elide.

Now could be seen the pale and wan features, the wild and vacant stare thrown upon each other and ever and anon, turning to view the fast receding remnant of the hulk, which had borne us so gracefully over the bosom of the ocean, as though it were possible that she could yet relieve us from the fate that seemed to await us, untill at last it sunk from our view beneath the horizon.

A chaotic memory trip, this journey toward what will have been mourning accomplished, because it is one not undertaken solely within the register of the visible and the tranquility of the fetish. Hoffman's cinema frequently guides us in the direction of what is off-screen, beyond the dimension of the frame. "The possibility of mourning lies in the unseen" (PH). And we might add: the silent, the unspeakable, the ungraspable, the foundered.

A distinctive feature of the film essay is that it gives its viewers access to a feeling of its "aboutness," but in such a way that any link between this "aboutness" and the manifest content of the film is broken, or at least seriously in question. Suppose I'm teaching a class dealing with, say, Martin Scorsese's *Cape Fear* (which is, I would argue, a film essay and not in any way, except satirically, a nostalgic repetition of the "B" movie whose namesake it is), and I ask "What is this film about?" The inevitable student response will be some sort of plot rehearsal, and occasionally something involving a more synthetic rendering of the drama, but each of these begs the next question: "What is it *really* about?" The possible answers are manifold and varied, but all would demand a careful scrutiny of those elements of the film that are likely to be missed (that is to say, unrecognized as significant) by an unsophisticated viewer attending mainly to the "story" (for example, and not exhaustively: the framing of the narrative within the daughter's "what I did last summer" class presentation; Max Cady's invocations of Silesius, the Epistle to the Galatians, and "the book between Esther and Psalms"; the obviously fake wreck of the houseboat; the name of the houseboat: *Moana*, after the Flaherty film; the daughter's encounter with Cady as a theatre arts teacher, etc.). Once attention is drawn to these elements, viewers are able to re-encounter them with new zest; the multiple vectors of the film are opened to interplay with whatever each viewer can bring to bear of his or her own intellect, emotion, experience, history in a voyage of interpretation and understanding that is not necessarily terminable. While this might prove another "risky crossing," the subject is no longer wholly "at sea."

The question "What is the film about?" is not, in the case of the film essay, to be divorced from the questions "What does the film do?" and "What can its viewers do with it?"

"Where I was born, you filmed" (from *passing through/torn formations*).

A primal scene? Somewhere east of Bratislava, a young girl romps along a fenceline in a steep meadow. Grown men are reaping, then stand to chat as they hone their scythes. The sexual menace that pervades here is only exceeded when the child enters a field and confronts a bull.

The male gonad: testis, testicle (L. *testis*, a witness [to virility]).

On tape, the girl speaks the Czecho-Polish dialect of this polyglot land. Hoffman's mother translates, haltingly: "Where I was born, you filmed." This girl could be her doppelganger, retracing the ground that Susie Kaczmarzyk trod in her own girlhood: one apparently fraught with penury, upheaval, illness, accident, leading eventually to emigration. When Sue returns after the war, she suffers "a hole in [her] leg that wouldn't heal." One night she's awakened and obliged to dance the Cassock in her bedclothes before an audience of Russian soldiers. At the beginning of the film, Chris Dewdney's voice over black leader: "The layers came apart easily."

We had travelld about three hours over the meadows and through the woods toward the hunting grounds, when we heard the most dismal howling set up before us, that can be imagined. We continued on our way untill we seemed to be approaching nearer and nearer the spot whence the dismal sounds came, when the two captains came to a full stop, looked at each other a few moments as though they wished to say something which each was ashamed to open first when they turned simultaneously around making good their retreat simply remarking that the walking was so bad and the sun so extremly hot they would return and take a cooler day for the excurcion.

The menace of sexuality gives way to the disaster of engenderment. There was a huge boil on Babji's neck while she was pregnant with Wally, "the boy born at the cone of our time's most explosive moment." The notion is put forward that one could be poisoned by history in the name of justice. Marian wondered if bad memories could cause illness. Like Blind Willie Johnson, Babji lived through the influenza epidemic of 1918. She wrote no songs, but contracted Parkinson's disease, the final stages of which she is suffering, comforted by her descendants, in the opening sequence of the film.

Wally, the wayward son, the black-sheep uncle, housebreaker, former dead-beat dad, accordion maestro, optics theorist, maven of the *mise-en-abyme*: "Are you taking a picture of us looking at the picture …? You're taking a movie of us watching a movie!" The mad genius constructor of the appalling "corner mirror," which corrects the lateral inversion of normal reflection, so that you can "see yourself the way others see you." He builds one as a gift for his estranged daughter Leesa Marie, the oddball spelling the result, she says, of "an identity crisis, I guess." We watch her struggle to put on makeup, her womanchild face bisected by the bead of solder conjoining the mirror's two panes; the vertical split-screen reverberating the pop-psych "schizo" trace of schizophrenia, possibly her father's affliction. Can a virus be transmitted if you see yourself seeing yourself (*en-abyme*) the way others see you? There's an eating sequence in *Destroying Angel*, shot up at Phil's farm, where Wayne is making dinner for Phil and Marian. "In the early 90s there was still such a fear of casual infection, you know, he could cut himself and infect us, but instead there's only celebration" (PH). How would others see you seeing yourself see yourself as others see you if you ate the poison mushroom?

Phil's trip to the motherland: the stop at Dachau with Zvia, the brutal silence of the *Muselmänner* ghosts who haunt the place provoking a wince at his patronym; the sudden violence on the Czech train; the encounter with the foreign relatives, the photos and the drinking and the amiable smiles and the eager messages to Susie; the recording of the story of Karol and Uncle Janyk. Was this legend of patricide the cryptic point of trauma for these family members scattered across two continents and four generations, each one of them, as Rilke would have it, "wet with the spittle of fate?" Can the poison of our secret histories invade us and operate within us—like a cancer: silent, invisible, ferocious—until we are consumed?

Who can be a burrower, a grubworm? Marian thought we must.

photo: Marian McMahon.

Susan Susie Sue Kaczmarzyk Hoffman translates an aunt's or cousin's account of Karol's murder of his father. The words refer to the unspeakable; they point to a gap. She falters, hesitates; Neil Schmitz once told me that stuttering is a form of knowledge. There are "remains in her trembling speech. This is where our forgetting, and the things we care not to tell, come to reside" (PH). "And Karol shot Uncle Janyk seven times." The re-filmed, black-and-white, video image of Susie's face, distant, now close, closer, close-up, its motion slowed down, slower, slow, as she switches off the machine and turns aside in anguish. Who can watch this? Who can film this? What's the difference between filming a death, and a cinema that by its nature, as Cocteau said, "films death at work?" Why is it so compelling? Why can I look at it forever? How can it be that it affords me some kind of feeling of comfort and peace? Is there something beyond the border of the frame?

Géricault's painting usually known as *The Raft of the Medusa* was actually called by its author *Scène de naufrage*, Scene of Shipwreck. I remember the press of the crowd before that picture in a gallery of the Louvre nearly thirty years ago now. What is the attraction, the fascination, of that image of disaster? My friend Pedro can't abide reading about the Holocaust, about the camps; he is too much assaulted by the ordinary human capacity for extraordinary brutality. Why do I go endlessly back to Claude Lantzman's *Shoah*, to Levi, to Elie Wiesel, and so many others? Is there an arcane sadistic enjoyment at stake when we witness scenes of shipwreck, maritime and otherwise, from positions of (I'll say relative) security? Would it be better to avert our eyes, stop up our ears? Do we or don't we put the camera down?

The constant and vivid lightning seemed to envelope us in a fearful blaze, and the awful thunder of an angry element threatened every moment our final extermination.

While on his deathbed, the maker of *Scène de naufrage* was asked to assess his masterpiece. He is said to have snorted with contempt: *"Bah, une vignette!"* Perhaps the unfortunate contemporary correlative of Géricault's painting is former Niagara Falls, Ontario resident James Cameron's *Titanic*. (Would he be a candidate for inclusion in the Escarpment School?)

To be human: to lend a voice to the inhuman.   photo: Marian McMahon.

Polyglot girlchild reclines in summerwhite meadowbliss. Whitenight brightsky,
hicon sunsparkled haystalks. Firephantom ghostgirl upjumps from supine girl-
body. Nightbright shadowgirl fencescampers rhythmrunning. Emulsionslash color-
bursts. Lyric, recuperative doppelganger. "I fell asleep and dreamed."

Early in *Kitchener-Berlin* there is an image of a backhoe with the word
"Zeppelin" painted on its arm. Then ... a countdown leader: "The Amateur
Cinema League presents ... The Voyage of the R-100: The Highway of Tomorrow
or How One Makes Two." The "first Canadian surrealist film" (PH) features the
trans-Atlantic voyage of a rigid airship, with twin brothers documenting the trip
from the air and the planetary surface. The ship arrives in Canada, "safe at last."
"Twin brother comes to visit me and finds me still dreaming." These twin brothers, staggering in their indistinguishability, seem to communicate by telepathy.

Later, a phantom form rises from a sleeping twin. "Have you people seen all I
have seen in my dream?" The words refer to the unspeakable; they point to a gap.

The psychoanalyst Nicholas Abraham describes the presence of the phantom
as indicating the effects in the descendants of something that had inflicted catastrophe on the parents. The phantom is equivalent to the drive: it has no energy of
its own; it pursues its work of disarray in silence; it eludes rationalization; it gives
rise to endless circulation and repetition. (PH: "I don't have a drive to repeat.") If
we are in possession of, or possessed by, the phantom, we are being haunted not
by ancestral ghosts, but by our ancestor's secrets, the nature of which we do not
know.

Sami Van Ingen, the great-grandson of Robert Flaherty, in *Sweep*: "What
have I inherited?" The ancestral weight of Flaherty, maker of *Nanook of the
North*, and perhaps only the most famous white man to go into the Canadian
Arctic and impose his whiteness on it, has compelled Sami to retrace his great-
grandfather's steps to "somehow get even with who I am."

The headlamps of miners emerging from the shaft; candles in a cave; cave drawings; dinosaurs; the miners again. Finally a little girl in a red dress, an extenuated image, a phantom, "slips into the emulsion" (PH). From the rocky meadowhills east of Bratislava, a generation or two ago? Or is she the remnant of my mother's secret, or your mother's? Or ours, twin brother?

Hoffman's cinema resides, is at home, with the chimerical, the phantasmatic, the spectral, the anomalous; its economy touches on the touch of the untouchable. (And with Cézanne it can say, "with each touch, I risk my life.")

Have you people seen all I have seen in my dream?

"Improbable accidents of an acausal nature, that is, meaningful coincidences, have entered the picture" (from *Sweep*).

PH: "The only guide I've had in my filmmaking are these so-called coincidences."

BLANCHOT: "The disaster: stress upon minutiae, sovereignty of the accidental" (*The Writing of Disaster*).

This day the wind has hauled to east south east, with torrents of rain falling, and at midnight had increased to an awful gale with a frightful sea, which seems to threaten our total anihilation.

The moment of inscription, two: in *Sweep*, Christopher Herodier, hotel manager and sometime second-unit cameraman, makes an offer to Sami and Phil. "Here are two pens. Write a story about me!" Herodier is a Cree filmmaker (*Chiwaanaatihtaau Chitischiinuu*) who understands, along with his French counterpart Robert Bresson, that cinema (even a cinema such as this, which seemingly privileges decoupage) is precisely cinematography, a writing. But under whose authorship? And what could authorship be?

HERMAN MELVILLE: "The names of all fine authors are fictitious ones" (*Hawthorne and His Moses*).

Richard Kerr, Jim McMurray, Rup Chand, Conrad Dubé, Mark, Dan, Robert Frank, Jack Kerouac, Neal Cassady, Peter Greenaway, John Grierson, Tucker Zimmerman, Chris Dewdney, Babji, Driououx, Walter and Leesa Marie Kaczmarzyk, Sue Hoffman, Uncle Janyk, Karol, Saugeen, Karol Witoya, Dent Harrison, Twin Brother, Richard Massey Williams, Gerry Shikatani, Robert Flaherty, Dante, Sami Van Ingen, Christopher Herodier, Wayne Salazar, Mickey, Marian McMahon. Phil Hoffman. Boneyard of names.

"The taut spring wound tightly tight. Tight" (from *?O,Zoo! (The Making of a Fiction Film)*).

PH (on *Chimera*): "The film doesn't insist that market people in Cairo's Khan Khalili and London's Portabello are the same, but that they share an energy related to colour, shape and form. That's why some of the film is abstract, to evoke these pleasures of sharing."

Melville: "Masonry—and is it man's? The lines of stone do not seem like courses of masonry, but like strata of rocks … These are the steps Jacob lay at" (*Journals*).

Chimera: cinema of intercontinental ballistic single-frame zooms, a film with no author at all, Hoffman suggests. A striking moment: Marian, sunshaded, in front of an Egyptian pyramid. Two modes of preservation, care for the departed. The layers come apart easily. "A terrible mixture of the cunning and the awful. It was in these pyramids that the idea of Jehovah was born" (Melville, *Journals*).

"Do you chance to look out? Can you make a different picture? Image yourselves into a place that lets you speak to each other, and to others, more closely?" (from *Sweep*).

And if you do look out, what sort of look could it be? Neither a furtive glance, nor a close perusal, nor a wideband scan, nor a lonely masthead watch by night; but let's say a reconnaissance. A risky crossing into enemy territory, a clandestine witnessing, a cracking of codes, a theft of secrets, perhaps the hard-won validation of information already possessed. Reconnaissance: exhaustively translated as a knowing again that we are born together. Where I was born, you filmed. To evoke these pleasures of sharing. Marian thought we must.

Jacques Derrida: "Any testimony testifies in its essence to the miraculous and the extraordinary from the moment it must, by definition, appeal to an act of faith beyond any proof" (*Demeure*).

Dewdney: "You are splashed by the other children, but move not" (from *passing through/torn formations*).

Howe: "Peace thereafter / Rest fathom over" (*Pierce Arrow*).

Pace Wayne Salazar, not peace before we die, but peace thereafter—so that not we, but rather our secrets, don't haunt the living after we're gone. "The dead carry on longer than the living, and it seems that the force of a life lived is stronger once it ceases to exert itself … its silence and mystery … majestic" (PH). Rest fathom over. Marian thought we must.

I can testify.

Melville: "So help me Heaven, and on my honor the story I have told ye, gentlemen, is in substance and its great items, true. I know it to be true; it happened on this ball; I trod the ship; I knew the crew; I have seen and talked with Steelkilt since the death of Radney" (*Moby-Dick*).

"I've never seen a whale" (Richard Kerr in *Road Ended At the Beach*).

The gusts of wind were very hard and the night very dark, but our little whaleboat glided away like a thing of life.

RR
CROSSING
AHEAD

NO EPITAPH

by Karyn Sandlos

When Ann Carson writes "… death lines every moment of ordinary time" (166) she suggests that mortality resides in the quotidian details of our lives. Time, as we know it, is a progression that is measured by clocks, calendars, the passing of days, the changing of seasons. When a loved one dies, the knowledge of time passing may allow us to briefly hover over the tumultuous reckonings of the present and imagine an afterwards—a prospective view that makes the immediate impact of loss bearable. But in the midst of bereavement, ordinary time is a view from the proximate clutter of a present that can't envision a future, a heightening of the minor drama of death that permeates the everyday. For Carson, the kind of death that "lines every moment" doesn't quite amount to an event, to the actual fact of Death. Rather than surviving death, we live it.

What took place every day was not what happened every day. Sometimes what didn't take place was the most important thing that happened.
Marguerite Duras, *Practicalities.*

Death is a recurring fascination in Phil Hoffman's oeuvre, a body of films that seem to rehearse a penultimate death that will take Hoffman to the outer and inner reaches of grief. In the film cycle that concludes with *Kitchener-Berlin* (1990), be it the figure of a young boy lying dead on a Mexican roadside or an elephant falling at the Rotterdam Zoo, death is an indelible presence that is, paradoxically, often left out of the frame. After 1990, by undertaking a series of collaborative works (*Technilogic Ordering* 1994, *Sweep* 1995, *Destroying Angel* 1998, *Kokoro is for Heart* 1999) and inviting audiences to order the progression of his *Opening Series*

films (1992 ongoing project), Hoffman explores, and in a sense instigates his own death as filmmaker. Phil's latest work, *What these ashes wanted* (2001), documents the abrupt death of his late partner Marian McMahon from cancer, and the film is a declaration of bottomless grief. But since assuming the role of familial custodian of memory at the age of fourteen, the death that Hoffman has been rehearsing is his own.

What these ashes wanted is populated by the familiar—even banal—images of home and family that I have come to expect from Hoffman, but here he makes use of the ordinary to evoke a profound experience of loss. Hoffman's iconography is the immediate material surrounding him: a garden alive in summer and dead in winter, the view from a hotel window, highway traffic signs, the stone wall of a Mennonite schoolhouse near his parent's cottage. In the unexceptional, *ashes* finds a gentle rhythm that acts as a refrain throughout the film, proposing a way of seeing how extraordinary loss illumines the daily practice of death-in-life. The film is not a story of surviving death, but rather of living death, of making life hospitable to the tremulous burden of mortality. Hoffman's carefully crafted attention to the minor details of loss makes the presence of death in the ordinary fabric of life acutely felt.

If you can read this you are standing too close.
Epitaph for Dorothy Parker.

Bereavement has become a thriving industry in Western culture, replete with therapeutic approaches and self-help strategies that instruct on how to grieve well and for discreet periods of time. Many forms of bereavement counseling treat life after loss as a healing strategy, a way to reach toward a time when grief will be less shattering, when the pain of loss will be less present. Funerals also act as occasions for shaping and articulating grief, and for marking the distinction between the mourner and the mourned, a kind of reality check that affirms what the mourner at once understands and resists knowing. And it may well be the case that loss is far too amorphous and terrifying without the formal containers into which we are compelled to pour it. Hoffman's project is, however, less committed to protocol and more concerned with a practice of bereavement that mixes psychic disintegration with the provisional solace gleaned from secular therapies or devout rituals of mourning. Early in *ashes* we partake of a playfully private moment shared between Phil and his late partner Marian McMahon, the first of several sequences that will draw us into the small circle of their relationship. Heavily bundled against the cold, they frolic, home-movie style, in the yard outside the schoolhouse, not far from Mt. Forest where they will later make their home. The camera moves erratically across the stone wall of the school house at close range, and an uncomfortable proximity is created as we observe an intimate game from which the burdens of the world seem to fall away. Phil touches the wire fence, feigns electric shock, and laughs. Filming this moment, the couple play at death while reaching for posterity—for permanence—bringing the underlying tension that haunts *ashes* to the surface.

People may die and be remembered, but they only disappear when they are completely forgotten, when no one ever uses their name.
Adam Phillips, *Darwin's Worms*.

It was Freud's observation that dreams are populated by incidental images and fragments of experience from conscious life. The death of a loved one, he noted, is often obliterated from the dreamscape only to return to memory with unusual force upon waking (78). Perhaps, then, in the midst of grief the unconscious makes itself known through a heightening of the minutiae of waking life, like a long, laborious swim under deep water where every movement, every sound, and every glimpse of color and light are attenuated. The irreconcilable clash between psychic longing for the lost loved one and the reality of absence is less an event than a palpable emptiness, a heightened view from the disruption of experience that seems to have fallen out of step with the continuity of time. In *ashes*, the rough-hewn fieldstones of the schoolhouse contrast the meticulously rendered brick facade and pillars of a more monumental structure, a relic of ancient history. A figure walks slowly past an Egyptian temple, appearing, disappearing and reappearing from behind the columns. When the body is absent, this sequence implies, the shadow remains.

Several years before her death Marian asks Phil, "If you had to make up your
own ritual for death what would it be? And would it be private, or shared?" Phil
responds that it should be shared, and his tone resonates with the force of this
deeply held conviction; for Phil, death is a lived practice that must necessarily be
shared if one is to live at all. It is often said that funerals are for the living; but
how, precisely, does ritual help us grieve and move on? With this question in
mind, I often visit cemetaries and wander amidst gravestones belonging to people
I have never met. Something troubles about the tone of epitaphs. The words say
that the loved one is gone. Etchings in stone mark the finality of death, but they
don't account for how life is inhabited by death—and still lived. The severing of
attachment and the abruptness of absence may be life's most shattering experience, yet loss itself has a lingering presence in life. Loved ones leave, but the
inevitability of death, if not desirable, is wholly enduring.

ashes is no epitaph, no tribute to the passage of time or the solace of monu-
ments. In his latest work, Hoffman remains in his own time, a daily practice of
loss lived precariously on the margin between disintegration and ritual. A voice
on Phil's answering machine quotes the poet Alfred Corn observing "in times of
great grief it is important to go through the motions of life until eventually they
become real again." When Phil films Marian making calls on her route as a home
care nurse, he rides in the back seat and watches her face in the rear-view mirror.
Caught up in the demands of the everyday and the immediacy of the task at hand,
Marian thinks out loud about how peculiar it feels to provide intimate physical
care to complete strangers. In illness, she observes, the body becomes public
property. The conversation takes on a heightened anxiety as Marian describes the
awkwardness of the situation, and her inability to talk with Phil about things she
really wants to talk about while he complains about the weight of the camera. The
nuances of Phil's response are missed in an exchange in which Marian teases him
for failing to appreciate the gravity of her insights. The conversation becomes a
speculation on the daily minutiae of loss—the disappointments, missed connections, and absences that act as small rehearsals for the larger drama of death.
Although I never met Marian McMahon, I remember her in a very particular
way. I was a new graduate student waiting for a meeting in the hallway outside a
professor's office. Wanting to absorb the culture of collegiality and ideas, I studied

my surroundings. The walls were plastered with memoranda: posters advertising political rallies, calls for papers, and cartoon strips—the clutter of academic life. What I recall most vividly is a poem that was taped to the door directly in front of me. Reading that poem, I felt a momentary break in time that I have yet to understand.

Perhaps there are no accidents. I had skimmed the eulogies on e-mail, and heard fragments of conversations in the hallways about a colleague who had passed away. She was a doctoral candidate, and she died of cancer just as her dissertation was approaching completion. The poem was written by one of Marian's professors, but it read as if her hand was urgently tracing his words … *I am still here.*

She might have spoken the words, or whispered them.

It is a common clinical experience that bereaved people fear that talking about the person they have lost will dispel their contact with them.
Adam Phillips, *On Flirtation*

ashes speaks most profoundly through a story that Hoffman struggles to put to words, not only because he cannot bear to articulate his loss directly, but because language itself can only approximate the void that is absence. In *ashes,* loss is evoked through a reordering of referentiality, a fragmentation of the details Hoffman depends upon to order his world. A window provides the only source of light for a darkened bedroom. Although the light fluctuates, it is impossible to determine when it is morning and when it is evening. The camera hovers on time lapse. Are seasons passing, or merely hours? Formless images, shapes, and shadows are intercut with lush scenes of the garden awash with the color of emotion, with the vividness of an image one might wish to have shared with a lover. Anecdotal remnants of Marian—her own voice on the answering machine as well as messages from friends and family before her death—procure the flavor of shared lives, recount daily events, confirm appointments, and announce the birth of a baby girl.

A nurse calls, wondering what to do with a blouse left behind at the hospital.

It is possible that we have no idea what secular grief is; what grief unsanctioned by an apparently coherent symbolic system would feel like.
Adam Phillips, *Promises Promises.*

Obsessing over the hidden meaning of a photograph taken from inside a cave, Marian reflects on learning to live life "from the inside out," from the midst of happenings yet to be understood, yet to be integrated into a coherent realm of experience. Transposed in text across the darkness of the cave's interior, her reflections on loss—in this case the loss of memory—resonate with Phil's own struggle to articulate his grief. The power of naming, Marian insists, gives experience its credibility. Attuned to the capacity of the symbolic to legitimize, Hoffman takes ritual as an entry point directly into the midst, the incoherent centre of sorrow.

"Seventeen's the number," Hoffman repeats. "One is for one, and seven is for doing." With childlike insistence, he translates a personal lineage of life and death into a number game. "She was born on May seventeen, and died on November seventeen. My Dad was born on April seventeen, my uncle was born on April seventeen, and my grandfather was born on April seventeen. Seventeen's the number. One is for one, and seven is for doing." Seventeen, we are told, is the number of Phil's hockey jersey, and of his seat on a plane, and it is the number entered in his log book on the day an elephant fell down at the Rotterdam Zoo. Seventeen is just a number, a minor detail easily discounted in the rush of daily experience. But in Phil's efforts to account for a series of happenings from the midst of bereavement, seventeen becomes the number, the numerology of loss.

Ladybug, ladybug, fly away home. Your house is on fire and your children are gone.

Hoffman's method is that of reiteration without redundancy; loss, we are reminded, is never just this loss. In *ashes* we learn that Hoffman is once removed in the order of his siblings from an older brother who died at birth. Because the child died so soon, the priest refused to perform the funereal rites that would have legitimized this life in the eyes of the church. But funerals are meant for the living, and this disavowal prompted Phil's father's departure from the church. Later, this man would have another son who would also be named Phillip. Upon completing his first film, *On the Pond* (1978), Phil changed the spelling of his name from Phillip to Philip, marking the distinction between his life and that of his lost brother with the absence of a single letter.

Good mourning, in Freud's terms, keeps people moving on, keeps them in time …
Adam Phillips, *Darwin's Worms*

What becomes of grief that traditional practices of mourning cannot, or will not, contain? *ashes* suggests that ritual serves us less as a remedy for grief, and more as a glimpse of ordered time from outside the midst of our daily reckonings with loss. When her mother died, Ann Carson scanned the pages of Virginia Woolf's diaries in search of something, following Woolf's own premise that there is pleasure to be derived from "forming such shocks into words and order" after the fact of Death (165). On the day after the funeral, Carson sat at her desk, books spread out before her, looking not for meaning, but for the comfort of structure. I turned to Carson the week I was finishing this writing, the day I had to pause, unexpectedly, to write a eulogy. How can I write my uncle's life? I wondered, barely upright before a blank screen, caught in the midst of this unexpected death, of my memories, his personal life, this public declaration, the faces of my family, my anguish, my rage.

He didn't just die, he was taken.

Sudden death doesn't begin to feel real until you see its impact etched across the faces of the people standing directly in front of you. Or, as in the case of my uncle's death, until I read the horrible truth in what would otherwise have been an ordinary newspaper headline, on an ordinary day. Even then, these were cues that only hinted at what I should feel. Everywhere it said that my uncle was gone, but I could not write of his life in the past tense. I could not write "My uncle was a committed painter for over three decades." In writing that "he has been painting all my life" … has been, and *will be*, I clung to the present perfect, the tense of continuity. *I do not release him*, my uncle's friend choked from the podium on the day of the funeral with an urgency that cut through my carefully measured sentences, my own attempt to fashion the expression of my grief. With those words came another break in time. If mourning requires our participation in the flow of time, *ashes* insists that we live with death in capricious ways that exist outside of this ordered progression. Perhaps learning to live "from the inside out" means learning to live while dying at the same time—learning to live *with* death and not despite it. Loss, it seems, is a persistent presence.

Works Cited

Carson, Ann.
Men in the Off Hours. New York: Alfred A. Knopf, 2000.

Freud, Sigmund.
The Interpretation of Dreams. Trans. James Strachey. London: Penguin Books Ltd., 1991.

NOTES ON CONTRIBUTORS

Sarah Abbott is a filmmaker at large.

Shary Boyle is based in Toronto, with the odd extended exception. Her practice revolves around drawing, painting, and the production of small book works. She is mainly concerned with articulating the personal.

Variably a chef, college lecturer, frame carpenter and web designer, **Mike Cartmell** divides his time between les bas fonds of Buffalo and his canoe in Temagami. Recently a number of friends encouraged him to return to filmmaking, and he is grateful.

Tom Chomont is a filmmaker turned video-maker currently living in New York City. He began making films in 1963 and videos in 1991.

Janieta Eyre is a Toronto-based artist who works chiefly in photography. The pictures reproduced in this volume derive from her first two major bodies of work. The first is entitled *Rehearsals*, which stages scenes of her own death. The second, *Incarnations*, features the artist alongside her doppelgangers in serial masquerade.

Su Friedrich is a New York-based filmmaker whose work has won numerous awards and is widely screened and broadcast throughout the U.S. and Europe. Since 1978 she has made thirteen 16mm films and one videotape. She has had several retrospectives, including one at the Whitney Museum. Friedrich is also a teacher and sometimes writes about film.

Chris Gehman is a Toronto-based filmmaker, film and video programmer, and occasional film writer. Chris has done extensive programming for organizations such as Pleasure Dome and Cinematheque Ontario. He is currently the Artistic Director of the Images Festival of Independent Film and Video.

Peter Greenaway is a celebrated UK filmmaker who began making short films in 1966, and entered the world of feature filmmaking with *The Draftsman's Contract* in 1982. Along with his films, he is a well-known photographer, painter and art curator.

Peter Harcourt has studied at the University of Toronto and at Cambridge University. He has worked for the British Film Institute and taught at Queen's University, York University and Carleton University. He is the author of *Six European Directors* (1974), *Movies & Mythologies* (1977), *Jean Pierre Lefebvre* (1981) and a personal memoir, *A Canadian Journey: Conversations with Time* (1994).

Ron Heydon has a degree in Communications from Concordia, and currently resides in New York City, where he works as an archivist of visual imagery and as a technical writer. He has kept a journal these last thirty years and intends, one day, to synthesize it down to a moderate size for publication—a sort of trip through the end of the 20th century—starting from Regina and ending in New York.

Mike Hoolboom is a prolific film and video maker, writer, and advocate for artists' film and video. He is the editor of *Inside the Pleasure Dome: Fringe Film in Canada* (1997) and the author of *Plague Years: A Life in Underground Movies* (1998).

Chris Kennedy is an American-born, Canadian-educated film and videomaker and writer who now spends his time in Toronto. His day job is Distribution Manager at V tape.

Richard Kerr is an associate professor at the Mel Hoppenheim School of Cinema at Concordia University. He began making films at Sheridan College in 1976, and has produced over a dozen short films and videos that have travelled the world. In 1993 he was the subject of a major retrospective at the MacKenzie Art Gallery, entitled "Overlapping Entries."

Robert Lee is interested in architecture.

Deirdre Logue is an independent curator and a film, video and performance artist living and working in Toronto. *"Enlightened Nonsense,"* a collection of short films, was exhibited at YYZ Artists' Outlet in 2000. She is currently producing an independent feature film made collectively by ten Canadian film and video artists from across the country. She has exhibited her film and video works internationally.

Brenda Longfellow is currently co-chair of the Department of Fine Arts, Atkinson College, York University, where she teaches film studies. She has written extensively about women's cinema in *Screen, Cine-Tracts,* and the *Canadian Journal of Film Studies.* She is an award-winning documentary filmmaker whose films include *Our Marilyn, Gerda, A Balkan Journey,* and *Shadow Maker.*

Roy Mitchell is a serious experimental filmmaker who would understand all the theory if he had studied harder.

Cara Morton is a filmmaker who merges personal experience and reflection into her art-making process. She has received her MFA from York University and is currently living in northwestern British Columbia.

Matthias Müller is a German filmmaker who has produced more than thirty experimental film and videos. In 1996, he co-curated the first German festival of diary films at the Bielefeld Kunsthalle.

Jeffrey Paull teaches movie making. Philip Hoffman was a student of his many years ago.

Gary Popovich is a Toronto-based artist who has made twenty films and videos.

Steve Reinke is an artist and writer best known for his work in video. Currently, he is a professor at the University of Illinois. His work has been exhibited widely and is in many collections, including The Museum of Modern Art (New York), the Pompidou (Paris) and the National Gallery (Ottawa).

Daniel Reeves began making video work in 1979. Combat experiences in Vietnam were the driving force behind his early videotapes, which developed from preparatory work in sculpture, photography and film, culminating in *Smothering Dreams* (1981). Subsequent tapes have addressed inhumanity, dispossession and social upheaval with a lyrical sensibility, and from an outlook informed by Eastern philosophy.

Jeremy Rigsby is the program director for the Media City Experimental Film and Video Festival in Windsor, Ontario.

Karyn Sandlos is a writer and filmmaker, and a doctoral candidate in the Faculty of Education at York University, Toronto. She is the chair of the Board of Directors of the Images Festival and a member of the programming collective for Pleasure Dome.

Polly Ullrich is a Chicago-based artist, writer and art critic.

Darrell Varga is a filmmaker and lecturer in Film Studies at various universities. He is currently writing a PhD dissertation in the Department of Social and Political Thought at York University, Toronto.

Michael Zryd teaches Film Studies at the University of Western Ontario and writes about avant-garde/experimental film and documentary.

LIST OF WORKS

Films

What these ashes wanted (56 min., 2001)
Opening Series 4 (10 min., silent 2000)
Kokoro is for Heart (7 min., b/w, 1999)
Destroying Angel (32 min., 1998) (co-maker Wayne Salazar)
Chimera (15 min., 1996)
Sweep (30 min., 1995) (co-maker Sami van Ingen)
Opening Series 3 (5 min., b/w, 1995) (co-maker Gerry Shikatani)
Technilogic Ordering (30 min., 1994)
Opening Series 2 (7 min., silent 1993)
Opening Series 1 (10 min., silent 1992)
Kitchener-Berlin (34 min., 1990)
river (15 min., 1979-89)
passing through/torn formations (43 min., 1988)
?O,Zoo! (The Making of a Fiction Film) (23 min., 1986)
Somewhere Between Jalostotitlan and Encarnacion (6 min., 1984)
The Road Ended at the Beach (33 min., 1983)
On the Pond (9 min., b/w, 1978)

All films are 16mm colour with sound, unless otherwise noted.

For information regarding Philip Hoffman's films, contact:

Canadian Filmmakers Distribution Centre
37 Hanna Avenue Suite 220
Toronto, Ontario, Canada M6K 1W8
Telephone: 416.588.0725 Fax: 416.588.7956 www.cfmdc.org

Video Installations

Parabolic Senses (with Gerry Shikatani) (30 min., video/film, FSAC, 1999)
Chimeras (50 min., multi-screen video/film, 1997)
Chimerae (17 min., video, 1996)
Ahead of the Rest (10 min., video, 1995) (installation at Union Station, Public Access, Toronto)
Technilogic Ordering (52 min., 1991)

a landmark work, sure to be a primary resource on Canadian and international artists' film and video of the 1990s

Lux: A Decade of Artists' Film and Video
edited by Steve Reinke and Tom Taylor

d by YYZ Books and Pleasure Dome 374 pages

www.pdome.org   f.416.656.5577 $20

Richly illustrated with essays and artist projects by such noted contributors as
Laura U. Marks, Janine Marchessault, George Kuchar, Peggy Ahwesh, Cameron Bailey, Elisabeth
Subrin, Colin Campbell, Barbara Sternberg, Mike Hoolboom, Lisa Steele and Kim Tomczak, Sally
Berger, Wrik Mead, Catherine Russell, Jan Peacock and many others.

Pleasure **Dome**

Canadian Filmmakers Distribution Centre

37 Hanna Ave., Suite 220
Toronto, Ontario
Canada, M6K 1W8
www.cfmdc.org   e-mail cfmdc@cfmdc.org   phone (416) 588-0725

A co-op dedicated to the distribution of the work
of independent filmmakers since 1967

MEMBER OF THE SCABRINI GROUP
Quebec, Canada
2001